SHEDDING
SHADOWS

SHEDDING SHADOWS

THE ASTROLOGY OF 2025

GAHL EDEN SASSON

ABOUT THE AUTHOR

Photo credits: Peter Vulchev

Gahl Sasson has been teaching workshops on Storytelling, Kabbalah, Astrology, and Mysticism around the globe for over 20 years. His first book, *A Wish Can Change Your Life*, has been translated into over eight languages and is endorsed by HH the 14th Dalai Lama (Simon and Schuster, 2003). His second work, *Cosmic Navigator*, is the essential reference guide to understanding your astrological makeup (Weiser, 2008). Gahl self-published a yearly astrology book since 2018. In his 2020 book he predicted the recession and pointed at the possibility of a pandemic.

He is a contributor to the Huffington Post, and Astrology.com, and has been named "Los Angeles' Best Astrologer" by W Magazine. He is a guest lecturer at USC, Tel Aviv University, and teaches at Esalen, Omega Institute, University of Judaism, Asia Yoga Conference, Alternatives in UK, and the Open Center in NYC. He has appeared on CNN, ABC News, KTLA-TV Los Angeles to name a few. In 2017 his academic article, *Symbolic Meaning of Names in the Bible* was published by the Journal of Storytelling, Self, & Society. He currently resides in Los Angeles but gives seminars and workshops globally. His web site is www.CosmicNavigator.com

ACKNOWLEDGMENTS

Special thanks to Belinda Casas for her unwavering support, Laura Day for her astute and insightful suggestions, Laurie Scheer for meticulous editing, Adina Cucicov for her exceptional formatting, and Rochelle Bolima for her inspiring cover design.

Heartfelt gratitude goes out to the talented baristas from Silverlake, Palm Springs, Istanbul, Fethiye, London, Zurich, Dubai, Tel Aviv, Haifa, and Sofia who participated in transmuting coffee beans into cosmic narratives.

FOREWORD

Get ready for a year of dramatic transformations and thrilling cosmic events! In 2025, we will experience a period of intense shedding and rebirth. The Year of the Snake sets the stage for a descent into the Underworld, guided by Lilith and Vesta in Scorpio—the sign of death and resurrection. Saturn, Uranus, and Neptune transition between signs, shedding and redressing. Adding to the cosmic storm, both Mars and Venus retrograde in the fiery signs of Leo and Aries, while mystical eclipses, guided by the Dragon in Pisces, illuminate our paths and accelerate events. And let's not forget the Grand Benevolent, Jupiter, who, after a challenging exile in Gemini, finally returns to his exalted sign of Cancer mid-year, bringing hope and renewal.

Astrology is rooted in the ancient alchemical axiom "as above, so below." 2025 showcases this mystical equation vividly with Neptune, Uranus, Saturn, Lunar Nodes, and Jupiter all shedding their signs, prompting us to undergo similar transitions. Additionally, the numerology of the year 2025 is 9, symbolizing endings and new beginnings. In the Kabbalistic Tree of Life, 9 is represented by the sphere *Foundation*—the vessel of magic, transformation, death, reincarnation, intimacy, sexuality, and the occult. The sphere's assigned name of God is *Shaddai* "God of the wilderness," or to paraphrase—God of the Wildlings.

These intense transits of 2025 represent the shedding of shadows, but what about the rebirth? For that, we need to look at Neptune, Saturn, and the North Node, who are transiting right over the first degree of Aries, the cusp that links the last sign, Pisces, with the first sign, Aries. The initial degree of Aries marks the Spring Equinox, the most sacred "real estate" of the zodiac wheel. The significance of this cosmic synchronicity is multifold and will take decades to unwrap, but with the help of Jupiter moving to his sign of exaltation in the second part of the year, we can expect a great deal of new beginnings rising out of the ashes. One thing is clear: to successfully navigate this uber intense year, we need to become witches and warlocks, wizards and enchantresses. This book is designed to be your cosmic GPS, helping you navigate the waves of probability as they collapse into reality.

Astrology is not a fortune-telling tool; rather, it is the confluence of fate and free will. Having analyzed thousands of astrological charts over the past three decades, I am convinced that we are not mere pawns to destiny. Instead, we co-create our futures, and astrology is the technical support the universe so kindly provided.

I sincerely hope that this book assists you in tapping into the year's potential and avoiding its pitfalls. Sending heartfelt wishes of light and love from the coordinates 33°N01' 035°E17' Mount Carmel, the place Homo Sapiens coinhabited along with the Neanderthals, Israel, Levant, Middle East, Asia, Earth, Milky Way, Creation, Oneness.

~ **Gahl**

ABOUT THE BOOK

This book is your cosmic GPS, guiding you through the waves of probability as they collapse into reality.

The first part of *Shedding Shadows—the Astrology of 2025* features a list of significant dates for each month as well as a directory of major retrogrades and eclipses. This section is designed to help you plan the year ahead, identifying auspicious dates for business ventures, romantic adventures, or starting a new health regimen. The second part presents the major trends and cosmic patterns of 2025, including dates to kick-start your New Year's resolutions, a lunar calendar that can help you manifest your dreams, the numerology and color of 2025, as well as major transits and how they manifest for each sign. The third part offers a month-to-month overview for each zodiac sign. I suggest reading both the chapters corresponding to your Sun sign and the one relating to your rising sign. If you don't know your rising sign, which outlines your life's path, you can generate your astrological chart for free on my website. Simply visit www.CosmicNavigator.com and click the tab LEARN, scroll down to FREE ASTRO CHART.

For more free guidance on navigating 2025's astrological landscape, tune into my weekly podcast—streamed every Sunday 10am PST, which is also available as a Zoom webinar, for which you can register through my website. I also post regular astrological insights on my Instagram: @ Cosmic_Navigator.

ABOUT THE COVER

The cover of this book features key symbols and astrological transits that define the year 2025. Central to the design is the Ouroboros, a serpent biting its own tail, representing the Chinese Year of the Snake. It encircles the cusp of Aries and Pisces, reflecting the powerful transits between the first of his kind, Aries, and the tail of the zodiac, Pisces. The color of the cover, "Future Dusk," echoes the year's official color, embodying the intense year's mood and energy. Encased within Ouroboros is a detailed chart of the planetary transits, including their retrogrades. This chart serves as a guide and reference as you explore Part II of Shedding Shadows.

CONTENTS

PART I

GENERAL GUIDES

Please note, all dates mentioned in this book
are set for 12pm UT/GMT.

LIST OF ARCHETYPAL CHARACTERS IN YOUR JOURNEY

The heavenly planets are the engines empowering the zodiacal archetypes. These planets can be exalted, ruler, fallen, or in exile, depending on the sign they are occupying. These terms define the planet's strength. When a planet is exalted, it channels its archetype optimally, full of its potential, like spending time with your best friend who pampers and treats you like royalty. When a planet is in its ruling sign, it manifests strongly, like the safety one feels in one's home. When a planet is fallen, it struggles to shine its qualities, akin to spending a night in a rundown shady motel in a city you despise. The sign of exile signifies that the planet is furthest from its home (always the opposite sign) and misses it; therefore, it's considered "sad" or "detached."

Below is a list of the most important heavenly bodies (like characters in a play) that will be mentioned in the book:

Sun—Ruler of Leo. The Sun represents you—the hero or heroine of the journey. In astrology, the Solar disk signifies your self-expression, the heart of your chart, the capital of your kingdom, and what you aspire to become. He's exiled in Aquarius and fallen in Libra.

Moon—Ruler of Cancer. The Moon symbolizes your instinct, DNA, ancestral memory, genetics, and how you react to unexpected situations in life. In astrology, she represents emotional expression, home, family, real estate, your perception of your mother, and how you need to be nurtured. She's exalted in Taurus, exiled in Capricorn, and fallen in Scorpio.

Mercury—Ruler of Virgo and Gemini. Mercury represents intellect, mind, communication, business, writing, information, relatives, neighbors, contracts, diet, work, employees, and service. He is exalted in Virgo, exiled in Sagittarius, and fallen in Pisces. When Mercury retrogrades, he takes on the role of the mischievous wily trickster, but more on that below.

Venus—Ruler of Libra and Taurus. Venus signifies money, talents, art, diplomacy, justice, values, relationships, self-worth, pleasure, and beauty.

She is exalted in Pisces, exiled in Aries, and fallen in Virgo. Alas, this year Venus will be retrograding (March 1—April 14).

Mars—Ruler of Aries and co-ruler of Scorpio. Mars represents vitality, passion, energy, war, leadership, desire, assertiveness, planting, and entrepreneurship. He is exalted in Capricorn, exiled in Libra and Taurus, and fallen in Cancer. Mars started retrograding on December 6, 2024, and continues his backward walking until February 25, 2025.

Jupiter—Ruler of Sagittarius and co-ruler of Pisces. Jupiter symbolizes luck, opportunity, morality, justice, education, travel, benevolence, generosity, and truth. Jupiter is exalted in Cancer (where he will be from June), exiled in Gemini (until June), and fallen in Capricorn.

Saturn—Ruler of Capricorn and co-ruler of Aquarius. Saturn, the father who devoured his own children, symbolizes hardships, karma, tradition, patience, focus, structure, strategy, ambition, and career. He is exalted in Libra, exiled in Cancer and Leo, and fallen in Aries (where he makes a short stop this year).

Uranus—Ruler of Aquarius, he symbolizes innovation, epiphanies, strokes of genius, revolution, individuality, science, AI, and technology. Known as the Great Awakener, he acts as the joker, the twister of fate. This year Uranus makes a brief transit in Gemini.

Neptune—Ruler of Pisces, representing mysticism, dance, poetry, imagination, dreams, meditation, and intuition. Also considered Venus' higher octave. This year Neptune makes a short visit to Aries.

Pluto—Ruler of Scorpio, stands for transformation, power, investments, death, research, the underworld, sexuality, and the occult. Also considered Mars' higher octave.

RETROGRADES & STATIONARY PLANETS

Inverted Magic

Retrogrades can be fun. While it may sound like an oxymoron, retrograde periods, when navigated correctly, can infuse your life with magic and excitement. In addition, I find that retrogrades can help you get out of energetic swamps. Retrograde planets add an important component to the cosmic navigation of your life—the ability to shift into "reverse" gear. I am certain you would never agree to drive a car that does not feature a reverse mode. The same goes for retrograde planets; life would be impossible without the contribution of the celestial reverse gear.

Just as we need to sleep, rest, dream, blink, and meditate to reflect and process our experiences, we need retrograde periods to assimilate whatever took place while the planet in question was in direct motion. In the three decades I have had the pleasure of casting thousands of charts, I have found retrograde periods to be filled with synchronicities and meaningful coincidences. Let's look at the gifts retrograde periods can bestow on us:

- Finding lost objects, people, and passions.
- Reigniting projects you failed to accomplish or dropped in the past.
- Increasing "magic" (something out of nothing) and synchronicities.
- Sharpening your intuition, psychic abilities, and prophetic dreams.
- Meditating, especially during stationary phases.
- Engaging in any activity that begins with the prefix "re," such as rewrite, reedit, revisit, reevaluate, return, reimagine, etc.
- Examining your projects, relationships, and values with a fresh outlook and trying new approaches to resolve old issues.
- Connecting to memories, people, gifts, insights, places, and lessons from previous lives. Retrogrades are periods for spontaneous past lifetime regression.

For these reasons, I find retrograde periods, especially those of the personal planets (Mercury, Venus, and Mars), to be exciting. These are times when we are asked to flip-flop the way we communicate and think (Mercury retrograde), relate to each other and deal with finances (Venus retrograde), and act (Mars retrograde). In 2025, we will have all planets retrograde, so you will get a lot of practice. If you are a yoga practitioner, retrograde periods are great for inverted poses like handstands and headstands.

This leads us to the last point: retrogrades (especially Mercury) are times when we experience "Inverted Magic." During the retrograde motion of a planet, things you want to manifest may go awry while things you haven't planed suddenly happen. For example, if you lost your keys, it might be hard to find them, but while searching for them, you might find something else you lost a while back. It won't help you unlock whatever the key was supposed to, but it could be valuable for something else.

Here are a few principles that could make your next retrograde period productive, meaningful, and even enjoyable:

- As a planet retrogrades, whatever it rules and symbolizes must be accessed from within, not from the outside. For example, when Mercury retrogrades, information and communication are accessed through intuition, dreams, insights, revelations, and visions. For this reason, during retrogrades, you may experience more magic, serendipities, and even encounters with the supernatural.
- Retrogrades are great times for therapy, healing, prayers, and enchantment. It's as if reason and normalcy are challenged by the magical and extraordinary.
- Play a game: "A Memory Never Recalled." I played this game from an early age to pass time. The goal is to try to recall a memory you have not thought about since the time it occurred. For example, think of your last birthday and challenge yourself to recall a scene from that day that you have not thought about since. Not only is this a good brain exercise, but it can also help you recall memories you might have shunned or repressed.

Stationary, Retro, Pre and Post Retrogrades

But would you kindly ponder this question: What would your good do if evil didn't exist, and what would the earth look like if all the shadows disappeared? After all, shadows are cast by things and people. Shadows also come from trees and living beings. Do you want to strip the earth of all trees and living things just because of your fantasy of enjoying naked light?
  – Mikhail Bulgakov, The Master and Margarita

Just like anything under the Sun possesses a shadow, so does a retrograde planet. The retrograde period of a planet features five stages: pre-retro shadow, stationary, retrograde, stationary, and post-retro shadow. The stationary periods last two days (though the actual duration depends on the velocity and orbit of the planet), while the length of the retrograde caught between them varies depending on the planet in question. Remember, the word we use in English for "planet" comes from the Greek word for "wanderer." When the planet retrogrades it acts counter to its nature. For example, if Venus is the matchmaker, then when she goes retrograde, she could assume the role of the divorce lawyer.

Pre-Retro Shadow: A few weeks before a planet retrogrades (two weeks in the case of Mercury, a month with Venus), it appears to slow down as it traverses the area in the zodiac where it will later retrograde through (hence the term "shadow"). During this time, you can still start projects and sign documents, but you must be extra vigilant, akin to driving at night. This period can highlight the areas in your life that might be subject to disruption during the coming retrograde.

Stationary: During the two stationary periods, we experience the pure essence of the planet, as though you are dealing with a concentrated version of the planet's archetype. Time seems to stand still—the quiet before the storm. I find the stationary stages an opportune time for relaxation, meditation, and spending time in nature. Psalm 46 advises us to "Be still and know that I am God," which is a godly suggestion to practice "stationing," embracing stillness, and connecting to the divine spark within us. Considering Saturn (patience and stability) and the North Node (good karma) are in Pisces (meditation) for the first time since 1876, I would say 2025 is the best time to deepen your meditations.

Retrograde Period: Be extra careful with starting new projects or engaging in activities related to the archetype of the planet. If it's Mercury, avoid signing documents or starting new businesses; if it's Mars, then stay away from sharp objects and avoid starting conflicts; in the case of Venus, refrain from initiating new relationships or making big investments.

Stationary: The planet stands still for two days once again before it begins its "direct" motion. You might feel impatient to start new projects but hold on for a bit longer.

Post-Retro Shadow: Go for it! A fresh stream of possibilities storms in. You should still tread carefully and, if you can, wait until after the shadow period to initiate important projects.

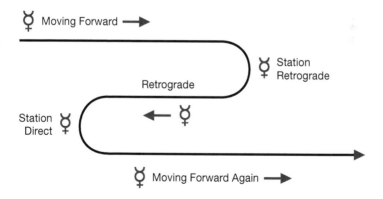

Mercury Retrograde

Undoubtedly, the most frequent and panic-inducing member of the retrograde gang is Mercury. Besides being the messenger of the gods, Mercury is also the god of scoundrels, thieves, tricksters, liars, and cheats. Even those who are skeptical or agnostic towards astrology admit to noticing something amiss when Mercury, the envoy of the gods and goddesses, appears to wander backward. The sign where Mercury retrogrades can often indicate the type of miscommunications and technical glitches one might experience.

In 2025, Mercury retrogrades in Aries, Pisces, Leo, Sagittarius, and Scorpio, which means a great deal of water (emotions) and fire (action). The mixture of these two elements can create quite a lot of steam, leading to thoughts within thoughts, panic, and anxiety.

Mercury is the ruler of both Gemini and Virgo. These two intellectual signs square each other and therefore have a rather tense sibling rivalry. While Gemini knows a little about everything, Virgo uses her Mercurial superpowers to know everything about something so little it's close to nothing. Most people focus solely on the Gemini qualities of Mercury retrograde, such as miscommunications and issues with electronic devices, but often neglect the Virgo aspects of Mercury retrograde, which can manifest as challenges in health, diet, workplace complications, employee misunderstandings, issues with pets, and disruptions in daily routines.

☿ Mercury (Communication, Business, Technology, Workplace, Health, Diet, Service)

- Pre-Shadow but Direct: March 1–March 13
- Stationary: March 14–15 in Aries (leadership, identity, your path in life, head, muscles, blood, eyes, vitality)
- Retrograde: March 16–29 in Aries
- Retrograde: March 30–April 5 in Pisces (intuition, meditation, dance, movement, empathy, imagination, dreams, hospitals, addictions, confinement, feet, lymphatic system, immune system)

- Stationary: April 6–7 in Pisces
- Post-Shadow but Direct: April 8–April 26

- Pre-Shadow but Direct: June 30–July 16
- Stationary: July 17–18 in Leo (children, love, creativity, sports, entertainment, happiness, ego, heart, spine, upper back)
- Retrograde: July 19–August 9 in Leo
- Stationary: August 10–11 in Leo
- Post-Shadow but Direct: August 12–August 25

- Pre-Shadow but Direct: October 21–November 8
- Stationary: November 9–10 in Sagittarius (travel, in-laws, foreigners, publishing, education, justice, truth, mass media, thighs, liver, hips)
- Retrograde: November 11–18 in Sagittarius
- Retrograde: November 19–28 in Scorpio (sexuality, intimacy, death, investments, partner's assets, shared resources, research, investigation, sexual organs, nose, bowels, reproductive organs)
- Stationary: November 29–30 in Scorpio
- Post-Shadow but Direct: November 31–December 17

Avoid: Signing documents, initiating new projects or diets, scheduling elective surgeries, publishing, or making big purchases.
Recommended: Editing work, backing up computers, practicing forgiveness, manifesting wishes, and exploring synchronicities.

♂ Mars (Action, Leadership, Research, Physical Strength, Warrior, Investigation, Passion & Sexuality)

- Retrograde: December 6, 2024–January 5, 2025, in Leo (children, love, creativity, sports, entertainment, happiness, ego, heart, spine, upper back)
- Retrograde: January 6, 2025–February 22, 2025, in Cancer (home, family, real estate, homeland, security, parenting, motherhood, womb, ribcage, hormones, breast, chest, stomach)

- Stationary: February 23—24 in Cancer
- Direct: February 25

Avoid: Undergoing elective surgeries (unless in an emergency), initiating wars (whomever shoots first loses), embarking on risky ventures, gambling, pushing individuals excessively (note to yoga instructors and personal trainers), starting a lawsuit or divorce, launching campaigns, making life-altering decisions, purchasing machinery (e.g., cars or appliances), commencing new intimate or sexual relationships, overtraining, overextending, or instigating fights and conflicts.

Recommended: Reassessing your fitness regimen, reconciling longstanding animosities or disagreements, embarking on new activities, finalizing pending projects, and revisiting your objectives, goals, passions, and strategies. This is an ideal time to modify behavior, as well as to learn the art of unwinding and relaxation. It's a prime moment to rally your troops and allies, reorganize, and rekindle bonds with those you consider sibling-in-arms.

♀ Venus (Relationships, Finances, Diplomacy, Justice, Law, Art, Values & Self-Worth)

This retrograde can create havoc with diplomacy, lawsuits, marriages and divorces, your relationships at work and personal life, art, design, and even our connection to Mother Nature. Expect interest rates to come down, as Venus retrograde is usually a good time to refinance and reexamine investments and loans.

- Stationary: March 1–2 in Aries (leadership, identity, your path in life, head, muscles, blood, eyes, vitality)
- Retrograde: March 3–26 in Aries
- Retrograde: March 27–April 11 in Pisces (intuition, meditation, dance, movement, empathy, imagination, dreams, hospitals, addictions, confinement, feet, lymphatic system, immune system)
- Stationary: April 12–13 in Pisces

Avoid: Starting a new relationship, abruptly ending a relationship, signing partnership agreements, making big purchases, plastic surgeries, buying artwork, getting married, getting engaged, overindulging, being tempted to return to exes, or starting a new lawsuit.

Recommended: Reevaluate your relationships, refinance your home, change your values, or reconnect with talents you might have abandoned or given up on.

♃ Jupiter (Travel, Truth, Education & Law)

- Retrograde: October 10, 2024–February 2, 2025, in Gemini (business, relatives, roommates, neighbors, communication, contracts, lungs, breathing, hands, nervous system)
- Stationary: February 3–4, 2025 in Gemini
- Direct: February 5—November 10 in Cancer (home, family, real estate, homeland, security, parenting, motherhood, womb, ribcage, hormones, breast, chest, stomach)
- Stationary: November 11–12 in Cancer
- Retrograde: November 13—March 11, 2026, in Cancer

Avoid: Since Jupiter retrogrades for an extended period each year, it's impractical to completely "close shop," but it's wise to steer clear of overoptimism, overconfidence, extravagance, gluttony, overindulgence, proselytizing, zealotry, dogmatism, neglecting legal matters, overpromising, and overcommitting. In short, be cautious of actions prefixed with "over." Additionally, be discerning of lies, deceptions, and half-truths. Neglecting kindness, hospitality (Jupiter was the protector of strangers), or denying aid to someone in need can unleash the furies upon you and backfire threefold.

Recommended: Revisit educational goals, study something you dropped in the past, and reconnect with your intuition.

♄ Saturn (Discipline, Career & Figures of Authority)

- Stationary: July 12–13 in Aries
- Retrograde: July 14–November 26 in Aries and Pisces
- Stationary: November 27–28 in Pisces

Avoid: If feasible, refrain from launching important long-term endeavors or clashing with superiors or parental figures. Additionally, don't be overwhelmed by feelings of melancholy or despondency; instead, go for a run or consider engaging in physical activities as an outlet.

Recommended: Focus on self-discipline, reevaluation of aspirations and goals, strategy adjustment, and revisiting past career objectives or ambitions that were overlooked or abandoned.

During Saturn's retrograde phases, his influence switches from external to internal. The discipline, persistence, endurance, focus, resilience, accountability, and pressure that characterize Saturn must come from within. Moreover, Saturn retrograde is a time to confront your karma (actions from past lives that reverberate in the present life). In other words, these retrograde periods present opportunities to settle karmic dues. Over the approximately four and a half months when Saturn retraces his path, it's vital to practice forgiveness, accept the imperfections of loved ones, and seek pardon from people you might have wronged.

SOLAR AND LUNAR ECLIPSES IN 2025

The etymology of the word "eclipse" in English is derived from the Greek word meaning "to leave out," and in Hebrew, the word for eclipse, "likui," suggests defect or lack. These rather gloomy connotations might be a bit misleading, as eclipses, both solar and lunar, are, in fact, periods when the New Moon (solar eclipse) and Full Moon (lunar eclipse) exhibit their fullest potential and influence, albeit untamed, unpredictable, and raw. There is a reason why eclipses have always been associated with terror, catastrophes, and mishaps. I prefer to look at eclipses as times when stagnation and inaction are replaced with a quickening, a heavenly awakening that shouldn't be classified as either good or bad. Eclipses are the wild card, the joker, the turbo function that shakes our lives and propels our life narrative forward.

Since the Sun and Moon's disks appear to be the same size, twice a year, when they perfectly align, they cover each other's faces, creating two occultation seasons, each having one solar and one lunar eclipse. The two weeks that separate the eclipses generate a great deal of synchronicities and stories that take about six months to unfold. In 2025, these seasons are between March 14–March 29 and between September 7–21.

- Lunar Eclipses (March 14 in Virgo and September 7 in Pisces) often signify the culmination of processes, evoking strong emotional responses. Typically, lunar eclipses influence employees, artists, parents, companies, communities, and groups. Lunar eclipses can unveil the more primal, instinctual aspects of your personality, like in the stories of werewolves transforming into their animalistic form under the Full Moon's eclipse.
- Solar Eclipses (March 29 in Aries and September 21 in Virgo) herald fresh starts and proactivity. They resonate with entrepreneurs, the self-employed, leaders, those considered untouchable (like Tucker Carlson, who was fired by Fox amidst the 2023 eclipses), and those with an active lifestyle. Generally, solar eclipses can introduce new life directions and serve as catalysts for personal transformations.

Dates of eclipses
- Total Lunar Eclipse: March 14 in Virgo. Easier on Scorpio, Capricorn, Taurus, and Cancer. Challenging for Virgo, Sagittarius, Pisces, and Gemini.
- Partial Solar Eclipse: March 29 in Aries. Easier on Aquarius, Sagittarius, Leo, and Gemini. Challenging for Aries, Capricorn, Libra, and Cancer.
- Total Lunar Eclipse: September 7, the Harvest Full Moon. Easier on Capricorn, Scorpio, Cancer, and Taurus. Challenging for Pisces, Sagittarius, Virgo, and Gemini.

- Partial Solar Eclipse: September 21 in Aries, a day before the Equinox. Since the eclipse is on the cusp of Virgo and Libra, it radiates challenging aspects for most signs.

PART II

SPECIAL GUEST STARS:

IMPORTANT DATES IN 2025

Although the dates provided below indicate the precise transits, the influence or effects of these planetary aspects often manifest a few days prior. In the part of the book dedicated to the signs, I provide interpretations of a few of the most important dates listed below for each zodiac sign. However, I suggest going over the dates listed here first to ensure successful planning for the year ahead.

JANUARY

- **January 1–5** (Mars opposite Pluto): Not a promising beginning to the year with the two rulers of Scorpio trading blows. With Mars also retrograde, take extra care as your actions might be misconstrued. There is an opposition between your will and that of your community, company, or friends. People around you might experience paranoia, resort to manipulation, conflict, and aggression.

- **January 3** (Venus in Pisces until February 4): Venus is exalted in Pisces, and you can now benefit from her mystical plunge. Opportunities to improve your finances, relationships, and artistic gifts manifest. Creative visualization can be extremely potent, and you can experience its fruits faster than normal. Faith healing, prayers, and any form of therapy are blessed. Divine love is in the air. Great for poetry, dance, photography, and meeting a significant other.

- **January 6** (Mercury square Neptune): The shady start of the year continues, with logic and intuition conflicting. Your gut tells you to do one thing, while your cortex rationalizes a reason not to do it. There could be deception and disillusionment. Hold your boundaries strong and steady.

- **January 6** (Mars retrogrades into Cancer until April 18): Mars doesn't like being in Cancer, his sign of fall. Be vigilant of accidents, falling (unless it is in love), and issues with water, leaks, and floods. Conflict can arise with family members.

- **January 7** (Eastern Orthodox Christmas): Happy Christmas to 12% of Christians who celebrate the holiday according to the Julian calendar. You are done with the 40-day fast and ready for the great feast!

- **January 8** (Mercury enters Capricorn until January 28): Serious thought, disciplined study, and lessons from mature and experienced figures. Slow your thought, speech, and writing. Be mindful of every word, take your time, and ground your ideas with discipline and strategy to bring them to fruition.

- **January 10–14** (Mars trine Neptune): At last, some good news. Action is supported by intuition, or perhaps your actions are your intuition.

A great day for yoga, spiritual activities, dreams, or any action by or in water.

- **January 12–13** (Sun trine Uranus): The positive trends continue with brilliance, clarity of mind, and original ingenious ideas. There could be good news regarding e-commerce, technology, your community, and science. A new friendship might be formed that leads you down an innovative path.

- **January 13** (Full Moon in Cancer): Today is Tu Be'Shvat, the fruit trees' New Year, according to Jewish scriptures. It could get emotional and a bit aggressive with family and loved ones due to the opposition of retrograding Mars and Pluto. You might feel overly emotional, so be careful of guilt casting.

- **January 14–15** (Venus squares Jupiter): Be mindful to avoid excessiveness, gluttony, and greed. You might experience immoderation and an attempt to appease everyone. There could be unexpected expenses.

- **January 15–16** (Sun opposite Mars): Conflict may occur from an unwelcome visit. Be careful not to over-assert yourself and come across as aggressive or pushy. You might feel or act more combative than you planned. Avoid choosing sides or being caught between warring factions.

- **January 18–19** (Venus conjunct Saturn): Things are getting serious in matters of the heart as well as finance. This is not necessarily a bad aspect as Venus is exalted and Saturn can ground your talents and help you use your gifts in a practical way. Whatever is going on in your personal and professional relationships is being galvanized and crystallized, for good or bad.

- **January 19** (Sun in Aquarius until February 18): We are all Aquarius for the next 30 days. It's a time to spend with friends and community, as well as immerse yourself in science, technology, and innovation. Make friends with AI and aliens, and don't be afraid to be original and somewhat quirky.

- **January 21–23** (Sun conjunct Pluto): Since Pluto is in the first degrees of Aquarius, as the Sun moves to the Water-Bearer sign, it activates the Lord of Death and Resurrection. There could be a meeting with a powerful or influential person or group of people today that holds the potential to transform your life.

- **January 23–24** (Mercury trine Uranus): The two most brilliant planets come together to bring new intellectual, business, and social connections into your life. Your IQ is getting a boost as well as your storytelling abilities. It's a great time for e-commerce and anything to do with futurism, AI, and innovation.
- **January 25–26** (Venus trine Mars): The two celestial lovers are meeting, bringing a new relationship or helping you harmonize your existing partnerships. It is a great day for dating, falling in love, connecting finance with passion, and creating practical art.
- **January 28** (Mercury in Aquarius until February 14): Mercury loves being in the fixed air sign of Aquarius. Ideas flow fast, and new friendships form with like-minded people. It's a great time to make new contacts and reconnect with old friendships.
- **January 28–29** (New Moon in Aquarius and Chinese New Year): Welcome to the Year of the Earth Snake. Jupiter is blessing this New Moon with wisdom and synchronicity. It's a great time to start a study group. You might join a group or meet an individual who can expand your horizons.
- **January 29** (North Node retrogrades into Pisces until August 19, 2026): Right on the New Moon in Aquarius, the North Node, aka "Dragon," retrogrades into the sign of mysticism, intuition, and imagination. For the next 18 months, we are asked to practice the positive qualities of Pisces: empathy, meditation, any form of trance, movement (yoga, dance, Pilates, martial arts), dreaming, poetry, imagination, and mystical experiences. At the same time, the South Node retrogrades in Virgo, asking us to let go of the overbearing qualities of Virgo such as criticism, perfectionism, and overanalyzing everything.
- **January 29** (Mercury conjunct Pluto): Obsessive thoughts can make this day a bit intense for your brain. On the other hand, it is a great time for transforming the way you perceive certain aspects of your life. It's great for research and investigation.

- **January 30–31** (Sun trine Jupiter): The Sun shines Jupiter's gifts. It's a day to feel good about yourself and your community. Wisdom, teaching, learning, and traveling are all blessed.
- **January 31–February 2** (Venus conjunct Neptune): A wonderful time for romance, art, and movement. Mysticism meets art. It's a wonderful time to ask the Universe for help in matters of the heart. Be careful of extramarital affairs.

FEBRUARY

- **February 1–2** (Venus conjunct Neptune): Venus kisses her higher octave, Neptune, and we experience their grace through artistic expression, romance, and mystical allure.
- **February 3** (Mercury trine Jupiter): Left and right brain are in balance, philosophy and logic interact. It's a great day for writing and conjuring pragmatic ideas. The two planets are in air signs, facilitating your communications, storytelling, sales, and connections with people (and pets) around us.
- **February 4** (Venus enters Aries until March 27): Venus is in her sign of exile, so she is not super thrilled. This can create conflict and strife with relationships and partners. Venus in Aries can make you feel a bit competitive with your partner, but she does favor action rather than words as expressions of love and devotion. Watch impulsiveness with your finances.
- **February 6–12** (Mars trine Saturn): What a treat! A weeklong of constructive action, stable effort, and sustained passion. This aspect can give you the endurance to complete a marathon or two. True, Mars is fallen and retrograde, but under the tutelage of Saturn and his leadership, the celestial soldier can fight your battles and bring about a few victories.
- **February 8–10** (Mercury conjunct Sun): Brilliance is in and around you. It's a great day for crafting words, smithing ideas, brainstorming, and finding an agent or a messenger to deliver your messages. With Mars and Saturn on good terms, these ideas and businesses, contacts and contracts can bring results.

- **February 10–12** (Mercury square Uranus): This challenging aspect brings about disruptions, uncertainty, explosiveness, and idiocy. I call this the aspect of populism—much ado about nothing.
- **February 12** (Full Moon in Leo): You might feel the pull and push between the gravitational forces of your children or romantic partner versus demands of friends or your company. The square with Uranus can cause disruption and lunacy during this lunation.
- **February 14** (Mercury enters Pisces until March 3): Mercury enters his sign of fall. Communications can be a bit challenged while intuition and mediumship are on the rise. Trust your gut more than your brain. Make sure to use the words "I feel" or "I imagine" or "I believe" rather than "I think."
- **February 18** (Sun enters Pisces until March 20's Equinox): We are all Pisces for the next 30 days. Imagination, dance, movement, dreaming, meditation, intuition, mysticism, and empathy are heightened. Just make sure to guard your boundaries and avoid addictions or self-destructive tendencies.
- **February 20** (Mercury squares Jupiter): You might be forced into writing or saying things you would later regret, so be extra cautious. In addition, thieves and robbers are on the prowl.
- **February 23** (Mercury trine Mars): A great day for business, negotiations, and walking the talk. The messenger of the gods and goddesses is in action mode, with speedy delivery of messages and ideas. Make sure your words are backed by action.
- **February 25** (Mercury conjunct Saturn): A great day for pragmatic mystical work. Dreams can be prophetic, and visions, practical intuition, and deep meditations are favored. However, words carry a great deal of karma. Serious thoughts and deep learning. There could be good rapport with mature people or superiors.
- **February 28** (New Moon in Pisces): A great day to start something new that involves your imagination, photography, movement, yoga, and meditation. There is a tendency to absorb negativity from others, so watch what you take in. Since Jupiter is squaring the New Moon,

there could be some conflict between reason and emotions. Be careful of overdoing or illusions.

- **February 28** (Ramadan begins until March 1): The ninth lunar month of the Islamic calendar commemorates Muhammad's first revelation of the Koran. This year Ramadan occurs in Pisces while both Saturn and the North Node are in the mystic sign, which means you too could receive a mystical call for action—a revelation.

MARCH

- **March 1–2** (Venus Stationary in Aries): Not only is Venus in her sign of exile, but now she is asked to walk backward in burning coals wearing her high heels. She is quick to anger, so make an effort to avoid conflicts or arguments with partners or lovers.
- **March 2–3** (Sun square Jupiter): Everything and everyone feels bigger than life. There is a danger of feeling overoptimistic as well as facing too many false opportunities. Make sure not to fall prey to deceptions and illusions.
- **March 3** (Venus retrogrades until April 14): Avoid getting married, starting new relationships, getting engaged, starting lawsuits, and signing partnership agreements. Exes or lovers from previous lives or this life might return. Be extra mindful with finances, as people tend to lose money or make bad investments. It's a good time to have money owed to you paid back as well as refinancing loans or mortgages.
- **March 3** (Mercury enters Aries until March 30): Mercury can be a bit impatient when in Aries and favors practical, short, and concise communication.
- **March 7–8** (Sun trine Mars): A great aspect for energy, determination, vitality, and leadership. It is a wonderful period for breakthroughs, taking control over life, and getting things done. Activities by and around water are recommended. Passion is in the air.
- **March 11–13** (Sun conjunct Saturn while Mercury conjunct Venus): Seriousness, focus, discipline, and planning can bring tactical or strategic accomplishments. It's a good time to connect with people

of authority and improve relations with superiors. Additionally, it's a good time to fix communication issues with partners in work or life.

- **March 14** (Pi Day and Lunar Eclipse in Virgo): Today symbolizes the intriguing blend of the infinite nature of Pi and its practical application in computing a circle's finite dimensions. It highlights the interplay between boundlessness and boundaries in the fabric of existence. How auspicious that today is also the Full Moon in the mathematically inclined Virgo. It's a great time to bring a project to an end and focus on diet, service, and combining your analytical and holistic aspects in life.

- **March 14–15** (Mercury Stationary): Here we go again, Mercury is standing still. It's a great time for reflection and meditation. Anything you need fixated and locked in, you can do today.

- **March 16–April 8** (Mercury Retrograde): You know the drill, avoid signing documents or starting new projects unless you have tried before and failed to complete. Be aware that the worst time of the retro (March 30–April 8) occurs when Mercury retrogrades into his sign of fall, Pisces. This could bring about melancholy, confusion, and disorientation. However, dreams and intuition are enhanced.

- **March 17** (Sun conjunct North Node): A powerful day for accessing skills and knowledge from past lifetimes. There could be an encounter with powerful and successful individuals or groups that can further your goals.

- **March 19–20** (Sun conjunct Neptune): Increased imagination, intuition, and channeling of information from above. You might feel a bit tired. A great deal of omens, synchronicities, and spiritual awakening.

- **March 20** (Equinox and the Sun in Aries until April 19): Happy New Year! The Astrological New Year is upon us. The most celebrated and holiest day in the Zodiac wheel, the March equinox incites us to spring into action despite the retrogrades. For the next 30 days, we are all Moses, Christ, Muhammad, and Da Vinci. It's a time to focus on your body, health, leadership, brand, and image. You are getting liberated from the slumber of Pisces, ready to heed the call of action.

- **March 22–23** (Sun conjunct Venus): A day of creativity, love, and balance. The collective unconscious is wide open for you to tap into your artistic side. A possible encounter with someone special, a significant other, or a lover. Today you look amazing!
- **March 24** (Sun conjunct Mercury): Another brilliant aspect of intellectual prowess. Messages from above and around are coming your way and can inspire you regardless of the Mercury retrograde.
- **March 26** (Mars square Chiron): The disobedient soldier. Watch out for injuries, accidents, and misuse of force.
- **March 26–28** (Venus conjunct Neptune): With Venus and Mercury retrograding, this conjunction brings you in contact with people, skills, gifts, and artistic abilities from previous lives. Let your imagination flow and you will experience a great deal of revelations in the next few days.
- **March 27** (Lilith enters Scorpio until December 20): Emotional intensity, powerful desires, fascination with the forbidden, shadow work, possessiveness, and jealousy. This unfortunate transit can bring about power struggles, manipulation, abuse, distrust, and criminality. Truly, the dark side of the Force. Stay clear of any form of gossip. It's a good time to place a heap of salt in the four corners of your bedroom for protection against negativity.
- **March 29–31** (Mercury conjunct Neptune): An interesting aspect that combines logic and intuition, reason and fantasy. A great book to read is the *Tao of Physics* by Capra, which combines modern physics with Daoism.
- **March 29** (Solar Eclipse in Aries): Eclipse season is upon us and events in the next two weeks are quickening and intensifying. Be mindful of unnecessary aggression and impulsiveness. Events and stories woven in the next two weeks can take six months to unfold.
- **March 30** (Mercury in Pisces until April 15): Mercury retrogrades into his sign of fall; communication can be extra hard as the messenger is not only retrograding but drowning in subjectivity. Talk and write from your heart rather than mind. Great for intuition and applying your imagination to overcome challenges.

- **March 30** (Neptune enters Aries until October 22): Perhaps the most important transit of the year. Confusion can lead to war, so be extra careful of fanaticism or aggression triggered by propaganda of misinformation. Watch your immune system, inflammation, and your head.
- **March 31–April 4** (Mars trine Saturn): A great aspect to close the month of Mars with the soldier under the tutelage of the general. Think of a Jedi in training. It's a great day for success and recognition.

APRIL

- **April 1** (Fool's Day): Today is a celebration of the Green Man, Idris, Mother Nature's son/lover. Plant a tree, go out to nature, and do something that connects you to your inner Druid. April 1st is the day of the Tarot card "The Fool," or "The Joker" of the playing cards. Both cards represent absolute potential as well as a leap of faith into something new. Making this day even more magical is the continuing Mars and Saturn trine that started March 31.
- **April 1–5** (Mars and Saturn sextile Uranus): A wonderful time for innovation and practical scientific breakthroughs in medicine and technology. A great time for brainstorming and coming up with pragmatic original solutions to old issues. The warrior is under the guidance of the brilliant general.
- **April 5–7** (Mars and Venus trine): Due to Venus' retrograde motion, she is back to forming a harmonious aspect with her secret lover, Mars. While she is exalted, he is fallen. While she is retrograding, he marches direct. They resemble Barbie and Ken, considering he's a professional "simply beach" dude, and indeed Mars is in Cancer, a water sign. These are great days for romance, increasing your income from talents you are passionate about, and better relationships with significant others as well as brothers and sisters in arms.
- **April 5–10** (Venus conjunct Saturn): Saturn can be a sugar daddy who is upset with Venus running around with dashing Mars. This aspect can introduce you to someone older who can be helpful with finance and developing your talents. This conjunction can also sit heavy over

your primary relationships. A time to reassess your close partnerships and how you make money.

- **April 6–7** (Mercury Stationary): We are at the tail end of the retrograde. I know you are impatient to engage with everything that was stuck, but please wait until after April 8.
- **April 8** (Mercury direct): All good to sign documents, make purchases, start new projects, etc. Let Mercury recover a bit as he is in Pisces, his sign of fall, until April 15. At that point, he returns to his former self while transporting in Aries.
- **April 7–16** (Mercury trine Mars): This is a great aspect for business, writing, marketing, sales, and any form of communication. An opportune time for making important decisions based on facts while linking your words and thoughts with action. Take control over the helm.
- **April 12** (Sun conjunct Chiron): A day of teaching, mentoring, healing childhood deep-seated wounds, and connecting to your inner warrior.
- **April 13** (Full Moon in Libra): One of the most powerful lunations of the year marking the story of Exodus, Passover, and the Last Supper. This is the day of liberation, coming out of constriction and negativity and marching towards your Promised Land. It is a magical Full Moon where you might connect to your inner Moses, guardian angel, or higher self.
- **April 14** (Saturn conjunct North Node): Positive interactions with groups of powerful individuals or people who are older. You are downloading some gifts or connections from previous lives. Good for joining new groups and organizations that share your long-term goals.
- **April 16–18** (Mercury conjunct Neptune): The planet of reason, logic, and objective communication must share bandwidth with the planet of intuition, channeling, and imagination. A day when your reptilian and cortex brains come together. A good time for faith healing, creative visualization, using imagination in your business and professional life as well as receiving messages from the beyond.
- **April 16** (Mercury enters Aries until May 10): A quick-tempered messenger, Mercury can speed things up but also show signs of impatience. Words can easily be weaponized. A good time to speak your mind and

assert your identity. You might experience aggression in your business and communication.

- **April 17–21** (Mars trine Neptune): Neptune is in trine with the ruler of the sign he is hosted by. This strengthens the connection between water and fire, reception and action, feminine and masculine. A great day to act according to your gut feeling or following omens, dreams, and vision quests. Activities in or around water are encouraged.

- **April 18** (Mars enters Leo until June 17): The knight in the service of the queen or king. Courtly love. Mars in Leo is called "Valor" and brings about a great deal of courage. Great for entertainment, sports, creativity, and reconnecting to your inner child.

- **April 19** (Sun enters Taurus until May 20): We are shifting gears into sensuous and luxurious Taurus, trading conquest for comfort, the yurt with a seven-star hotel. This month you are to indulge your six senses. It is a good month to tap into your artistic talents and perhaps discover new ones. Pay extra attention to your values and self-worth. This transit helps you connect with the Hierophant (one of the Tarot cards of the year) and ground sacredness.

- **April 20** (Easter): A day where you are coming out of the cave (womb) and reconnecting to the spark of God in you. A woman might be able to help you connect to your divine aspect just as Maria Magdalena was the first to see Jesus' resurrection.

- **April 22** (Earth Day): Always celebrated on the second or third day of Taurus, being the sign of Mother Nature. Spend time outdoors or gardening.

- **April 22–24** (Sun square the rulers of Scorpio—Mars and Pluto): This can bring about a great deal of letting go, death, and intense sexuality. Watch your steps these days, things can turn ugly or violent.

- **April 25–28** (Mars squares Pluto): The winds of war are in the air. The nasty aspect from April 22 continues, therefore, please be mindful not to add to the challenges and conflicts in the world and around you. Humanity seems to need a good dose of anger management therapy. Manipulations can turn aggressive.

- **April 27** (New Moon in Taurus): The exalted New Moon in Taurus is a giver of gifts. A great time to start a new artistic or financial project. Spend time in nature, connect to your senses, and do something that can symbolize rooting yourself. You are connecting to the Tree of Life today, a wonderful new beginning.
- **April 30** (Venus enters Aries until June 6): Venus doesn't like being under the sweaty and military Aries regiment. There could be a bit more conflict and aggression in your primary relationships. In her sign of exile, Venus might be somewhat snappy and can cause hasty decisions and actions with finances and love.
- **April 30** (Pluto squares Lilith): Darkness, manipulation, strife, and challenges. Take extra heed. You might be demonized and misunderstood.

MAY

- **May 1–3** (Venus conjunct Neptune): Happy Maypole Day (Whitsun)! A time to dance (Neptune) and fall in love (Venus). This tradition started in Roman Britain when soldiers would dance around decorated trees or poles with ribbons in honor of the goddess Flora and the arrival of spring. This year, a 2000-year-old tradition is colored by Venus, the planet that rules Taurus (Mother Nature), dancing with her higher octave, Neptune, the planet of imagination and mysticism. The first days of May are indeed blessed if you can find it in your heart to connect to your inner mystic and artist. This day of intuition can benefit your talents as well as your relationships and finances.
- **May 10** (Mercury enters Taurus until May 26): A sense of worry and anxiety, do not fret about things you have no control over. A good time to communicate and market, as well as sell, your talents and gifts. Speak your mind without attachment or inflexibility.
- **May 12** (Mercury square Pluto): This is not an easy aspect that can bring about obsessive thoughts and compulsive behaviors. However, it's a good time to get to the bottom of issues as well as investigate the root causes of problems. Great for therapy.

- **May 12** (Full Moon in Scorpio): The Full Moon in May is when the Lord Buddha was born, attained enlightenment, and died. While the Moon in Scorpio is fallen, it is great for shadow work, dealing with temptation, and discovering the light within you. Because the Moon falls on the 22nd (Master Number) degree of Scorpio, we can build something out of the rubble of an older project or relationship. In this lunation, you feel the tug of war between "mine" and "yours." A great deal of passion and sexuality, just make sure you channel it the right way. Since Uranus is also involved in this lunation, take extra heed as there is a Wild Card in this Full Moon that can bring about an unexpected event or situation.
- **May 17–18** (Sun conjunct Uranus): Everyone's IQ is getting a temporary elevation. A fantastic day for humor, jumping into the unknown, and embracing the original and innovative. Spend time with friends or in a group.
- **May 17–18** (Mercury squares Mars): Spend time with friends while being aware that some of them might make you angry or say things they would later regret. There is intellectual aggression and people could show their nastier side.
- **May 20** (Sun enters Gemini until June 21): We are all Gemini for the next 30 days, channeling the spirit of intelligence, communication, and bridge-building. This is a great month for business, contracts, improving relationships with relatives, roommates, neighbors, and folks you consider siblings. Find your message, your way of delivering it, as well as your audience.
- **May 20–24** (Venus trine Mars): Once again (due to the back and forth of the retrograde Venus), Venus and Mars are going on a date, and we are influenced by their glowing stardust love. Romance, love, and harmony (the daughter of Venus and Mars) are around you, as well as an ability to see people's beautiful side. It's a great time for making money from things you are passionate about.
- **May 24** (Mercury conjunct Uranus): A day of ingeniousness. You can get new insights and ideas that can help you in business, communication,

and better connect with people around you. Do something intellectually stimulating and share your thoughts and ideas with your peers.

- **May 24–25** (Sun trine Pluto): This powerful aspect is all about energy, strength, and the ability to manifest things you desire. The Sun and Pluto are both in air signs, therefore your friends and community can help you bring your projects to fruition. It's also a good time for therapy, transformation, magic, intimacy, and sexuality.

- **May 25** (Saturn enters Aries until September 1): Saturn moves to his sign of fall for the first time in 30 years. This round he is just testing the fire, so to speak, and in February 2026 he will move there permanently for two years. Saturn in Aries wishes to rectify how we deal with our identity, body, anger, and vitality. While Saturn is in Aries, we are all asked to assume the role of a leader and liberator, prompting us to become a Moses, Christ, Muhammad, or Da Vinci, all proud Aries.

- **May 26** (Mercury enters Gemini until June 8): Mercury is back to his domicile, and he is happy to unpack and chill. Information, opportunities, connections, and words flow effortlessly.

- **May 27** (New Moon in Gemini): A great day to start something new in connection with communication, networking, businesses, marketing, sales, and written projects. This New Moon is blessed by Pluto and Neptune, making it possible for you to link passion and reason, emotions and intellect. There is a great deal of intimacy and a possibility for a lover coming into your life.

- **May 29–30** (Sun conjunct Mercury): With both the Sun and Mercury in Gemini, it is an opportune time to deliver your messages, build bridges, write, start new businesses, and make new connections. There could be a connector around you, like an agent or an angel that can bring you to your destination.

JUNE

- **June 4–8** (Venus, Jupiter, Mercury, and Mars in minor benevolent aspects): The month kicks off with short-lived graceful windows of opportunities that can improve sales, communication, writing, health, education, and art.

- **June 6** (Venus enters Taurus until July 4): Venus is happy to be back home to her sign and could lend a helping hand in matters of art, finances, and security. You will experience your five senses in a much stronger way than usual, perhaps getting a glimpse of the sixth one as well. It's a great time to connect to an artistic project or talent and relink your gifts to the way you generate your income.

- **June 8** (Mercury conjunct Jupiter): The philosopher and engineer come together to offer help with studies, teaching, writing, travel, and mass media. It's a great day for communication and publishing, but be aware that Saturn is tainting this aspect with frustration and delays. The two intellectual guides, Mercury and Jupiter, are conjoining in the last degree of Gemini. While Jupiter is impatient to finally move into his sign of exaltation, Mercury laments that he needs to leave his domicile in Gemini and dive into emotional Cancer. Therefore, use these transits to look at things from above and connect the dots instead of being too binary or particular.

- **June 8** (Mercury enters Cancer until June 26): Mercury in Cancer favors "I feel" over "I think." It is not a terrible position for Mercury; after all, it is easier to recall information if it carries an emotional component. It's a great transit for healing relationships with family members. Don't be afraid of expressing your feelings.

- **June 9** (Mercury squares Neptune and Saturn): Two challenging aspects come together. It's a day you should relax and avoid big projects. There is deception, lies, theft, and disinformation. Monkey mind is out of the cage, causing us to jump from one subject or project to the other.

- **June 9–10** (Venus squares Pluto): The challenges of the day are emphasized by this hard aspect. Breakups, manipulation, and discord with people of power.

- **June 9** (Jupiter enters Cancer until June 30, 2026): This is great news for us all. Wherever you have Cancer in your chart (planets or houses) will experience breakthroughs and opportunities. Jupiter leaves his sign of exile where he could not share his bounty freely and moves into his sign of exaltation, thus the king of the gods and goddesses is able to bestow his grace upon us. This is a great year for real estate, healing familial relationships, connecting to fortune and abundance, and opening new doors. Be careful of overdoing and overcommitments.

- **June 10** (Saturn conjunct Neptune until August 23): Two and a half months of a challenging aspect connecting Saturn (karma) and Neptune (self-destruction). The conjunction takes place on the cusp of Pisces and Aries. Like everything in life, it is a blessing and a curse. While your intuition, ability to meditate, and connect to your dreams is enhanced, so would your self-destructiveness, addictions, and escapism. Tread carefully, and watch out for fanaticism or being too attached to your beliefs.

- **June 10–20** (Jupiter squares Saturn): Jupiter (opportunities) is stifled by Saturn (restrictions). There is a tendency to place your energy, love, and creativity in the wrong places. Limiting circumstances, your work goes unappreciated, and you might feel sadness and despondency. However, it is a good time to change direction and try a new way of approaching your goals.

- **June 11** (Full Moon in Sagittarius): A blessed Full Moon in a challenging month. Jupiter, ruler of Sagittarius, is exalted, creating what is called "Mutual Reception" with the Moon. This is an auspicious aspect and can facilitate your personal as well as professional life. It's a wonderful time to complete a cycle of learning and get ready for something new. Great for travel, especially by water or to a location close to the water. Mars gives a boost of energy to the lunation. Stay away from inauthenticity to receive the magic of the Moon.

- **June 13–16** (Mars squares Uranus): Mars and Uranus are joining the already difficult aspects of June with their own set of challenges. Be extra careful of accidents, impulsiveness, explosive behaviors, and misplaced energy. Mars is out of control and seeks freedom. There is a strong urge to break free.

- **June 15–21** (Jupiter square Neptune): The two rulers of Pisces are arguing while Neptune is also conjunct the Lord Karma, Saturn. If you were a pilot, I would tell you to ground your plane, and if you were a captain, to return your vessel back to port. There could be a sense of overwhelmed emotional distress. We are drowning in a sea of confusion. It is vital to meditate and spend time in nature. Whatever helps you focus, this is the time to do it. June is a tough month, but crisis always brings opportunities if you are willing to change direction and try new approaches.

- **June 17** (Mars enters Virgo until August 6): Mars in Virgo gets things done. He is the watchmaker, the engineer, the organizer—here to protect and serve. Conflicts can arise if you are too critical of yourself and others. It's a good time for diets and a new health regimen. You can make things happen as long as you stick to a strict routine.

- **June 21** (Sun enters Cancer until July 22): Happy Solstice! One of the four holiest days of the year. Today is dubbed the "Gateway of Humanity," the original concept of baptism and purification of the waters of compassion. For the next month, we are all Cancers. Use "I feel" instead of "I think," and open your heart to your family. Perhaps you might meet family members from past lives. It's a great month to renovate and remodel your home, relocate, move in with someone, get a new property, or start a family.

- **June 24–25** (Sun conjunct Jupiter): There is help coming your way, a mentor, teacher, or guide. This aspect feels like a lighthouse in a stormy month.

- **June 25** (New Moon in Cancer): The Moon returns home to Cancer, providing a new beginning that involves home and family, real estate, security, and emotional support. With Jupiter exalted in Cancer, blessing the union of the Sun and Moon, this is a great time to start new projects. Besides Pluto, there are no planets retrograde, so full steam ahead!

- **June 26** (Mercury in Leo until September 3): This Mercury transit can be extremely creative, entertaining, and exciting.

- **June 27–28** (Mercury trine Saturn and Neptune): Another window opens for some light to come.

JULY

- **July 4** (Venus conjunct Uranus): Venus revisits Uranus, the revolutionary mad professor. Relationships can be exciting and full of unpredictability. There is a need for freedom and exploration of new frontiers with your finances, relationships, and artistic expression. Embrace the original and unique. Be extra aware of potential volatility in the market.

- **July 4** (Venus enters Gemini until July 31): Venus begins her flirtation with Gemini. Since the Tarot card of Gemini is "The Lovers," these next few weeks can bring you in contact with a potential lover or work partner. Art and communication link, making this a great time for marketing, sales, design, and making new connections.

- **July 4** (Neptune retrogrades until December 12): Be extra careful with deceptions, illusions, confusion, and relapses of past addictions and codependent relationships. However, it's a good time to return to meditation, yoga, dance, or any movement or mystical practices that served you in the past. Keep a dream journal; you might get many messages from your subconscious.

- **July 6–7** (Venus trine Pluto): This aspect is great for investments, productions, working with other people's money and talents, and participating in larger-than-life projects. Improved relationships with significant others and work partners.

- **July 7** (Uranus enters Gemini until November 8): The planet of technology moves to the binary sign of Gemini for the first time in 84 years. Everyone's IQ is augmented, and we can expect significant scientific breakthroughs, especially in healthcare, computing, AI, quantum technology, aerospace, and possibly communications with aliens (from 2026, Uranus will settle in Gemini for seven years).

- **July 10** (Full Moon in Capricorn): The lunation can bring about an opposition between your need to focus on home and career. The Moon is exiled in Capricorn and can create a sense of emotionality and longing for a paradise lost. However, Mars is sending his troops to help, and with a bit of action, determination, and a clear mission, you can disperse the emotional confusion of the Full Moon and get things done.

- **July 12** (Saturn retrogrades until November 29): Lord Karma is retrograding, taking us back in time to previous lives. Actions from your current life and past ones are creating a reaction. It might be harder to connect to discipline. Your goals might need to be adjusted and refined. There also could be issues with superiors and authority figures.
- **July 17–18** (Mercury stationary in Leo): As Prince suggested in his song *Positivity*, "Hold on to your soul, we got a long way to go!" A good time for meditation and anchoring things in your life that you want to keep going for a while.
- **July 19** (Mercury retrograde until August 12): The Queen (Leo) of Hearts (the organ ruled by Leo) is screaming, "Off with their head!" You know the drill. Avoid signing documents and starting new projects. Watch your relationships and communication with kids, lovers, and people with big egos.
- **July 21–24** (Venus squares Mars): The celestial lovers are filing for divorce. All types of relationships can be challenged these days, whether personal or professional. Find it in your heart to have compassion for your significant others and those surrounding you. However, you might find that some of these challenges lead you to new talents and income potential. Don't make rash decisions regarding breakups or unions with partners.
- **July 22** (Sun enters Leo until August 22): Connect to your inner lion during these 30 days. Engage in creative, joyful, and heartwarming activities. Generosity, nobility, chivalry, sportsmanship, and enthusiasm guide us this month. It's a great time to connect to a hobby or a new sport.
- **July 23–25** (Sun trine Saturn and Neptune): One good thing about the conjunction of Saturn and Neptune is that when the Sun trines one, he also trines the other. This means we have a wonderful flow of vitality, intuition, healing, and the ability to bring new structure into our lives. This is a glorious aspect, and you can benefit from creative visualizations, meditation, dance, and any form of self-expression.
- **July 24** (New Moon in Leo): This is not an easy New Moon since it is opposite Pluto and can bring about confrontations with powerful figures

whose motivations are unclear. With Mercury retrograding in Leo, it's not the best time to start something new, but you could initiate a project you already tried before and failed to complete.

- **July 30** (Chiron goes retrograde until January 4, 2026): The Wounded Healer retrograding allows us to go deeper into our healing and overcome issues with identity and self-expression. It's a time to connect to shamanism, herbology, and physical therapy.

- **July 31** (Sun conjunct Mercury): This is a great aspect for intellectual clarity and the ability to express yourself and your ideas. Either you or someone around you can serve as an angel or a messenger. There is a great deal of logic and intuition, objectivity and subjectivity.

- **July 31** (Venus enters Cancer until August 25): Venus is putting on her swimsuit and jumping into the waters of Cancer. In the Tarot cards, the Two of Cups, dubbed "Love," is the best description of this transit. Marriage, social events with family members, and harmonious flow with family members.

AUGUST

- **August 1** (Sun conjunct Mercury): Another day of intellectual clarity and mindful deliberation. While Mercury is retrograde, much can still be achieved. It's a great time to try new strategies and connect to sources of information and data that can help your business and writing.

- **August 1–2** (Venus square Saturn and Neptune): Watch out for deception, illusions, and fantasies in your primary relationships and financial dealings. Not the best time to start a new relationship. Rapport with people who are older than you can be fraught with discord. Try a new approach to an old problem.

- **August 6** (Mars enters Libra until September 22): Mars the warrior is asked to surrender his sword. Not Mars' favorite position, but he could excel in fighting for peace. There could be legal issues coming up. However, it's a good time for compromises and finding resolutions to conflicts.

- **August 7–9** (Mars trine Uranus): Brilliance and originality are in the air. Mars is stepping into a spacecraft, very much like the character

Han Solo from Star Wars. Search for innovative and original solutions. Connections with friends can thrive. Action is guided by new approaches.

- **August 8–10** (Mars opposite Saturn and Neptune): Saturn is trying to take down Mars' spacecraft before it has a chance to leave the atmosphere. There could be accidents, mishaps, and physical challenges, especially since Mercury is retrograding. Avoid arguments with superiors, stay calm, and try to do less. The opposition with Neptune adds more hardships to an already difficult period. Stay away from stormy seas (metaphysically and physically speaking). Nightmares and panic are inside and around you.

- **August 9–11** (Mars trine Pluto): Mars resurrects with the help of Pluto, his Scorpio co-ruler. This is a great aspect for investments, financial gains, inheritance, and retrieving money or assets that belong to you. Sexuality, passion, and letting go of grief. Just be mindful that Mercury is stationary, so it's not a good time to start anything new.

- **August 9** (Full Moon in Aquarius): Welcome to the Biblical Day of Love. It's a day traditionally spent with lovers, best friends, and children. You might feel a push and pull between the need to have quality time with lovers or your children and demands presented by your friends or company.

- **August 10–11** (Mercury Stationary): The last days of the retrograde can be especially hard, so a bit of patience is needed.

- **August 12** (Mercury direct in Leo): The lioness is released from captivity and ready to hunt. Remember we still have the post-retrograde shadow for about a week or so, but still, it feels like things are moving forward full steam ahead.

- **August 12–13** (Venus conjunct Jupiter): One of the best aspects this year, the coming together of the two benevolent planets. Luck, flow in finances, new relationships, and maybe a novel love.

- **August 12–October 27** (Uranus trine Pluto): A powerful aspect that can bring about transformation through technology, science, social movements, and revolutions. Changes in government that can, in the long run, bring more prosperity.

- **August 22** (Sun in Virgo until September 22): We are all Virgos for the next 30 days. We are asked to focus and refine our diet, health, routine, work, and how we serve. It's an ideal time to eliminate impediments to health and productivity.
- **August 23** (New Moon in Virgo): A great time for a new diet, work project, or service. It's recommended to reorganize your home and office or home office. A bit of chaos is added by a square to Uranus that can awaken the critic and perfectionist in you. Try to channel these propensities into something productive at work.
- **August 23–24** (Sun square Uranus): This aspect of unpredictability and revolution can bring about unnecessary change. Do not become a rebel without a cause. However, this can also awaken a new original way of expressing yourself.
- **August 25** (Venus enters Leo until September 19): The planet of love in the sign of romance is always good news. Just be careful of extramarital affairs. It's a very creative time with your inner child active and playful. It's a great time to reconnect to a hobby you had in your teens. Be careful of pointless drama.
- **August 25–27** (Venus trine Saturn and Neptune): A delightful aspect of art, design, justice, and romance. Long-term plans and relationships are favored.

SEPTEMBER

- **September 1** (Saturn in Pisces until February 13, 2026): Saturn returns to Pisces, where he has been transiting since March 2023. Expect a rise in religious fanaticism, confusion, floods, and conflicts about water or in locations close to seas, lakes, and rivers. Ground your mystical practices, dreams, and intuition.
- **September 2** (Mercury in Virgo until September 18): Mercury, in his sign of exaltation, is in full thrust, pushing words, sales, ideas, and information. This is a great time for projects that demand precision, micromanagement, organization, and information. A wonderful opportunity for detoxing and cleansing.

- **September 3** (Mercury square Uranus): A somewhat peculiar day. Ingenious ideas or impractical people might take center stage. Information could be scattered, and you might feel absent-minded. Laughter, humor, and thinking outside the box are recommended.
- **September 3–6** (Mars square Jupiter): There is a tendency to overdo, overreach, and take on too many things at once. Anger and discord could flare into full conflicts, so be mindful of what you do, say, and write.
- **September 5** (Uranus retrogrades until February 5, 2026): Uranus retreats to his lab, prompting us to reevaluate our connections with friends, affiliates, clubs, groups, and companies. Revolutions, riots, and issues with governments may arise.
- **September 7** (Full Moon in Pisces): Welcome to the Harvest Full Moon and Lunar Eclipse! Momentum builds towards closure, especially in work and personal affairs. It's time to harvest the fruits of your labor from March/April. Mercury provides a touch of reason to an otherwise very emotional lunation.
- **September 10** (Sun opposite North Node): A talent you have worked on for many lifetimes might make an appearance. It's also time for a fresh outlook on all aspects of life, especially primary relationships. Let go of familial patterns from your father's side of the family.
- **September 12–14** (Sun conjunct Mercury): Enjoy clear thinking, effective marketing, and precise communication, making it a prime time for forging new connections and plans. Jupiter and Venus bless the union of Apollo (Sun) and Hermes (Mercury), who were good friends as well as half-brothers. It's a good day for business, contracts, writing, and hanging out with friends.
- **September 17–18** (Mercury opposite Saturn and Neptune): Reflect deeply on your long-term aspirations, adjusting if necessary. You or someone close might come across as stubborn or biased. Avoid disputes with colleagues or superiors. You might feel an opposition between intuition and reason. Integrate what your gut and brain are telling you.
- **September 18** (Mercury in Libra until October 6): Mercury seeks peace, compromise, and beauty. It's a great time for healing

relationships and harmonizing the workplace. Link artistic talents with your business and work. Revamp your website, redesign your logo, and come up with new ways to brand yourself and your projects. Compromises, negotiations, diplomacy, and mediations are welcomed and reinforced.

- **September 19** (Mercury trine Uranus and Pluto): An aspect of intelligence, science, and community. The three planets form a golden triangle of protection and luck. Neptune and Saturn assist the flow, and since this benevolent aspect is happening in Virgo, it can improve your health, diet, and work.

- **September 19** (Venus enters Virgo until October 13): Venus doesn't like to be in her sign of fall, like a fashion influencer asked to wear a nun's uniform and join a monastery. You might feel overcritical about your art or partners and feel the criticism of others directed toward you. Gain from being solo or practicing self-sufficiency. It's a good time to be frugal, balance your expenses and income, and detox.

- **September 20–24** (Sun opposite Saturn and Neptune): Connect to discipline and focus on endurance, persistence, and strategy. There could be pushback from people of authority or demanding bosses. However, the opposition with Neptune can add intuition, imagination, and a dreamlike quality to the mix.

- **September 21** (Solar Eclipse in Virgo): Right before the equinox, this lunation is granted much more power. Balance your diet, start a new work project, and get the energy you need to reach the finish line. The Eclipse pushes the planets to bestow their gifts: Pluto (power and intimacy), Saturn (focus), Neptune (imagination and intuition), and Uranus (innovation).

- **September 22** (Sun enters Libra until October 23): Happy Equinox! The masculine phase of the year transitions gracefully into its feminine counterpart. As one of the four sacred days in the astrological calendar, commemorate it by celebrating relationships, justice, beauty, and art. Over the next 30 days, everyone should embody Libra traits—diplomacy, equilibrium, justice, and attentiveness to partners.

- **September 22** (Mars enters Scorpio until November 4): Mars is thrilled to be back in his sign, propelling us into action. It's a wonderful time to collaborate on big projects that demand a lot of energy and resources. Passion, intimacy, and sexuality are on the rise. Great for physical activities in water or reconnecting to sports you are passionate about. It's an opportune time for research and investigation, as well as fighting for what you believe in.
- **September 23–24** (Sun trine Uranus and Pluto): A great deal of ideas, creativity, innovation, and invention, not to mention exciting new friends and connections. It's great for e-commerce and social media businesses.
- **September 23–25** (Mars square Pluto): The two rulers of Scorpio are in battle, forcing us into actions we might later regret. Be extra careful of aggression or manipulative folks. Take extra heed in general. Actions can be easily misconstrued.

OCTOBER
- **October 1–2** (Mercury square Jupiter): Words are cheap these days, so better listen rather than talk. Be careful not to waste ideas, time, money, or connections on mindless endeavors or chitchat.
- **October 6** (Mercury enters Scorpio until October 29): An ideal period for research, finding lost objects or people, and expressing intimacy. Mercury is known as the psychopomp—the guide of souls to the realm of the dead. It's a good time to move on, let bygones be bygones, bury the zombies in your life, and explore investments and collaborations with other people's assets and talents. Mercury can be your private investigator and expose hidden information.
- **October 7** (Full Moon in Aries): This Full Moon, bordering on a lunar eclipse, is a tad challenging. With Chiron's involvement, it's an occasion for learning, teaching, and shamanistic journeys. While there's an aggressive undertone, it's a good moment to conclude matters and move on. There could be conflicts with partners in life or work.
- **October 11** (Venus opposite Saturn): This is not an easy aspect for your relationships or finances. There is emotional frustration with partners, especially long-term ones.

- **October 13–14** (Venus opposite Neptune): The challenges in relationships continue with Neptune creating illusions as well as dependency and codependency. There might be disappointment with someone you placed on a pedestal only to learn they are not what you expected. Be careful of unwarranted expenditure. However, you can use this aspect to connect mysticism and art.
- **October 13** (Venus enters Libra until November 6): Venus is so happy to be out of the cloister just in time for fashion week. She is back in her sign and can now help us connect to beauty, diplomacy, justice, relationships, and harmony.
- **October 14–15** (Venus trine Uranus and Pluto): Taking place while the Sun transits in Libra, ruled by Venus, it's a great treat to have Venus receive such praise from Pluto (intimacy, sexuality, power) and Uranus (innovation, technology, friendships). This is a powerful time for igniting, transforming, balancing, and solidifying partnerships in work and personal life.
- **October 15** (Pluto direct): The planet associated with banking, sexuality, passion, intimacy, and death begins its direct motion after retrograding for nearly half a year. Investments that were held back begin to flow again, as does your personal power, magic, and healing abilities.
- **October 16** (Sun square Jupiter): Be careful of excessiveness and over-commitments. There are many inflated egos around you, so make sure you are not one of these balloons. However, this aspect can give you the courage and strength to deal with hardships.
- **October 19–21** (Mercury conjunct Mars): A good time for campaigning, starting a new business, and taking on a leadership position. Be mindful of how you communicate since you might come across more aggressively than intended.
- **October 21** (New Moon in Libra): Dubbed the "Moon of Peace," the Libra New Moon is a great time to start a relationship or an art project. However, both Jupiter and Pluto are squaring off with the Sun and Moon, creating uncomfortable situations. Be extra cautious and focus on breathwork and meditation.

- **October 22** (Neptune enters Pisces until January 27, 2026): Neptune is back to his sign for the last time in 165 years. This is the last chance to start a deep meditation practice facilitated by the ruler of mysticism. Dreams, imagination, channeling, mediumship, poetry, and art are enhanced.

- **October 23** (Sun enters Scorpio until November 22): For the next 30 days, we are all Scorpios. Focus on being true to your passion. It's a month of healing, transformation, magic, occult, and assisting others in their talents, finances, and endeavors.

- **October 24–25** (Sun square Pluto): This aspect brings intense energy, which can be harnessed for good or bad. Avoid manipulative individuals with dubious reputations, as they might be drawn to you or you to them. We are entering the realm of Scorpio, and Pluto, its ruler, takes the intensity to the next level.

- **October 24–26** (Mercury trine Jupiter and Saturn): This aspect mitigates some of the intensity and brings about communication flow and intellectual clarity. This aspect creates a triangle of protection when we need it most. An older individual can come to your aid. Long-term projects and endeavors involving foreigners or education can be extra successful.

- **October 26** (Mars conjunct Lilith): Be extra careful today as the Mother of Demons hires an assassin. This is a violent and aggressive aspect. Tread cautiously.

- **October 27–30** (Mars trine Jupiter and Saturn): Full force ahead with Mars (energy) lending his skills and power to Jupiter (opportunities) and guided by Saturn (focus, career). Another positive grand aspect is taking off with Pluto (power) leading the way. This is an opportune time to collaborate on big projects. There is also a sense of closeness with people, shared resources, and common purpose.

- **October 29** (Mercury enters Sagittarius until November 19): Mercury in his sign of exile makes you feel absent-minded and distracted. It's a good time for traveling and doing business with foreigners. Stick to the truth and avoid liars and half-truths. Great for education and publishing.

- **October 30–31** (Jupiter trine Saturn): This is another promising aspect right for Halloween, the day when the veil between reincarnations is the thinnest. You can truly make your wishes come true. You might encounter a teacher or a mentor who can take you to the next level. Happy Celtic New Year!

NOVEMBER

- **November 1–December 4** (Jupiter trine Saturn): This aspect started on October 30 and will continue throughout the month. Sometimes we need to thank our lucky stars for retrograding since this is the reason we enjoy this helpful aspect for such a long time. Jupiter provides opportunities while Saturn lends his focus and manifestation skills to bring these blessings into reality. You find joy in your chores. Despite the looming Mercury retrograde, this month can bring a great deal of success and positivity.
- **November 2–3** (Venus square Jupiter): Beware of issues in finances and love, indulgence, and gluttony. You might feel enslaved to pleasure or a need to satisfy someone who can never get satiated. This aspect can bring about wastefulness and needless expenses.
- **November 3–5** (Mars opposite Uranus): Be extra careful of accidents and mishaps involving aggression, impatience, speed, or sharp objects. You might experience erratic behavior that doesn't make sense, as well as gadgets and machines breaking or malfunctioning. The robot is out of control.
- **November 3–5** (Mars trine Neptune): While Mars might not get along with Uranus the scientist, he is having a ball with Neptune, the mystic. Another benevolent aspect is forming, helping us soar into mystical heights. Action is guided by empathy and intuition. You might do things that, in hindsight, appeared guided by psychic premonition. This is a great aspect for any form of movement that can balance and connect you to your true self.
- **November 4** (Mars enters Sagittarius until December 15): Mars loves Sagittarius, where he can practice riding horses, motorbikes, or

anything that allows him to travel at speed. This is a call for adventure and an expedition. Your Mars wants you to conquer, hunt, and expand your knowledge.

- **November 5** (Full Moon in Taurus): This is a powerful exalted Full Moon. It's an opportune time to bring something into completion. Since the lunation is on the 13th degree of Scorpio, it carries a powerful connection to love and oneness (the Gematria value of 13). Spend time in nature and indulge your five senses.

- **November 6** (Venus enters Scorpio until November 30): Venus in her sign of exile can cause us to feel alone or unwanted, possessive, and jealous. However, it's a good time to focus on your partner's money and talents rather than your own. Look into your investments as there might be a need to make some adjustments.

- **November 7–8** (Venus square Pluto): This aspect can create tension in your primary relationships and contacts. Manipulation, power struggles, and breakups. Navigate your intimate relations with caution and choose your investments of time, energy, and money wisely.

- **November 8** (Uranus returns to Taurus until April 26, 2026): Uranus was in Taurus from 2018, and this is his final visit to Taurus in the next 84 years. Expect changes in finances, fluctuations in cryptocurrency, and new ways of expressing artistic talents.

- **November 9–10** (Mercury Stationary): Here we go again, things are starting to stand still. It's a great day for doing things you want to last forever, so be mindful.

- **November 11** (Mercury retrograde until December 1): Avoid signing documents or starting new projects. This retrograde dances on the cusp of Sagittarius (where Mercury overthinks) to Scorpio (where he's secretive). Avoid signing documents, starting new projects, and initiating anything unless you tried to do so before and failed to accomplish.

- **November 12–13** (Mercury conjunct Mars): Mercury in exile is aggravated by Mars, which can cause us to communicate in an aggressive way. It's a good time for therapy, reflecting on your anger issues, and voicing yourself in a different way.

- **November 16–17** (Sun trine Jupiter and Saturn): A beautiful triangle of protection in the middle of a chaotic month. The Sun brings vitality and power to your projects. This aspect can help in physical healing and deliver a new sense of direction. Philosophy and wisdom abound.
- **November 19** (Mercury trine Neptune): Logic and reason are in service of intuition and empathy. This is a great aspect for communicating in an imaginative and creative way. You will feel like you are channeling information from beyond. You are gaining a deeper understanding of life.
- **November 19** (Mercury enters Scorpio until December 10): Mercury returns to Scorpio as he retrogrades back into the Underworld. Good for investigations and finding lost objects and people.
- **November 20** (Sun conjunct Mercury): This continues the positive aspect of communication and business that started on November 19. Intellectual clarity and good connections with powerful people.
- **November 20** (New Moon in Scorpio): A great time to investigate your passions, what you really want in life, and what you wish to transform. It's a good New Moon to initiate projects that need shared resources, talents, or funding. However, since Mercury is retrograde, you can only start things you already did in the past and failed to bring to completion. This is an opportune time to initiate healing, therapy, a shamanistic journey, or an investigation. The New Moon is getting a boost from Saturn, Jupiter, and Neptune, which bless this lunation with structure and focus, imagination and inspiration, and a great deal of open-mindedness.
- **November 21** (Sun Opposite Uranus): Revolutions, calls for change, and disruptions. Leaders, bosses, and the self-employed could have a problematic day. On the other hand, there is a great deal of originality and innovation.
- **November 22** (Sun enters Sagittarius until December 21): For the next 30 days, we are all centaurs, shooting arrows to the stars. Sagittarius is the time of the year when we have the strongest connection to our higher self or guardian angel. This is a month for teaching, mentoring,

learning, speaking your truth, mass media, publishing, and connecting to foreigners and in-laws.

- **November 23** (Sun trines Neptune; Mercury trines Jupiter and Saturn; Jupiter trines Saturn): What a busy day, and mind you, busy at being great. Today you can further your goals in almost all aspects of life.
- **November 25** (Mercury conjunct Venus): A great day for relationships, generating possibilities that can augment your finances, talents, and gifts. This is a blessed day for promoting yourself and expressing how you can make the world a better place.
- **November 26–27** (Venus trine Jupiter and Saturn): It's a great time for relationships, especially with teachers or people who are older than you. This is an opportune time for improving your position with bosses and superiors. This aspect brings luck and fortune.
- **November 28** (Venus conjunct Lilith): Be extra careful with all your relationships and partners in work or personal life. A three-sided relationship might form around you. Beware of stalkers, gossip, enemies, and lawsuits.
- **November 29** (Venus opposite Uranus): Meetings with highly intelligent but rather strange people might occur. There could be some unexpected challenges and oppositions with partners or relations.
- **November 30** (Venus in Sagittarius until December 24): Venus is putting on her safari outfit and is ready with her overpacked luggage for an exotic journey. This is a great time for connecting with educators, foreigners, and travel abroad. It's an opportunity to improve relationships with in-laws.

DECEMBER
- **December 1–7** (Jupiter trine Saturn): The auspicious connection between the archetype of expansion and that of focus continues to help you accomplish your goals.
- **December 4** (Full Moon in Gemini): This is an optimal moment to finalize projects. As this is the year's last Full Moon, it's a good time to begin the year's closure.

- **December 5–6** (Mercury trine Jupiter): A positive flow between the messenger and the teacher enhances your ability to learn, teach, travel, and publish. This is a good aspect for marketing, sales, signing documents, and leaving a mark on the world. A lucky triangle forms between Mercury, Jupiter, and Saturn, providing protection and a sense of direction.

- **December 8–9** (Mars squares Saturn): This is a party-pooping aspect. Right when the triangle was bestowing luck and opportunities, Mars comes to cause trouble. I call it the fascist aspect—symbols and sigils abused in the service of war and intimidation. People are fortified in their ideas, actions, and beliefs.

- **December 10–11** (Mercury opposite Uranus): While it is an aspect that can bring about a great deal of originality, there is also madness, unpredictability, and disruptions. Be extra careful of people promising things they cannot deliver.

- **December 11** (Mercury enters Sagittarius until January 1, 2026): Mercury is not happy in Sagittarius, and you might experience this transit as a latent Mercury retrograde. However, it is good for traveling and businesses abroad as well as for education.

- **December 13–15** (Mars squares Neptune): We are entering a season of squares, so tread slowly. This is an aspect that can reduce the immune system and your emotional defense. There is a great deal of deception and illusion. Be careful of sharp objects. There is also a tendency to relapse into old addictions, dependency, and codependency. Self-destruction is also an issue these days.

- **December 15** (Mars enters Capricorn until January 26, 2026): Mars is exalted and happy to march forward. Make sure you give him a mission—something you need help conquering or mastering. This is a good aspect for leadership and initiation. A call for action is coming, make sure not to refuse the call.

- **December 16–17** (Sun square Saturn): Issues with father figures or bosses, a sense of repression and heaviness, sadness, and depression. The Sun is covered with a layer of clouds.

- **December 20** (New Moon in Sagittarius): This is a difficult New Moon with Neptune and Saturn sending squares all over the place. It's not the best time to start new projects. Be careful of aggression and anger. There is a sense of war approaching. Lay low and be vigilant.
- **December 20** (Lilith enters Sagittarius): We are better off with Lilith, the Mother of Demons, in the sign of optimism and luck than having her where she was most of the year, in deadly Scorpio. There could be discord with students and teachers, as well as foreigners. Take extra care when traveling. Lilith can generate xenophobia, misinformation, disinformation, preachiness, and religious fanaticism.
- **December 20–21** (Sun square Neptune while Venus square Saturn): As mentioned, the end of December is challenging, so make sure you do your holiday shopping before. This aspect can demonstrate wastefulness, discord in primary relationships, misleading intuition, nightmares, daydreaming, and a general sense of laziness.
- **December 21** (Sun enters Capricorn until January 20, 2026): Celebrate the Solstice, the "Gateway of Gods." As one of the four sacred astrological days, your spiritual connection peaks. The ensuing month calls for Capricorn-like discipline and focus. Strategize the year ahead, bearing in mind that patience is vital.
- **December 23–26** (Venus squares Neptune): Not the best aspect for Christmas. It feels like the Grinch is stealing the holiday season. Moodiness, betrayal, extramarital affairs, loss of money, and unexpected expenses. Go to sleep and ask your prince (or princess) charming to wake you up next year.
- **December 24** (Venus enters Capricorn until January 17, 2026): This transit of Venus can help you improve relationships with people who are older, long-term partnerships, and bosses and superiors. This is a time to connect art and design to your professional life.
- **December 30** (Mercury square Saturn): The Grinch continues with some negative thoughts and a feeling of loss. Words taken out of context, false accusations, and disinformation.

PART III

INTRODUCTION TO ASTRO TRENDS

MAMA MIA

I noticed that in many cultures, when we are facing imminent danger, we do not call out for our father but rather our mother. In English, we instinctively say "Mommy!" In Hebrew, "Ima'le!" In Italian, "Mama mia!" In Spanish, "¡Madre mía!" In French, "Oh ma mère!" In Bulgarian, "Ma-le," In Portuguese, "Minha mãe!" In Greek, "Μάνα μου!" (Mana mou!), In Russian, "Мама моя!" (Mama moya!), In Dutch, "Mijn moeder!" In Polish, "Matko moja!" In Czech, "Matko Boží!" In Arabic, "يمأ اي!" (Ya Ummi!), In Hindi, "माँ रे!" (Maa re!), In Vietnamese, "Mẹ ơi!" In Romanian, "Mamă dragă!" And the list goes on. If you noticed, most of the words for mothers contain the syllable "ma." One reason could be that it's one of the first sounds babies can make when learning a language. The "m" sound is a bilabial nasal consonant that's easy for newborns to produce simply by closing their lips and allowing their voice to resonate.

But why? Why do we reach out for our moms instead of our dads? After all, the father is supposed to be the guy with the muscle, sword, gun, or an axe. One reason could be that our mother is the Moon, who shines upon us in times of darkness, at night, when the predators are on the prowl.

This call for the Moon is found deep within our DNA. In fact, the earliest form of stargazing could very well be moongazing. The first evidence dates back to the Aurignacian Culture of Europe, around 32,000 BCE. According to Alexander Marshack's research revealed that Late Upper Paleolithic cultures in Europe had advanced mathematical and astronomical knowledge. He discovered that marks carved into animal bones and cave walls, arranged in crescents or lines, were records of the lunar cycle. These marks were carefully made to correspond with lunar phases and were often laid out in serpentine patterns, possibly representing snake deities. In astrology, the Moon is considered fallen in Scorpio, the sign of all things serpentine. It is as if the Moon has "fallen" down to our awareness via Scorpio, the sign of occultism and magic.

For this reason, before we go any further in our exploration of the astrology of 2025, the Year of the Snake, let's focus on our mama and plan our Moon magic for the year ahead.

MOON CYCLES AND MOON MAGIC

Below you will find a list of the New Moons of 2025 and the best types of wishes you should manifest based on their sign's archetype. However, feel free to choose whatever you want to work on. You don't always have to use the zodiacal "dress code," so to speak.

In general, on the New Moon, you should formulate the wish for the next lunar month, but I recommend beginning to work on the wish the day after the New Moon. After seven days, the Moon reaches her first square with the Sun, a time of tension, where you might be forced into action. This square is the first sign of resistance and pushback, either from within you or from the universe. It could come in the form of regret (why did I ask for that wish?), skepticism (this is all BS), unworthiness (I don't deserve it), etc. Don't give up. A square is a challenging aspect (90 degrees) between the active principle of the Sun and the receptive quality of the Moon. The best way to deal with this tension is to be active while receptive and receptive while active—easier said than done.

As the Moon grows, she takes on the shape of the letter D. She appears pregnant, carrying your wish. This is a time you should add things to your life, for example, hire someone, acquire something, infuse your life with novelty, and say "yes!" to what life or the Moon offers.

Fourteen days after the New Moon, the Moon reaches her full term. Something has come to completion—ready for picking. The Full Moon is also a time for practicing gratitude, meditation, and healing. There is a reason why Passover, the celebration of social and personal liberation, takes place on the Full Moon, as well as Wesak, the day the Buddha was born, died, and attained enlightenment.

After the Moon passes her fullness and begins to shed light, entering her waning stage, she takes the form of the letter C. Now begins the phase of ridding yourself of whatever hinders you, in general, or in connection with your wish. The waning moon is an opportune time to let go or dismiss someone from your life or work, get rid of destructive attitudes, or embark on a detox journey.

A week after the Full Moon, the Lunar disk once again squares off with the Sun for the final showdown. This is the climax of your lunar journey. It might manifest as external and internal forces conspiring to prevent you from manifesting your project. Just as the Buddha or Jesus confronted their three temptations before their enlightenment, so will you face your final trials.

A day before the next New Moon, if you chose the right wish and did all the work, you should experience a shift or change in your life and be ready to embark on the next lunar journey.

The New and Full Moons of your Sun sign, Moon sign, and Rising sign are the most important cosmic landmarks on your yearly journey. Your Rising sign's New Moon can serve as a pathfinder of the year, supporting wishes that relate to your health, personality, direction in life, body, and identity. For example, if your rising sign is Leo, on the Leo New Moon, you should start working on a wish to improve your health, rebranding, and reinventing yourself. Your Sun sign's New Moon should be used for wishes concerning vitality, unraveling your destiny, creativity, romance, sports, children, hobbies, and happiness. On your Moon sign's New Moon, you can start working on projects that relate to home, family, parenting, pregnancy, real estate, or any emotional healing you might need.

To find your own Moon sign, you can visit my web site www. CosmicNavigator.com and click on LEARN and scroll down to the FREE CHART to cast your chart and find your Rising and Moon signs.

NEW MOON OF 2025
(Dates for 12pm UT/GMT)

January 29 (New Moon in Aquarius): An opportunity to revisit and refresh your New Year's Resolution. It heralds a fresh start with friends, groups, and organizations and is an ideal moment to update or upgrade your digital friends, gadgets, and reconnect with new technology. This lunation is blessed by Jupiter and receives a warm hug from Mercury and Pluto, which lends a great deal of wisdom and intellect to the powerful New Moon. It's a great time to make new connections with locals and foreigners, as well as a mentor and a guide. Coinciding with the Chinese New Year, when billions globally extend New Year blessings, you can harness this surge of positive energy to bolster your own intentions.

Wishes related to: Friendships, technology, science, clubs, groups, governmental projects or issues, altruism, community engagement, social media, innovation, or any aspirations for the future.

February 28 (New Moon in Pisces): Ideal for starting practices like yoga, meditation, swimming, or any water-based activity. Dance or other movement forms are also favored. Activate your imagination and delve into your subconscious to uncover hidden treasures. This ethereal New Moon could lead to vivid dreams. However, this New Moon is aggravated and challenged by Jupiter, the traditional ruler of Pisces, which can bring about overdoing, smothering, over-emotionality, and different manifestations of escapism.

Wishes related to: Dance, yoga, movement, healing, mysticism, intuition, imagination, photography, and poetry.

March 29 (Partial Solar Eclipse & New Moon in Aries): As the first New Moon (and eclipse) of the astrological year, this is a potent time for beginnings. However, with both Mercury and Venus retrograding, you should only initiate projects previously attempted but left incomplete. However, with Venus and Neptune conjunct, it is a good time to reconnect to a hobby or artistic project from the past. With Pluto sending a blessing to the New Moon, there is potential for a surge of power and magic coming from a friend, a new group or organization, or new technology.

Wishes related to: Past endeavors, sports, physical activities, leadership, identity, rebranding, health, and short-term projects.

April 27 (New Moon in Taurus): With the Moon exalted in Taurus, this is a powerful time for new beginnings, especially with Venus, the ruler of the lunation, exalted in Pisces. An older or experienced person can lend a helping hand. However, Pluto and Mars in opposition are squaring the lunation, which means the help can cost a great deal financially or emotionally.

Wishes related to: Finances, art, design, talents, skills, technology, e-commerce, self-worth, nature, and the environment.

May 27 (New Moon in Gemini): Excellent for starting a new business, making connections, launching projects, or adopting the role of a messenger. Joining the union of the Sun and the Moon are Mercury, Uranus, and Jupiter, making it a chattering lunation. With the blessing of Saturn and Neptune, this is an auspicious New Moon bringing about a great deal of potential in many different aspects of life. It's important to breathe, engage in some cardio activity, heal relationships with relatives and neighbors, and find new ways to communicate your message.

Wishes related to: Marketing, business, sales, contracts, writing, communication, bridge-building, networking, relationships with relatives, attracting a partner or lover, and starting new writing projects.

June 25 (New Moon in Cancer): The Moon returns to its domain. Perfect for initiating endeavors related to home, family, relocation, buying a car, or even changing offices. With no retrograding planet, this New Moon is a wonderful time for new beginnings, especially for projects you are emotionally connected to.

Wishes related to: Family, parenting, security, vehicles, home, real estate, and emotionally resonant projects.

July 24 (New Moon in Leo): Since Mercury is retrograde in dramatic Leo, you should only start something you tried in the past and failed to accomplish or start a project that has to do with editing or refining. Both Neptune (intuition) and Saturn (focus) are blessing the New Moon, adding practical mystical elements to the creativity of Leo.

Wishes related to: Fun, happiness, children, romance, love, creativity, sports, entertainment, recreation, and hobbies.

August 23 (New Moon in Virgo): With Mercury now direct, this is a prime time for work projects, health regimens, and service endeavors. Since the lunation takes place in the first degree of Virgo, it is far more potent. It's also apt for cleansing and detox. Uranus is creating disruptions and chaos; therefore, being extra focused and disciplined can help deal with the unpredictability presented by the Awakener.

Wishes related to: Diet, health, routine, employees, organization, cleanse, detox, service, editing, accounting, fixing broken things.

September 21 (Partial Solar Eclipse and New Moon in Virgo): As a solar eclipse, this lunation promises powerful new beginnings. And yes, this year we have two New Moons in Virgo, and this one takes place at the cusp of Virgo, a day shy of the eclipse, adding to its potency. With Saturn and Neptune opposing the eclipse, we are downloading a great deal of karma from previous lives. There is a great deal of deception and confusion. Please be careful with this New Moon.

Wishes related to: Diet, health, routine, employees, organization, cleanse, detox, service, editing, accounting, fixing broken things. But because the lunation takes place by the equinox, it can help with wishes related to balancing your life and relationships.

October 21 (New Moon in Libra): The New Moon of justice and relationships. A good time to balance your life, add an element of artistic expression, harmony, and peace. A good time to start activities you could do with a partner. The Moon is challenged by both Jupiter and Pluto, so tread carefully.

Wishes related to: Relationships, diplomacy, art, design, partnerships, justice, law, harmony, and peace.

November 20 (New Moon in Scorpio): With Mercury retrograde in Scorpio, be mindful not to start anything new unless you tried in the past and wish to revisit it. The New Moon is fallen and in conjunction with the Black Moon Lilith, so it is very Halloweenish and feels like a horror movie. This is a rather dark New Moon but can still help you in researching, investigation, and unveiling hidden issues. A good time for tantra, intimacy, and therapy. While it is a retro New Moon, it is also creating a wonderful protective triangle with Jupiter, Saturn, and Neptune. A great time to start a deep meditation practice or a new healing practice.

Wishes related to: Healing, the occult, investigations, shamanic journeys, magic, sexuality, passion, investments, and shadow work.

December 20 (New Moon in Sagittarius): The last New Moon of the year offers an opportunity to start working on whatever you need to get done before the year's end. A great time for travel, education, and healing relationships with in-laws. With Venus conjunction the lunation, we have a great deal of opportunity to discover new relationships, especially with foreigners or people who grew up in different settings than you. Just be careful of deception and illusions coming from the square with Neptune and Saturn.

Wishes related to: Travel, higher education, teaching, relationships with in-laws, wisdom, universities, mass media, truth, and authenticity.

Alas, this year we do not have a New Moon in Capricorn, as in 2024 we had two of them. No worries; in 2026 we will have one right at the onset of the year.

THE DEMOCRATIC NATURE OF ASTROLOGY

I often wondered why democracy was assigned to the zodiac sign Aquarius, the same sign that is associated with astrology, humanity, Artificial Intelligence, and the Future. After years of teaching and practicing the wisdom of the stars, I concluded that there are a few reasons for astrology sharing the same heavenly folder as democracy. For starters, while your Sun sign might be Pisces or Libra, your horoscope boasts all twelve signs, with each ruling one of your houses. The twelve houses represent a different aspect of your life, for example, there is a house of relationship, health, career, children, etc. In fact, your rising sign is the ruler of your first house, the house of personality and body. Since there are twelve houses and twelve signs, each of your houses is represented by one of the zodiac signs, like an assembly or parliament of archetypes. You might feel an aversion from this sign or that, but like it or not, that sign might be in charge of an important part of your life, perhaps the house of finances or the house sexuality. Better make peace with all members of the zodiac round table so you have a functioning and governing chart.

To share the second reason for the connection between astrology and democracy, we must travel back in time. There is no astrology without history, simply for the fact that history repeats herself in accordance with the cycles of planetary motion.

As you might know, Astrology was conceived in Sumer, the real startup nation and first civilization. Those remarkable people bequeathed humanity with agriculture, mathematics, the wheel, boats, time, writing, science, maps, sailboats, cities, and astrology. We suspect that the first proto-astrological symbols likely represented seasonal tasks. There was the time for shearing the sheep (Aries) gathering shellfish (Cancer), harvesting (Virgo), fishing by net or line (Pisces), managing water reserves (Scorpio), hunting (Sagittarius) etc. The Babylonian took astrology to the next level and used her also as a tool for divination. However, it was mostly used for the king or the nation, which meant that not that many charts were cast, and therefore, less samples of the perceived connection between the above and below. That all changed with Alexander the Great, one of the only folks in history that truly deserve the honorific title "Great." After Alexander the Great's conquest of Babylon, Babylonian astrology merged with the Egyptian celestial tradition of Decanic astrology and resulted in what we still use today—horoscopic astrology. Horoscope is a Greek word denoting the scope of the hour (of birth) resulting in the development of the 12 houses system. Within a century or two, Alexandria, the crown jewel of Alexander's empire, became the center of knowledge as well as astrology. The Ancient Greek, with their keen understanding of the natural world, philosophy, and mythology, provided the perfect environment for astrology to thrive and evolve. Democratizing astrology, the Hellenistic world began casting charts not only to royals (Leo) but to anybody who was interested (Aquarius). This was a significant leap for astrology since the more charts were cast, the more opportunities astrologers had to link the cycles of the planets with life on Earth. In the same way that Artificial Intelligence (also ruled by Aquarius), needs large samples of data to perfect itself, so does astrology. As the Theory of Evolution suggests, when a trait is beneficial to an organism, it survives and evolves. Same goes for the study of astrology. Erroneous assertions were deleted from the growing body of the wisdom of the stars, while correct ones were reinforced and passed on. In no time, astrology spread across Europe, the Middle East and all the way to India.

Since Aquarius is the sign of all things to come (astrology does deal with the future) as well as democracy and Artificial Intelligence, perhaps in the next two decades, as Pluto (transformation and power) transits through Aquarius, astrology would take another leap forward. Who knows, maybe universities would start offering degrees in cosmic studies, and perchance quantum mechanics would be able to provide a glimpse into how our celestial environment correlates to our lives.

ECLIPSES OF 2025:
AMPLIFIERS OF CHANGE

E clipses are New Moons (Solar) or Full Moons (Lunar) on steroids. They tend to quicken and thrust forward whatever is going on in your life or lurking under the surface. If you, your projects, or relationships are heading in the right direction, the eclipses will deliver you faster to your destination. However, if you are off course, then the eclipses could drive you further away from your goals. For this reason, a fortnight before the eclipses, get your life in order and present the eclipses with projects or processes you wish to amplify and propel.

The sign where the eclipses fall is determined by the whereabouts of the Lunar Nodes, also known as the Head and Tail of the Dragon. The North Node, which I will call from now on the "Dragon," points at the sign or archetype we are collectively asked to master. In January 2025, we are changing signs from Aries (which the Dragon was flying since July 2023) to Pisces. The South Node always falls on the opposite sign and marks the archetype we are supposed to unlearn or discard as we overused or even abused it in the past. In 2025, the tail of the Dragon wiggles in Virgo.

From July 13, 2023, until January 29, 2025, the Lunar Nodes were traveling backward through Aries (North Node) and Libra (South Node). The collective lessons in 2024 were related to Aries' need to assert one's identity and fortify the sense of self. For example, a client of mine told me the rise of antisemitism following the war in Gaza made her assert her identity as a Jew. Aries' keyword—I am—made her decide that she is first and foremost

Jewish. However, there was also a dark side to the tribal tendencies of the North Node in Aries as the South Node in Libra made it almost impossible for many to connect to the—I Balance—the keyword of Libra. For example, most of Israel's main media refrained from showing images of the devastation the war in Gaza caused the Palestinians, opting instead to focus on their own pain. At the same time, many of the pro-Palestinians demonstrators in Europe and US universities resorted to violence and abuse of students or faculty that didn't share their beliefs.

NORTH NODE IN PISCES (JANUARY 29, 2025–AUGUST 18, 2026)

As mentioned, the Dragon (North Node) points at the archetype we are collectively asked to master. Every 18 months, the Dragon soars to a different sign, thus completing the full Zodiac in about 19 years. In 2025 and the first half of 2026, we are instructed by the Dragon to learn the lessons associated with Pisces, the sign of imagination, mysticism, intuition, channeling, empathy, dreams, sleeping (siestas are encouraged), movement, dance, yoga, meditation, photography, religion, and shamanism. In order to connect to these ethereal Piscean traits, we must let go of the less flattering qualities of Virgo, which include but are not limited to—criticism, perfectionism, overanalytical propensities, obsessive thoughts, compulsive behaviors, and what I call the "Inch-Worm Syndrome," when one is busy counting the flowers instead of enjoying their smell. The South Node in Virgo does not mean we have to discard Virgo altogether, rather eliminate the hindering element of the super nanny sign. You still must take care of your diet, serve, work, and connect to routine, but do it with a Piscean flair. While Virgo tends to say, "No!" Pisces exclaims an enthusiastic "Yes!"

The North Node in Pisces wants us to dip our feet (the organ associated with Pisces) in water, metaphorically as well as practically. We are asked to dissolve the walls and barriers we have erected over the years that keep us safe but also prevent us from feeling other people's pain and suffering. The Dragon in Pisces wants us to surf life's synchronicities and soar up to heights that only our imagination can elevate us. As Mother Mary (Virgo) suggests, "Let it be, oh, just let it be."

One of the monumental additions to this year's transit of the Dragon is the fact that Saturn, for the first time in 30 years, is also swimming in Pisces. The two come together in April, forming a rare aspect which in the last 500 years occurred only in 1877, 1672, 1523, and 1466. Therefore, around April 2025, we are assimilating knowledge we have accumulated in this lifetime and previous ones, given the tools to use it practically in all aspects of our lives.

One good thing about the South Node being in Virgo is that it can help us break patterns, habits, and routines that might be ineffective and fail to serve us. The tail of the Dragon in Virgo can also aid in changing how we work, serve, or deal with coworkers and employees. Many of us might change our workplace or find new ways to serve our community.

Below are the dates when the North Node was in Pisces. See if you can identify recurring lessons or important events that took place in your life during those periods in order to deduce what is expected of you in 2025 and the first half of 2026:

- June 20, 2006–January 7, 2008
- November 8, 1987–May 28, 1989
- March 29, 1969–October 16, 1970
- August 17, 1950–March 6, 1952
- January 6, 1932vJuly 26, 1933

Let's look at the four eclipses in 2025. I have listed the body part associated with each eclipse as well as the Sabian symbol and location on the planet where the lunation will be visible.

MARCH 14 (TOTAL LUNAR ECLIPSE IN VIRGO)
Part of Body: Capsule and ligaments of the liver.
Sabian Symbol: Mary and her white lamb.

The last Full Moon of the astrological year, this eclipse pits the binary options of open (Pisces) and closed (Virgo) circuit. You might feel a tug of war between the need to agree and disagree, open yourself to a new experience, or shun away from it. Since it is a South Node eclipse, it is recommended to use the lunation to let go of something that hinders your health, diet, work, or ability to serve your community. Saturn sits heavy on the eclipse and can create some challenges with superiors, bosses, or a father figure. However, Uranus is blessing the eclipse with a touch of excitement, innovation, and scientific discovery. You might meet someone that inspires you to see things differently. Be aware that Venus is retrograding and can create challenges with your significant others.

Key Concepts: Completion, innovation in work, diet, health, work, service, routine, employees, and coworkers.

Eclipse Path: Europe, East North Asia, Eastern Australia, much of Africa, North America, South America, Pacific, Atlantic, Arctic, Antarctica.

MARCH 29 (PARTIAL SOLAR ECLIPSE IN ARIES)
Part of Body: Eyeball.
Sabian Symbol: A scholar creates new forms for ancient symbols.

If it wasn't for the Mercury and Venus retrograde, it would have been a powerful time to ignite a project in your personal or professional life. You can still start something new if you already have tried to do it before and failed to bring it to completion. In many traditions, this New Moon also marks the New Year (Babylonia, Sumer, and Persia), therefore this day holds a special ancestral memory for many of us who reincarnated in Mesopotamian cultures or have a genetic connection to the "Land Between the Rivers." Check to see if there is something you are refusing to see in your life. The eclipse can help you see things more clearly.

Key Concepts: Initiation, leadership, embracing adventure, tracing new paths, pioneering, battling inner and outer demons, reigniting past battles, changing tactics and strategy.

Eclipse Path: Europe, North Asia (Russia), North/West Africa, Northeast America, Atlantic Ocean, the Arctic.

SEPTEMBER 7 (TOTAL LUNAR ECLIPSE IN PISCES—HARVEST FULL MOON)

Part of Body: Cruciate ligaments of the right foot.
Sabian Symbol: In a quiet moment, the flow of inspiration.

Not only is this the Harvest Full Moon, one of the most powerful and bright lunations of the year, but this is also a total Lunar eclipse! The eclipse may induce feelings of tension between professional life and personal demands; detox versus intoxication; setting boundaries or eliminating them; analytical versus holistic attitudes towards life. The eclipse can bring clarity about work, health, and diet, as well as increase your connection to mysticism, meditation, intuition, dreams, and imagination. This is a North Node eclipse and can connect you to like-minded people. Be open to new experiences. With Mercury exalted, this is a great eclipse for receiving and spreading information.

Key Concepts: Cleansing, reorganization, harvesting results of prior actions, rapid karmic outcomes, dance, yoga, meditation, practical intuition, creative visualization, manifestation.

Eclipse Path: Europe, Asia, Australia, Africa, East Brazil, Pacific, Atlantic, Indian Ocean, Arctic, Antarctica.

SEPTEMBER 21 (PARTIAL SOLAR ECLIPSE IN VIRGO)

Part of Body: Hepatic duct.
Sabian Symbol: Having an urgent task to complete, a man doesn't look to any distractions.

A South Node eclipse and the second New Moon in Virgo allow you to start something new by letting go of something that was blocking your path. Shiva, the remover of obstacles, is riding the Dragon with you. It's a time to confront karma or issues you carry from your ancestors. There could also be some conflict at work with superiors. It's a great time to start a diet, a new job, and take on a novel routine. Since the eclipse takes place right on the equinox, it is magnified and more potent. A tidal wave of energy is coming your way. Make sure you hold on tightly to your surfboard and remember the mantra of surfers—No Fear! Interestingly, the only place the eclipse passes is Southeast Australia, New Zealand, and Antarctica (poor penguins).

Key Concepts: Diet, health, new jobs, service, reorganizing your life or work, balancing relationships (especially professional), justice, harmony, functional art.

Eclipse Path: Southeast Australia, New Zealand, and Antarctica.

SATURN IN PISCES
(March 7, 2023–Feb 13, 2026)

And God said: "Draw not nigh hither; put off thy shoes from off thy feet, for the place whereon thou stand is holy ground."

– Exodus 3:5

One of the most important trends in the astrology of 2025 is the North Node or Dragon swimming laps in Pisces alongside Saturn. While Saturn entered Pisces in March of 2023, the North Node joins the plunge in January 2025. Below you will find a list of the areas of life Saturn is rectifying for your sign this year.

Saturn likes to ask "Why?" For example, if you are a Virgo, Saturn is contracted to fix your relationships, therefore, he would ask: "Why is this person your partner?" or "Why are you not in a relationship?" For Taurus, it would be "Why are you associated with this company or these friends?" But unlike 2023 and 2024, in 2025 the North Node provides clues and answers to Saturn's queries, especially during the eclipse seasons (March and September)

On April 14, Saturn and the Dragon meet in Pisces for the first time since 1877, allowing us to benefit (North Node) and ground (Saturn) the positive and constructive qualities of Pisces. An interesting anecdote that promises some hope of a similar contraption: in 1877, Thomas Edison invented the phonograph, which quickly became the most popular home entertainment device of the century.

The union of the Dragon, which is associated with fate and karma with Saturn, Lord Karma, offers us a unique opportunity to delve deeper into our intuition, dreaming, imagination, and meditation. Not only can this conjunction shed light on talents and gifts you have brought from past lifetimes, but it can also help you navigate whatever Necessity, or the Fates, have planned for you. I suggest practicing being a stranger in a strange land this year. Try to engage in activities, hobbies, sports, and endeavors where you might feel like you are in unfamiliar territory. Since the South Node is dialing down the Virgo tendencies of self-criticism and perfectionism, this year can offer a way to explore new frontiers in your life.

As part of the planetary changes this year, Saturn makes a short stint into Aries between May 25 and September 1, which we will cover in the next section.

SATURN IN PISCES FOR YOUR SIGN (JANUARY TO MAY AND SEPTEMBER 2025 TO FEBRUARY 2026)

- **Aries**: Saturn is asking you to practice letting go as well as detox from foods, friends, companies, activities, or attitudes that don't serve you anymore. Saturn is grounding your mystical abilities, connecting you to gifts and memories as well as people from previous lives. Be disciplined about sleep and meditation. There is an enduring feeling of confinement, as well as the need to deal with other people's suffering.
- **Taurus**: Saturn suggests you focus on your friendships, companies, groups, clubs, and any group you belong to. There could be a need to fix your relationship with government officials. Technology, science, and your digital friends are in the spotlight; it is time to upgrade your gadgets.
- **Gemini**: Career and your relationship with people of authority are in the spotlight when Saturn sits at the Zenith of your chart. There might be an extra workload or a need to change your career or dive deeper into your chosen profession.

- **Cancer**: Saturn is pointing at your education, teaching, and learning, as well as how you relate to the truth, justice, and morality. It is a time to be authentic and truthful to yourself and others. Saturn could present you with challenges or a need to fix your relationship with in-laws or people of foreign origin.
- **Leo**: In the Thoth Deck, your card is called "Lust," and Saturn in Pisces is suggesting you dive deeper into tantra and examine your passion, sexuality, and what you are attracting. Additionally, he is asking you to bury the zombies, all these half-dead relationships, friendships, and attitudes in your life. Saturn is rectifying how you view death and the occult. A great time to become a healer as well as healing.
- **Virgo**: Saturn wants you to fix all your primary relationships, especially partners in work or in life. Saturn is opposing your Sun which can also create issues with father figures or older folks in your life. Watch out for lawsuits, enemies, and competitors.
- **Libra**: Saturn is asking you to investigate your health, work, routine, diet, and how you serve yourself and others. This is the time to practice being a super nanny, a healer, and a therapist to those around you.
- **Scorpio**: Saturn wants you to practice happiness, fun, and connect to your inner child. A great time to become a parent and look deeper into your relationships with your kids as well as children of the mind, as in your baby projects. Romance and love can be complicated; however, falling in love with mature or older people can be beneficial.
- **Sagittarius**: Saturn wants to ground you in your home and connect you to your familial responsibilities. It is a time to invest in real estate, form a family, and take on responsibility over your kinfolk. Some aspects of ancestral traumas can become evident via genetics, gifts, as well as curses that run down the generations.
- **Capricorn**: Saturn, your ruler, is asking you to rectify your relationship with relatives such as siblings, nephews, cousins, as well as neighbors or roommates. Some contracts you signed or agreements you made might need to be fixed or reexamined. A good time to focus on new businesses and marketing yourself or your projects.

- **Aquarius:** Saturn, your traditional ruler, is asking you to invest and look deep into your talents, finances, self-worth, and values. It is a great time to invest time, energy, and faith in your gifts and find new ways to increase your income.
- **Pisces:** Saturn is in your sign, and we are all there with you. It is a time to redefine yourself. A new look, address, image, or brand. It is time for a new version of yourself. Look deep into how you deal with your body and health. You need to awaken and take charge of your life. If you are born between March 8 to 21 or have a rising sign or Moon between 18 degrees Pisces to 29 degrees Pisces, Saturn will make his heavy presence felt in your life. You could experience a feeling of overload and extra pressure. Guard against excessive self-criticism, and although you might feel abandoned, you are not. Still, it's a great time to mature, take responsibility, and get help overcoming long-term obstacles. The secret to navigating this phase successfully lies in discipline, maintaining focus, drafting meticulous plans, and seeking guidance from experienced or older people.

SIT DOWN!

Around the time Saturn moved into the water sign Pisces, I started taking cold showers. I was always aware of the health benefits of cold plunges: from improving circulation and boosting the immune system (ruled by Pisces) to increasing alertness. These torturous showers may also enhance mood by triggering the release of endorphins and reducing symptoms of depression and anxiety. But it wasn't until Saturn, ruler of Capricorn, the sign that is the initiator of icy winter, moved into Pisces, that I began my cold hydrotherapy. Having done it now for two years (also when I was in Edinburgh in January), I can truly attest to its benefits. However, the swift showers somehow influenced my morning meditations, which also were fast and furious—wham bam, thank you ma'am—and I was done, ready for my coffee (alas, drugs are ruled by Pisces).

That all changed last March, right as the Sun transited into Pisces, and for some instinctual reason, an inner voice demanded that I stop playing hooky with the timeless tradition and give it the attention and endurance it deserves.

So here we go, the most important and transformative advice I can give in this book for the transit of Saturn (root chakra) in Pisces (meditation)—as the Psalmist suggested: "Be still and know that I am God." Start meditating. No, I don't mean maybe, or okay, I will someday. I am talking about a genuine commitment. What I did last March was promise Saturn that from this day on, until the day or night I die, I will meditate every day (or night) for at least 15 minutes. I said 15 minutes since it is a quarter of an hour (1/4), and in astrology, a square represents an action we must take but might not want to. I have five planets in fire signs, so hey, it ain't easy sitting still, but if I can do it, so can you.

Some people think meditation is beyond them. Some clients told me, "But I can't stop thinking; I can't still my monkey mind." Well, I was born in the year of the monkey, so I know a thing or two about furry primates. No one expects you to stop thinking; after all, our species is called Homo sapiens sapiens—the double-thinking man. Even Descartes, a celebrated primate, recognized that he thinks, therefore he is. You don't have to stop thinking; you can use your moments of silence and stillness to connect to your breath (Jupiter in Gemini, which rules breathing and the lungs, can help). If you've never meditated, I suggest using what is called Box Breathing (4-4-4-4) meditation: inhaling for the count of 4, holding your breath for the count of 4, exhaling for the count of 4, and holding the breath out for the count of 4. This gives your monkey mind something to do while the rest of you can meditate. Set your alarm for 10 minutes and start breathing. While meditating, you might suddenly realize you forgot to count. Great! That means you entered the deeper stages of meditation. You cannot fail; if you stopped counting, you are achieving your goals, and if you continue counting, you are also achieving the objective. The combination of Jupiter in Gemini and Saturn in Pisces, while it is a square, can be helpful to our meditating endeavor. I soon discovered 15 minutes is not enough, and now it stands at 30. I promise you similar results. Scientific research suggests that using this meditation can dramatically improve your sleep (ruled by Pisces).

Since you had to deal with Saturn being in Pisces for most of 2023 and 2024, you should already be familiar with what Saturn might need from you and your sign. However, since Saturn in 2025 is mostly transiting the last decan of Pisces, which is associated with Scorpio, the water is getting choppy, literally speaking, since Scorpio is the sign of death and transformation, symbolized by the very serpent of the 2025 Chinese Year. The last stint of Saturn in Pisces is the most intense. Be aware of your addictions, lack of boundaries, fantasies, blind faith, cognitive dissonance, dependent and codependent relationships, all forms of delusion, deceptions, hallucinations, procrastination, laziness, excessive receptivity, lack of initiation, defeatism, and escapism.

SATURN RETURNS TO 1995 AND THE FIRST QUARTER OF 1996

Below you will find the dates when Saturn navigated the waters of Pisces in the last hundred years. Try to identify the major challenges, lessons, and events that transpired in your life during those periods. Pay special attention to the second half of 1995 and the first quarter of 1996, the second half of 1966, and the end of 1936 and 1937, as these years correspond with Saturn's position in 2025. If you were born during these years, you are experiencing your Saturn Return—a period of reckoning and solidifying your identity. If something significant happened during those dates (marriage, move to a new place, health issue), there is a revisiting of that lesson and an opportunity to start a new cycle relating to similar situations.

- February 14, 1935–April 24, 1937
- October 17, 1937–January 14, 1938
- March 23, 1964–September 16, 1964
- December 15, 1964–March 3, 1967
- May 20, 1993–June 30, 1993
- January 28, 1994–April 7, 1996

GUNS AND ROSES
SATURN IN ARIES
(May 25–September 1)

As an Aries with five planets in the sign of the Ram (one being Saturn), for years I had wanted to visit the Valley of the Roses in Bulgaria. Roses, assigned to Aries, are also one of my favorite things (along with schnitzel and strudel, but more on that when Saturn enters Taurus in 2028).

The Rose Valley, historically known as the Valley of the (Thracian) Kings, is a UNESCO World Heritage site. The valley surrounds the quaint town of Kazanluk in central Bulgaria. The area is renowned for its unique Thracian burial mounds dating back to the 4th century BCE. The most celebrated Thracians were Spartacus, who led a major uprising against the Romans (73-71 BCE), a true warrior befitting Mars, ruler of Aries, and Orpheus, who armed with his lyre and talent could charm the hounds guarding the Underworld. However, Mars was also the god of vegetation, and from the 17th century, the Valley of the Kings became known as the Valley of the Roses, still under the domain of Aries, boasting thorny Mars-like flowers imported from the Levant. Most likely brought to the West by a crusader, the Damask roses found a new home in the Balkan. The valley's climate and soil composition were the perfect conditions for the flower of Aries to bloom, and by the 21st century, the region was responsible for half of the world's production of rose oil.

The idiom "wake up and smell the roses" is astrologically correct. Aries is the alarm clock that wakes us up from Pisces' slumber, and when I traveled to the Rose Valley at the end of May, right as the flowers reached their fullest bloom, I learned another interesting fact about the Valley of the Kings: it is also the center of Bulgaria's thriving arms production industry, estimated at $2 billion a year. There you have it—where there is one aspect of Aries (warrior tombs and roses), there would be another facet of the Martial sign (guns and ammunition).

In 2025, Saturn, the Lord Karma, is making a three-month visit to Aries, the sign where he is considered fallen and weak. One might argue that if the Lord Karma, the bringer of challenges, is feeble, it should be a cause for celebration. Nope. We want all planets to be as dignified as they can. If Saturn is fallen, it simply means we have a harder time accessing the aspects Saturn rules, such as discipline, planning, strategy, endurance, and persistence. We might suffer from Arian ADHD—start projects yet fail to complete them. This year, roughly between June and August, we get a sample of what is to come when Saturn settles in Aries from February 2026 to 2028.

Saturn's journey in Aries will be short and intense for the simple reason that he will be hovering over the first two degrees of the sign, which happens to be the Spring Equinox, the most powerful day of the zodiac. For the Sumerians and Babylonians, the inceptors of Astrology, the first degree of Aries was considered the most sacred of days, their New Year, and a time to reset the cosmic clock—a moment one could erase the past and start writing a new story. When Saturn is in Pisces, we are asked to seal, complete, resolve, or let go of the issues we have been dealing with for the past 30 years. Pisces is the last of the signs, and Aries is the first. Pisces are the feet, while Aries is the head. Therefore, between the end of May and the first day of September, you will catch a glimpse of what would be the main themes that would color your next 30 years.

Dates of Saturn on the Cusp of Aries (Equinox)

- April 1996
- March 1967

- April 1937
- March 1908

Here are a few incidents that happened last time Saturn was hovering over the cusp of Aries and Pisces (1996):

- **Port Arthur Massacre**: In Tasmania, Australia, a lone gunman killed 35 people and wounded 23 others in a mass shooting. This event led to major changes in Australian gun laws.
- **Qana Massacre**: During the Israeli military operation in Lebanon (Grapes of Wrath), an Israeli artillery strike hit a U.N. compound, killing 106 civilians.
- **Burundian Civil War**: Massacres of Hutus by Tutsis in Burundi took place, with more than 450 killed in a matter of a few days.
- **First Liberian Civil War**: Fighting broke out in Monrovia, Liberia, between various rebel factions struggling for power in the country's interrupted civil war. Several foreign nationals left the nation.
- **PLO Change of Policy**: Yasser Arafat, head of the Palestine Liberation Organization, dropped the clause in the Palestinian National Covenant that called for the removal of Israel. The Israeli government reciprocated by dropping a similar clause concerning Palestine.

SATURN'S LESSONS BETWEEN MAY 25–SEPTEMBER FOR EACH ZODIAC SIGN

In general, between May 25 and September 1, you are called to focus on self-discipline, refine your leadership abilities, redefine your identity, image, and relationship to your body, slow down your pace, overcome impatient tendencies, and take responsibility for past decisions.

- **Aries**: Saturn is in your sign. Get ready for it, since he returns to your sign between February 2026 and April 12, 2028. The Lord Karma is scrutinizing all aspects of your life. Especially if you are born between March 20 and 22, you will feel his teachings more strongly. Have a plan, form a strategy, decide what you want to conquer, and connect to discipline, and you will benefit from this transit.

- **Taurus:** It is time to practice letting go, flexibility of the mind and body, and marching into unknown territories such as the subconscious, your imagination, memories from past lifetimes, and mysticism. You might feel trapped at times or under siege, but it is only to help you weed out what is not authentic or necessary in your life. It's a great time for meditation and spending time alone.

- **Gemini:** A change is coming to your friends' circle, companies, groups you belong to, and your tribe. You might make a move that results in a change of your friendships. A friend might need your help, and in addition, you might feel the need to let go of friends as well as welcome new ones. Friends from past lives or from your past in this lifetime might return. A time to reexamine your relationship to technology and the digital world.

- **Cancer:** It is time to focus on your career advancements and professional life and be disciplined about your trajectory in life. There could be issues with bosses or father figures. You might feel a pull and push between responsibility towards your home and career. This Saturn position is especially challenging as it squares your Sun and forces you into actions you would rather not take.

- **Leo:** This Saturn position is easier than others and can provide a good opportunity to go back to school, study, teach, learn a new language, and perhaps move to a different country. However, there could be issues with in-laws as well as lawsuits. Hold on to your truth and be as authentic as possible.

- **Virgo:** Saturn is asking you to visit the underworld and look into your passions, sexuality, and intimate relationships. Your partners in work or in life might have a harder time with their finances, and you might need to step in and help organize their life. There could be a need to deal with death and inheritance. It's time to let go and bury all that was half-dead in your life.

- **Libra**: Saturn in your opposite sign can create tension and extra responsibilities. Especially vulnerable are your primary relationships and your partnerships in work and life. Pay extra attention to your competitors and enemies as antagonism and aggression can be experienced. You are asked to practice your sense of justice and diplomacy more than ever.
- **Scorpio**: Watch your health, diet, routine, and work. There could be issues coming up with coworkers or employees. There is a need to reorganize your life, especially your professional life and health. It's a time to examine how others serve you and how you need to serve others.
- **Sagittarius**: Saturn transiting a fellow fire sign is much easier on you. It is a good time to focus on children, romance, creativity, sports, hobbies, and changing how you enjoy life. Saturn might present a romantic love but at the same time creates some challenges in making it happen.
- **Capricorn**: Saturn is your ruler and expects a great deal from you. However, the transit of Saturn in Aries is challenging for you and forces you into actions you would rather not take. It is vital to focus on home, family, real estate, and healing ancestral karma. Some members of your family might go through a hard time that demands your intervention.
- **Aquarius**: Saturn, your traditional ruler, is asking you to look deep into how you communicate, write, deliver messages, and deal with your businesses. There could be challenges in your relationship with relatives, siblings, neighbors, roommates, and people you have contracts with.
- **Pisces**: You are all too happy to let go of Saturn for a few months and hand it over to impatient Aries. Life feels a bit lighter for a few months, but you will have to wait until your birthday in 2026 to completely lift the yoke of Saturn. Focus on your finances, talents, self-worth, and values.

NEPTUNE IN ARIES

(March 30–October 22 and
January 27, 2026–March 23, 2039)

HOLY WARS

Like Saturn, Neptune is marching out of Pisces and into Aries. In 2025, Neptune spends almost seven months in Aries, only to return to Pisces for one final dip before blazing back into Aries for 13 years. Since 2012, Neptune has been happily transiting in Pisces, his sign, but all good things never last, and it is time for Neptune's waves to be heated by Aries' flames. Neptune in Aries is like a jacuzzi—great for 10 minutes, but not for 13 years.

Neptune's orbit around the Sun takes 165 years, spending about 14 years in each sign. Neptune is Venus' higher octave and is associated with imagination, empathy, intuition, dance, dissolution of boundaries, poetry, yoga, meditation, ideals, dreams, and mysticism. However, when out of balance, Neptune can lead to addiction, escapism, illusions, nightmares, self-destruction, and suicide. Often dubbed "The Great Dissolver," Neptune in a tribal sign, like Aries, can bring about self-annihilation and narcissism. Globally, Neptune (water) in Aries (fire) could manifest as melting ice sheets and the acceleration of rising sea levels, especially due to our own self-destructive tendencies. Additionally, Neptune, the god of earthquakes, could bring more tremors and volcanic eruptions.

Neptune in Aries can also inspire holy (Neptune) wars (Aries), floods and droughts, tidal waves, arms races, and the development of new types of weapons, and conflicts around water. It can also lead to the dissolution and breaking down of old, outdated systems and institutions.

Historically, Neptune in Aries has coincided with significant religious conflicts. The "Great Schism" (1054) split Christianity into the Roman Catholic and Eastern Orthodox faiths, and the "Western Schism" (1378) divided the Roman Catholic Church, with no less than three men simultaneously claiming to be the true Vicar of Christ.

Right when Neptune entered warlike Aries in April 12-13, 1861, the opening battle of the American Civil War, took place. However, it was also during Neptune's transit in Aries, when the Emancipation Proclamation (January 1, 1863) declared that all slaves in Confederate territory were to be freed.

We can also expect significant changes in leadership (Aries) as Neptune (dissolver) melts away governments that were frozen in time. For example, the Meiji Restoration (1868) in Japan brought down the military government and restored the emperor (the Tarot card of Aries is "The Emperor"), leading to rapid modernization and westernization and transforming Japan into a military powerhouse.

There is also a sliver of hope as the idealism and imagination of Neptune could get a big boost from the fiery passion of Aries, resulting in increased interest in mysticism, art, spirituality, faith healing, literature, and other cultural pursuits.

Dates when Neptune graced Aries

- September 3, 1710–April 22, 1711
- December 8, 1711–February 12, 1712
- April 13, 1861–October 1, 1861
- February 14, 1862–June 8, 1874
- October 1, 1874–April 7, 1875
- March 30, 2025–October 22
- January 26, 2026–March 23, 2039

ON A PERSONAL LEVEL—VISIONARY ACTION AND CHANGE

Below are a few suggestions of how to manage Neptune (water) mixing with Aries (fire)

- **Welcome change and dissolution of old patterns**: Open your heart and mind to new ideas and ideals. Let go of old limiting beliefs, blind faith, and orthodoxy, and welcome new constructs and attitudes.
- **Follow your dreams**: Ask your nightly journeys and dreams for guidance. Pursue these insights with the courage and determination typical of warrior-like Aries.
- **Connect to movement**: This is a great time for walking meditations, trance work, martial arts, or any activity that helps you connect your body (Aries) to your subconscious.
- **Active intuition**: Listen to what your intuition tells you and receive messages from the world through action. For example, if you find yourself buying a lot of toilet paper, maybe your intuition tells you a pandemic is on the horizon. Pay attention to how you act.
- **Cultivate creativity**: Find a way to use your imagination in practical ways. Engage in creative visualization, art, and new forms of creativity. It's a time to do things for the first time without scrutiny or judgment.

NEPTUNE AND SATURN IN ARIES

In 2025, both Neptune and Saturn hover over the cusp of Pisces (ruled by Neptune) and Aries, aligning with the Spring Equinox, the holiest of holy days. Their conjunction should be especially significant as Saturn galvanizes and crystallizes whatever planet he meets. This year, their conjunction takes place in Aries from May 25 to August 31, marking a pivotal time.

PERSONAL IMPLICATIONS

On a personal level, the conjunction of Saturn and Neptune could help you manifest (Saturn) your dreams and inspiration (Pisces) as well as blend joy with responsibility. The conjunction might challenge you to let go of unrealistic and confused endeavors or relationships, bringing a sense of pragmatism. Taking action (Aries) and being disciplined (Saturn) in relation to your dreams, inspiration, and intuition (Neptune) is highly recommended.

Be extra careful of inflammation, lowered immunity, autoimmune disorders, lethargy and laziness, disabling confusion.

SUGGESTIONS FOR MANAGING NEPTUNE AND SATURN CONJUNCTION

- Manifest your dreams: use the energy of Saturn to turn your dreams and imagination into reality. Set realistic goals and create a plan to achieve them.

- Blend joy with responsibility: Find ways to incorporate creativity and joy into your work and responsibilities. Balance your professional and personal life.
- Initiate new projects: The first degree of Aries provides assertive and fiery energy to start new endeavors. Just be mindful of the Mercury retrograde period from mid-July to early August.
- Integrate creativity and work: Blend your creative pursuits with your professional life. Use your imagination to enhance your work and bring innovative ideas to the forefront.

NUMEROLOGY OF 2025: DEADLY NINE

In numerology, the year 2025 is reduced to the number 9 (2+0+2+5=9). This archetype is rather deadly, and since 2025 is also the Year of the Serpent, one of the symbols of Scorpio, ruler of Death and Transformation, the year ahead promises to be one of endings, culminations, conclusions, and letting go.

On the Kabbalistic Tree of Life, the blueprint of creation, there are ten spheres (sephiroth) or vessels that encapsulate archetypal energies. The ninth sphere, called *Foundation*, is ruled by the Moon and represents the astral plane—the foundation of creation. The Hebrew word for the sphere, *Yesod*, means "Foundation," but it is also composed of two parts: Ye (God) and Sod (secret). This sphere, being the 9th, encapsulates the secrets of the divine, the keys of esoteric wisdom.

Here is an excerpt from my book on the Kabbalistic Tree of Life, *A Wish Can Change Your Life*, discussing the meaning of 9:

Nine signifies completion, the final number before we start repeating the numerals that came before. In many cultures, nine denotes the "Foundation" of everything. One Egyptian myth recounts the birth of nine primordial gods that then created and ruled over the material world. The Greeks dubbed them the *ennead*, meaning "the great nine," the foundation of the universe. Nine judges sit on the Supreme Court, the foundation of justice in the USA. G.I. Gurdjieff, the noted 20th Century Greek-Armenian spiritualist, says that the enneagram—a nine-pointed star—contains all knowledge within its boundaries just as Foundation embodies the energies of all the other spheres. Odin, the king of the Norse, hung himself upside-down for nine days to achieve his ultimate transformation. It also takes nine months—nine moons—for a baby to gestate in the womb before it surfaces as a fresh member of the Kingdom, the fetus terminates its gestation and resurrects and a baby, given a name, and begins a life.

This year, you experience a great deal of dying and rebirth, shedding shadows and redressing. And if we are on the subject of death and resurrection, we better discuss the planet ruling these processes.

– Pluto, Lord of the Underworld

PLUTO IN AQUARIUS

Pluto, ruler of Scorpio, represents power, riches (hence Plutocracy—governance of the rich), sexuality, passion, death and resurrection, therapy, the occult, investigation, privacy, intimacy, and magic. If he sounds rather dark, well, it's because he is. Pluto is the patron-planet of the underworld, crime, as well as policing. I guess it takes one to know one.

Let's examine the last three transits of Pluto, so that you can better understand what the Lord of the Underworld does whenever he enters a new sign.

In 1995, the year GenZ made their initial entrance to the planet, Pluto transited into Sagittarius, the most popular sign associated with optimism, luck, and opportunities. The Soviet Empire collapsed (when Pluto was in Scorpio), and Francis Fukuyama published *The End of History*, optimistically suggesting that Western liberal democracy and human evolution had reached its zenith. Globalization gained ground under Pluto's transit in Sagittarius, the sign of traveling and foreign cultures, and the world felt like it was getting safer. That optimism reached banks and financial institutions, which started taking their belief in the "American Dream" a bit too seriously, issuing loans to people that otherwise wouldn't have been able to secure one. "You need half a million dollars to buy a house? No problem! We believe in you. Oh, you don't make any income now? Not a problem, we trust in your potential." That is indeed noble, and Sagittarius is a principled sign. And all was going kinda well, stocks up, bubble growing, until Pluto entered practical, pragmatic, frugal, budget-savvy, and realistic (some argue pessimistic) Capricorn in 2008.

Being an earth sign, Capricorn took one glance at the banks' spreadsheet and said "Wtf!" Pluto in Capricorn, ruled by Saturn, the Lord of Karma—action and reaction. The world entered the Great Recession—a global correction, or according to Kabbalah, *Tikkun*—rectification.

But that is not all that Pluto (investments, finances) in Capricorn means. On January 3, 2009, perhaps as a reaction to the Great Recession, an alternative decentralized coin was minted, right when the Sun, Pluto, and Mars (rulers of Scorpio, sign of investments) as well as Jupiter (abundance) were in Capricorn—Bitcoin. At first, the digital marvel would be met with skepticism (one of the traits of Capricorn) but by the time Pluto was getting ready to leave Capricorn and move into Aquarius, financial powerhouses like BlackRock's iShares Bitcoin Trust (IBIT) accumulated close to 300,000 bitcoins, each valued around 70,000$.

From March 2023 to November 2024, Pluto had been hovering over the cusp of Capricorn (past) and Aquarius (future). At the end of 2024, Pluto finally settled in the Water-Bearer sign where he will remain for the next two decades. Since Pluto's main theme is transforming the sign that hosts him, we can expect a great deal of changes in relation to the aspects of life associated with Aquarius: governments, corporations, humanity, revolutions, independence, technology, Artificial Intelligence (LLM and Generative), Quantum Technology, science, patents, altruism, sainthood, and nonconformity.

Another aspect that Pluto in Aquarius can bring about is actual contact and encounter with extraterrestrials. Not only because the Tarot card of Aquarius is "The Star," but simply because Aquarius is the sign of community, and aliens share the cosmos with us. They are sentient beings that have souls and can, and probably do, reincarnate as humans, just as you could reincarnate on a different planet. And if this sounds too weird for you, welcome to Aquarius, the sign that is associated with outlandish ideas, the genius, and the Fool (the Tarot card of Uranus, ruler of Aquarius).

PLUTO AND THE WATER BEARER

The last time Pluto visited Aquarius, from 1777—1798, the Aquarian motto *Liberté, égalité, fraternité* (liberty, equality, and fraternity) heralded a new age of human history. Given that Aquarius symbolizes humanity, democracy, hope, and revolution, it's no coincidence that during Pluto's transit through this sign, the Industrial Revolution extended its reach from England to the rest of Europe. Concurrently, the nascent United States ratified her constitution, commencing with the distinctly Aquarian phrase: "We the people." It was also during this cycle of Pluto in Aquarius, that the planet Uranus—the modern ruler of Aquarius—was discovered.

Since Pluto (power, assets, shared resources) will be in Aquarius for two decades we can expect crypto currencies to explode and the blockchain they are built upon to merge with AI, quantum technology, and other futuristic technology to provide a decentralized alternative to the current ancient financial systems.

AQUARIAN SEXY TIME

As Pluto (sexuality, intimacy) transited into Aquarius (technology and AI), sex doll brothels began emerging around the world. Patrons are offered the opportunity to rent and interact with life-sized sex dolls, often designed to mimic the appearance and feel of a human partner. Some of these sex dolls, dubbed "Sex Robots," are equipped with Artificial Intelligence and robotics to provide interactive experiences, such as conversation, responsive touch sensors, and movement. The Artificial Intelligence aspect is especially intriguing, as some of these sex dolls are programmed to say things like, "I don't feel like doing it tonight, I have a headache."

In the next twenty years, as Pluto delves deeper into the uncharted technological territories of Aquarius, we can expect the emergence of ethical and moral issues. Do these advanced AI systems have any rights? Some of them, in the future, might be as intelligent as humans, if not more so. Would it be legal to buy AI sex dolls that look, behave, and talk like teenagers or children? Since 90% of sex doll clients are men, would this contribute to the dehumanization of women? Does having your first sexual experience with a sex robot count as losing your virginity? As promised, Pluto in Aquarius just gets weirder and weirder.

PLUTO IN AQUARIUS FOR THE ZODIAC SIGNS

- **Aries**: Transformation of Community and Technology
  As the leader of the flock, you will experience deep transformations within your clan, social circles, friendships, community, and how you relate to technology, science, your digital footprints, and technology in general. It is time to embrace the geek in you and update and upgrade your workflow. You must strive to become a pioneer in technological advancements and implement them in all aspects of your life. This is a time to realize and manifest your hopes and aspirations and become a beacon of light to humanity. Altruism and working with nonprofits can benefit you and others.

- **Taurus**: Career, Status, and Public Image
  Pluto's transit in Aquarius, your square sign, can be challenging, forcing you into action you might prefer to avoid, especially in your professional life. It is a time for major transformation in your career, public image, and how you deal with superiors, bosses, father figures, and authority. You might also be called to change the way you boss others. Don't be afraid to take risks in your career, perhaps go solo, or find greater freedom in your chosen field. Innovation and trying new approaches will be beneficial.

- **Gemini**: Philosophy, Wisdom, Truth, and Travel
  While your ruler, Mercury, was the god of liars and thieves, the next two decades are about truth and authenticity. You will be called to change and adapt your beliefs, philosophies, as well as how you teach, learn, and educate yourself. This is an exciting time to relocate to a new country, travel, and earn money abroad. New friends and intimate relationships can be forged with foreigners as well as your in-laws, who might feel familiar from a past life.

- **Cancer**: Shared Resources, Passion, Intimacy, and Shamanism
Pluto is taking you down to his realm, the Underworld. Like Orpheus, you are descending into the shadow, ready to reclaim your healing abilities, as well as passion and sexuality. Of all the signs, you are the only one invited by Pluto into his domain, and he is ready to initiate you into the secrets of the occult and tantra. While you are known for being the midwife and bringer of life, the next twenty years you will serve also as a doula of death, helping people die and let go. You will also be asked to transform how your partners or friends manage joint assets, talents, and gifts.

- **Leo**: Relationships, Partnerships, and Enemies
Since Pluto is in your opposite sign, he will challenge you to reassess all your primary relationships, reconnect with your artistic talents, and deal with enemies and competitors. Be extra careful to avoid unnecessary lawsuits and antagonistic attitudes. Make sure you have a good lawyer. This period is designed to transform your personal and professional relationships, trying to infuse them with more intimacy and authenticity. If you were born in the first few days of Leo (July 22-24), this aspect can be extra challenging, transforming many aspects of your life, so be ready for a major shedding.

- **Virgo**: Work, Diet, Health, Service, and Routine
As the watchmakers and engineers of the zodiac, Pluto will be transforming very familiar aspects of your life—health, routine, workplace, diet, and how you serve as well as how others serve you. It is a good time to get a pet, or if you have one, expect major transformations in your relationship with your furry friends. Try to connect to new, innovative, or forward-thinking ways of doing your work. This is a great time to connect with AI, e-commerce, and futuristic practices in work and health habits. There could be some transformations with employees and coworkers.

- **Libra**: Children, Romance, Recreation, and Creativity
Libras, you are asked by Pluto to transform how you define and experience happiness. Engage more in team sports and hobbies you can do

in a group or with your digital friends. It is a time to connect creativity with innovation. Additionally, you will undergo transformations in your connection to children, as well as baby projects. Explore innovative ways to create, entertain, and enjoy what life has to offer. Romance is in the air but be careful not to fall in love with love itself instead of with a person, or to get addicted to the dopamine releases.

- **Scorpio**: Home, Family, Parenting, and Real Estate
Pluto, your ruler, is in a sign that is square to yours, making it a bit uncomfortable and potentially forcing you into actions you'd rather not take, especially at home or with family members. Be extra careful to avoid unwanted pregnancies unless you are planning for it. Pluto can bring about transformations in your home life, family dynamics, and where you feel safe. It is a good time to relocate to a place with a strong community or closer to friends. This is a great time for remodeling your home and office, or changing cars, especially to an electric vehicle. Ancestral traumas or intergenerational karma might arise, necessitating healing. It's a good time to change parenting techniques.

- **Sagittarius**: Communication, Relatives, and Messaging
As the sign of mass media and publishing, Pluto is eager to transform the message you wish to publish to the world. While you usually excel in world travel, the next two decades will ask you to travel within your own country, focus on your own language, and refine your methods of communication. If you were a country, you would be transforming your harbors, airports, highways, train system, and fiber optics. Additionally, Pluto changes your relationships with your neighbors, siblings, relatives, and roommates. Embrace innovative, futuristic, and even rebellious ways of thinking and expressing yourself.

- **Capricorn**: Finances, Talents, Values, and Self-Worth
From 2008 until 2024 you were tasked with hosting Pluto and this year you are happy to let Aquarius deal with the Lord of Death and Transformation. Nevertheless, Pluto asks you to bring changes to how you earn your income, deal with your finances, and project your self-worth. Additionally, you will find yourself open to changing and

reshaping your values and core attitudes. Ensure that the way you make money is tied to your true talents and congruent with your values. Working with other people's money and talents can enhance your own.

- **Aquarius**: Identity, Image, and Body Transformation
  Of all the signs, you were chosen to host Pluto for the next twenty years. This means that all aspects of your life are going through major transformation. It is vital that you keep up with the times, upgrade and update yourself, and find ways to bring the future to the here and now. This is especially a time to transform your body, image, brand, and personal identity. Be yourself, express your individuality, and consider changing your hairdo, wardrobe, logo, and brand. Surrender to change and embrace your newfound freedom.

- **Pisces**: Mysticism, Imagination, Past Lifetimes, and Letting Go
  Pluto is asking you to connect with what you were designed to do: be the mystic, intuitive, dreamer, and empath of the zodiac. Of all the signs, only you and your opposite, Virgo, were given the task to enhance and transmute your own archetype, promising success and recognition by simply being yourself. This is the time to travel to your subconscious, past lifetimes, astral plane, dream time, and the collective unconscious to bring your tribe the boon, the gifts only you can access. Pluto encourages you to use your imagination, creative visualization, and intuition to help us all in these dire times.

URANUS IN TAURUS AND GEMINI

The Great Awakener Changing Signs

U ranus, the restless rebel, is getting jittery. He has been in Taurus since 2018 and feels the urge to explore a new sign. In 2025, Uranus, the Awakener, will attempt to lift off from Taurus, where he was grounded, and soar to Gemini heights. However, like a newly hatched eagle, his flight attempts this year are hampered by gravity, and only in 2026 will he be able to move to the binary sign for seven years. In the following chapter I will cover the areas in your life which Jupiter blesses in 2025 based on your sign.

URANUS'S JOURNEY BETWEEN TAURUS AND GEMINI—LIFT OFF?

Uranus in Taurus: 2018 until July 6, 2025, and from November 8, 2025, until April 25, 2026.

Uranus in Gemini: From July 7, 2025, to November 7, 2025, and from April 26, 2026, until 2032.

As you can see, Uranus, as well as Neptune and Saturn, are hovering over the cusp between signs. In 2025, we get a taste of things to come in 2026.

Given that Taurus is Mother Nature's sign, having Uranus within her archetype for most of the year encourages us to change (Uranus) the way we treat or interact with Mother Nature, or face the rude awakening (Uranus) in the form of climate disasters (Uranus is the god of the sky), zoonotic diseases (such as COVID), and other unpredictable calamities that are yet to manifest.

The World Meteorological Organization stated in a report published in 2024 that there is an 80% chance that in the next five years, we will cross the symbolic threshold of 1.5 degrees Celsius above the pre-industrial global average. Until 2015, the chance of this happening was negligible. As Uranus moved into Taurus in 2018, it rose to 20%, and last year to 66%. Another report, published by the Copernicus Climate Change Service, the European Union's climate research center, stated that May 2024 was the hottest May ever recorded.

Uranus' four-month flight into Gemini could bring news regarding Artificial Intelligence and perhaps the dawning of true Generative Artificial Intelligence. However, Uranus can also create unpredictable and erratic issues between siblings and relatives that could result in civil wars.

On the New Moon in Taurus, when Uranus was conjunct the Sun and Moon, along with Venus and Jupiter in the same sign, a study was published in Nature written by 21 leading scientists entitled *A Meta-Analysis on Global Change Drivers and the Risk of Infectious Disease.* The scientists isolated a few factors that contribute to the risk of the world suffering from another pandemic such as COVID:

- **Climate Change**: Alters habitats and migration patterns, affecting pathogen transmission (Uranus is associated with climate).
- **Land Use Change**: Deforestation, urbanization, and agricultural expansion increase human-wildlife interactions, facilitating disease spillover (Taurus is the sign of Mother Nature).
- **Globalization**: Enhances the spread of pathogens through increased human movement and trade.

The analysis suggests implementing policies to reduce greenhouse gas emissions, mitigate climate change impacts, and develop adaptive strategies for healthcare systems to handle climate-related disease outbreaks.

However, as long as populist politicians are elected around the world who deny the contribution of human action to climate change, we will have to endure many more years of suffering until Uranus wakes up all those that resist change.

In June 2024, as I am writing this section, AP reported that: "Each of the past 12 months ranked as the warmest on record in year-on-year comparisons," according to an EU report, while U.N. Secretary-General António Guterres called for urgent action such as a 30% drop in fossil-fuel production and use to avert "climate hell." Alas, let us hope it is not too late for a change.

URANUS IN GEMINI

"Everything is holy! Everybody's holy! everywhere is holy! everyday is in eternity! Everyman's an angel!"

– Allen Ginsburg (a proud Gemini)

As the ruler of Aquarius and paragon of innovation and technology, Uranus' flight in curious binary Gemini brings about a scientific revolution. My prediction is that in the next seven years, AI and quantum computing will converge and begin changing our lives in many tangible ways. That is, if Saturn in Aries (2026—2028) won't drag us into needless wars.

For those born between May 14 and May 23 (from 23 degrees Taurus to 3 degrees Gemini), 2025 is noteworthy as Uranus aligns with your Sun. Since this happens once in 84 years, it's a resonating wake-up call. This could manifest as a personal revolution, a big switch, a significant transition, perhaps an upgrade which could upend your life. It's a time to liberate yourself from parental influences or other external pressures and embrace one's unique individuality.

Binary Gemini in collaboration with Uranus' technological savvy brought to the world in 1943/1945 the Colossus Computer, developed by British codebreakers and used by Alan Turing to crack the Nazi's Enigma code, thus quickening the end of WWII.

Here are some of the key events that took place the last time Uranus was in Gemini (1942–1949):

- **Holocaust**: Systematic genocide of Jews, Romanos, LGBTQ, and other minority groups by Nazi Germany.
- **Warsaw Ghetto Uprising (April-May 1943)**: Jewish resistance against Nazi efforts to transport the remaining ghetto population to concentration camps.
- **D-Day (June 6, 1944)**: Allied invasion of Normandy, France, marking the beginning of the liberation of Western Europe.
- **Atomic Bomb Development (1945)**: The Manhattan Project culminates in the successful detonation of atomic bombs, leading to their use in Hiroshima and Nagasaki.
- **Computer Advances (1945)**: The Electronic Numerical Integrator and Computer (ENIAC), one of the first general-purpose computers, is completed in the United States.
- **Germany Surrenders (May 8, 1945)**: Official end of World War II in Europe (V-E Day).
- **Atomic Bombings of Hiroshima and Nagasaki (August 1945)**: U.S. drops atomic bombs, leading to Japan›s surrender.
- **United Nations Established (October 1945)**: Formation of the international organization to promote peace and cooperation.
- **Invention of the Microwave Oven (1946)**: Percy Spencer invents the microwave oven, revolutionizing cooking and food preparation.
- **Development of Transistors (1946)**: John Bardeen, Walter Brattain, and William Shockley invent the transistor at Bell Laboratories, paving the way for modern electronics.
- **Partition of India (August 1947)**: British India is divided into India and Pakistan, leading to mass migrations and violence.
- **Marshall Plan Announced (June 1947)**: U.S. initiative to aid European economic recovery.
- **State of Israel Established (May 1948)**: Declaration of the independence of Israel, leading to the Arab Israeli war.

- **Universal Declaration of Human Rights (December 1948)**: Adopted by the United Nations General Assembly.
- **NATO Founded (April 1949)**: North Atlantic Treaty Organization established as a military alliance.

As Uranus returns to Gemini, we can expect significant advancements in technology, communication, and social structures. The intersection of AI and quantum computing will likely redefine our daily lives, pushing the boundaries of what is possible. However, we must remain vigilant against the potential for conflicts and upheaval, balancing innovation with responsibility.

SOME GOOD NEWS—PLUTO AND URANUS AGREE TO AGREE

Throughout August and September, Uranus and Pluto are positioned in what is called a "trine," creating an auspicious aspect that can help channel the best qualities of Uranus (innovation, friendships, originality) and Pluto (power, transformation, shared resources). This is a great time to forge new friendships, collaborate with shared resources, think outside of the box, and have the power to practically use new ideas. Since the two planets are in air signs, this is especially good for science, technology, relationships, friendships, connecting to new organizations and companies, writing, business, as well as healing relationships with relatives.

PRACTICAL SUGGESTIONS FOR URANUS IN GEMINI

- **Be curious**: Embrace your curiosity. Engage in activities that stimulate your mind and explore new interests.
- **Learn new skills**: Take up a new language or any intellectual pursuit that involves learning and working with your brain.
- **Embrace humor**: Surround yourself with humorous people and seek to be funny yourself. Laughter is great for mental stimulation and social bonding.
- **Update technology**: Keep up with technological advances. Upgrade your gadgets and ensure you're using the latest tools and platforms.

- **Read and write:** Engage in extensive reading. Express yourself through writing, posting, and texting. Mental stimulation is essential.
- **Innovate communication:** Allow changes in the way you communicate and deliver messages. Experiment with attracting different clients or targeting new audiences.
- **Expand social circles:** Seek to enlarge your friend circles. Connect with new people and stay connected. Networking can lead to exciting opportunities.

JUPITER RAISES
TO HIS EXALTATION

JUPITER EXILED IN GEMINI (JUNE 11, 2024–JUNE 10, 2025)

Jupiter, king of the gods, symbolizes expansion, opportunities, synchronicities, generosity, adventures, enthusiasm, and luck. He takes 12 years to orbit the Sun, meaning he lingers in each sign for about a year, completing the entire zodiac wheel every duodecennial.

As mentioned before, planets have different dignity or strength of expression, depending on the sign they occupy. From June 11, 2024, to June 9, 2025, Jupiter flies through Gemini, and since it is his sign of exile, his guidance and grace are not fully active. I always say that Jupiter in Gemini is only good for Gemini. Think back to 2020, when Jupiter was in his sign of Fall, Capricorn, far from being able to answer our cries for help. However, in December 2020, as Jupiter moved into social Aquarius, we began to return to some sort of normalcy. By the way, Jupiter was also fallen when the Great Recession started.

Nevertheless, even in Gemini, Jupiter can still help us in the first part of the year—delivering our messages, facilitating writing projects, enhancing communication skills, aiding business pursuits, and potentially mending and strengthening relationships with relatives, especially siblings, as well as neighbors and even neighboring countries. Jupiter's propensity to weave remarkable synchronicities remains robust.

Below is a list of dates when Jupiter resided in Gemini. Reflect on those periods and try to recognize the boons and blessings Jupiter gave you in those years. By doing so, you'll gain insight into Jupiter's cyclical waves of abundance and can set your expectations for the coming year:

- August 1976 to October 1976
- April 1977 to August 1977
- December 1977 to April 1978
- July 1988 to November 1988
- March 1989 to July 1989
- June 2000 to July 2001
- June 2012 to June 2013

JUPITER EXALTED IN CANCER (JUNE 10, 2025–JUNE 29, 2026)

Something good is starting to happen on June 11, as Jupiter moves away from his sign of exile to his sign of exaltation, where his benevolence is expressed in the strongest way. Jupiter sailing in Cancer can help in all aspects of Cancer: family, parenting, real estate, healing from genetic ailments, tapping into ancestral gifts through both nature (genes) and nurture, emotional support, regaining a sense of security, and allowing a full range of emotional expression, especially compassion and unconditional love.

SUGGESTIONS FOR JUPITER'S TRANSIT IN CANCER

- **Expand your family**: This is a great time to grow your family, settle down, domesticate yourself, become a parent, or relocate to a place where you feel safe and secure. It's a time for nesting.
- **Healing familial feuds**: Jupiter can help mend lingering issues within your family of origin (especially parents) and your own family.
- **Heal yourself and become a healer**: This transit of Jupiter is a favorable time for therapy, emotional support, overcoming addictions, and physical as well as emotional rehabilitation.
- **Use "I Feel" rather than "I Think"**: As Jupiter transits from Gemini (I think) to Cancer (I feel), try to use the key word of Cancer when you

speak. For example, say "I feel you need to listen to my suggestions" instead of "I think you should adhere to this recommendation."

- **Meditate**: The Tarot card for Cancer is "The Chariot," which in Kabbalah (Merkava) is the code for "meditation." The esoteric meaning of "The Chariot" (thus also meditation) is the ability to travel without movement. We all meditated for nine months in our mother's womb (both mother and womb are associated with Cancer), traveling wherever our mother went without moving away from her womb.

- **Real estate**: The real estate market may see growth, with more people investing in property and land, particularly homes and family-oriented spaces. It is also a good time for remodeling.

Jupiter in Cancer Dates

- May 24, 1954–June 13, 1955
- September 21, 1965–November 17, 1965
- May 5, 1966–September 27, 1966
- January 16, 1967–May 23, 1967
- August 20, 1977–December 31, 1977
- April 12, 1978–September 5, 1978
- March 1, 1979–April 20, 1979
- July 31, 1989–August 18, 1990
- July 13, 2001–August 1, 2002
- June 26, 2013–July 16, 2014

JUPITER'S GIFTS FOR EACH ZODIAC SIGN IN 2025

Aries

- **Jupiter in Gemini (until June)**:
  Communication, writing, business and learning: Focus on expanding your knowledge and improving communication skills. This is an excellent time for learning, teaching, writing, and networking. A favorable period to heal relationships with relatives, neighbors, and roommates. Engage in social activities and build new friendships. Short trips and local travel can be particularly beneficial.

- **Jupiter in Cancer (from June):**
  Home and family: Shift your focus to home and family matters. Consider improving your living situation, whether at home, the office, or your car, spending quality time with family, and creating a nurturing home environment. Additionally, pay attention to your emotional health and seek activities that bring comfort and security.

Taurus

- **Jupiter in Gemini (until June):**
  Financial opportunities, talents, values and self-worth: Focus on increasing your income and managing your finances. Look for new ways to boost your earnings through sources that are consistent with your values. Improve your resource management skills and invest in valuable assets.

- **Jupiter in Cancer (from June):**
  Communication, writing, business and learning: Engage in learning new skills and enhancing your communication abilities. This is a great time for education, writing, and sharing knowledge. Get involved in your local community and build stronger connections with neighbors. Local travel is encouraged. Great for new contracts and contacts.

Gemini

- **Jupiter in Gemini (until June):**
  Personal growth: Focus on personal development and self-improvement. Embrace opportunities for growth and expansion in all areas of your life. This is a time for rebranding yourself and embracing leadership roles. It's a time for new ventures and taking bold steps toward your goals.

- **Jupiter in Cancer (from June):**
  Financial stability, talents, values and self-worth: Shift your focus to financial security and stability. Look for ways to improve your financial

situation and manage resources wisely while being true to your values. Work on building your self-worth and confidence.

Cancer

- **Jupiter in Gemini (until June):**
  Introspection, imagination, mysticism, past lives and healing: Focus on introspection, healing, and spiritual growth. This is a time for self-reflection and addressing unresolved issues. It's a wonderful time for meditation and exploring gifts from previous lives. Engage in activities that support others from behind the scenes.

- **Jupiter in Cancer (from June):**
  Personal growth and reconnecting to your body: Embrace opportunities for personal growth and expansion. Focus on your goals, desires, and overall well-being. Rebrand and improve yourself. Embrace new beginnings.

Leo

- **Jupiter in Gemini (until June):**
  Social networks, technology and altruism: Focus on expanding your social networks and building new friendships. Engage in group activities and collaborative projects. Set and work toward achieving your long-term goals and aspirations. Update and upgrade your workflow and life by implementing new technologies.

- **Jupiter in Cancer (from June):**
  Introspection, imagination, mysticism, past lives and healing: Turn your focus inward for introspection and healing. Address unresolved emotional issues and engage in spiritual practices. Rest, rejuvenate, and prepare for new beginnings starting June 2026 as Jupiter moves to your sign.

Virgo

- **Jupiter in Gemini (until June):**
  Career advancement and professional life: Focus on career growth and professional development. Seek opportunities for advancement and

recognition in your field. Heal relationships with superiors, bosses, and authority figures. Enhance your public image and reputation through hard work and dedication.

- **Jupiter in Cancer (from June)**:
Social Networks, technology and altruism: Engage with social groups and build stronger connections with friends and colleagues. Participate in community activities and collaborative projects. Be altruistic and help your community. Friends can be a source of joy and connections. Set future goals and work toward your long-term aspirations.

Libra

- **Jupiter in Gemini (until June)**:
Education, truth and travel: Focus on expanding your horizons through education and travel. Seek opportunities for higher learning and cultural experiences. Jupiter, the philosopher and teacher, is helping you become one. Engage in activities that broaden your philosophical and spiritual perspectives. Your relationships with in-laws can improve.
- **Jupiter in Cancer (from June)**:
Career advancement and professional life: Shift your focus to career growth and professional development. Look for opportunities to advance and achieve recognition. Enhance your public image through dedication and hard work. Improve relationships with bosses and superiors.

Scorpio

- **Jupiter in Gemini (until June)**:
Shared resources, sexuality and transformation: Focus on managing shared resources and finances. Engage in joint ventures and investments. Experience heightened passion and intimacy, as well as magic and transformation. Jupiter is enhancing the very things your sign is associated with.
- **Jupiter in Cancer (from June)**:
Education, truth and travel: Expand your horizons through education, travel, and cultural experiences. Seek opportunities for higher learning

and spiritual growth. Jupiter, the teacher and philosopher, is trying to help you become a sage. Engage in activities that broaden your philosophical and spiritual perspectives. Improve relationships with foreigners and in-laws.

Sagittarius

- **Jupiter in Gemini (until June):**
  Partnerships, justice, design and marriage: Focus on building and improving partnerships, both personal and professional. Engage in collaborative efforts and strengthen relationships. Expect good luck in legal matters and protection against enemies. Be careful not to overextend yourself. Find balance in your relationships and personal life.

- **Jupiter in Cancer (from June):**
  Shared resources, sexuality and transformation: Focus on managing other people's money and talents. Engage in joint ventures and investments. Experience heightened passion and intimacy, as well as magic and transformation. Your healing abilities are enhanced. You could also receive an inheritance or good news from investments.

Capricorn

- **Jupiter in Gemini (until June):**
  Health, Diet, Work, service and daily Routine: Focus on improving your health and daily routine. Engage in activities that promote physical well-being and efficiency. Expect a promotion and improved relationships with employees or coworkers. This is a great time to get a pet.

- **Jupiter in Cancer (from June):**
  Partnerships, justice, design and marriage: Shift your focus to building and improving partnerships, both personal and professional. Engage in collaborative efforts and strengthen relationships. Work on finding balance in your relationships and personal life. Expect added protection against competitors and enemies.

Aquarius

- **Jupiter in Gemini (until June):**
  Creativity, children, romance and fun: Focus on creativity, fun, and self-expression. Engage in activities that bring joy and allow you to express your unique talents. Explore romantic opportunities and enhance your love life. This is a great time to connect with your children or inner child and create.

- **Jupiter in Cancer (from June):**
  Health, Diet, work, service and daily routine: Focus on improving your health and daily routine. Engage in activities that promote physical well-being and efficiency. Expect a promotion and improved relationships with employees or coworkers. This is a great time to get a pet.

Pisces

- **Jupiter in Gemini (until June):**
  Home and family: Focus on home and family matters. Improve your living situation and strengthen family bonds. This is a great time for real estate and remodeling. Pay attention to your emotional health and seek activities that bring comfort and security.

- **Jupiter in Cancer (from June):**
  Creativity, children, romance and fun: Focus on creativity, fun, and self-expression. Engage in activities that bring joy and allow you to express your unique talents. Explore romantic opportunities and enhance your love life. This is a great time to connect with your children or inner child and create.

TRINES: THE SACRED
MOUNTAIN OF ASTROLOGY

Astrology is an esoteric library composed of different fields—alchemy, numerology, history, geography, as well as sacred geometry. In fact, the aspects I keep mentioning in the book (square, opposition, conjunction) derive their meaning from the ancient art of sacred geometry. The aspects found in your chart represent the distance in degrees between the planets. The square, which is a challenging aspect, appears whenever two or more planets are located 90 degrees apart, while an opposition is formed whenever two planets are 180 degrees apart. These sacred shapes highlight the relationship between the two planets and therefore how well their energies mingle.

The trine is the most auspicious aspect in astrology and is formed when two or more heavenly bodies are 120 degrees apart. If three planets are distanced 120 degrees from each other, they form a perfect triangle, creating what looks like a mountain, allowing us to reach the heights of our potential. It is said that King David had two of these triangles forming a perfect hexagram, a six-pointed star, or Magen David, Hebrew for "the shield of David."

In 2025, we definitely need protection, and we are granted a few of these throughout the yearly journey. Below are the dates when we receive a protective shield. Since the trine connects the three water signs (Cancer, Scorpio, Pisces), they would benefit from it the most, and to a lesser degree, also the earth signs (Capricorn, Taurus, Virgo). The rest of the signs would also be granted protection but indirectly.

- September 17–September 30
- October 20–December 5

THE YEAR OF
THE EARTHLY SNAKE

Jan 29, 2025, to Feb 16, 2026

Every twelve years, in accordance with the cycles of Jupiter, the Chinese Lunar calendar circles back to the same animal sign. Since there are five elemental phases, every 60 years, the same combination of animal and element returns. This 60-year cycle also mirrors the infamous "Second Saturn Return," which is a time of focus, pressure, and lifechanging events. To truly grasp the significance of 2025, we must look back to 1965 and 1905, which were Earth Snake years. One of the greatest contributions of the Year of the Earth (practical) Snake (wisdom) was 1905, Albert Einstein's *Miracle Year Papers*, which laid the foundation for modern physics.

Chinese sages tell us that what you do at the beginning of a Lunar New Year determines your luck for the coming year. Adhering to the Law of Beginning, which is also why we cast your astrological chart based on your first breath, Chinese astrologers suggest staying up on Chinese New Year's Eve (January 28, 2025), and instead of a kiss at the end of countdown, as we do in the West, focus on blessing the people you love. By the way, an international study conducted in 2015 titled *Is the Romantic-Sexual Kiss a Near Human Universal?* (W. Jankowiak and S. Volsche) discovered that less than half of the world's cultures associate kissing with romance or love, so you don't have to feel pressure to kiss anyone at 12am on New Year's.

The snake is a complicated symbol; it universally generates fear, shared by other primates as well. The serpent represents wisdom, esoteric studies, and temptations. The snake kills yet symbolizes healing. Considering this year's numerology is 9, associated with death, shedding shadows, and transformation, as well as the fact that Saturn, Lunar Nodes, Jupiter, Uranus, and Neptune change their astrological signs, 2025 can indeed be a year of practical (Earth) transformation (Snake).

Since it is the Chinese New Year, we should examine the snake through the lenses of our friends in China, where the serpent represents wisdom, intuition, mystery (keeping thoughts and feelings to themselves), caution (poisonous), resourcefulness, determination, charm, and magic. Combined with the pragmatism of the Earth element, we can conclude that 2025, viewed from a Chinese perspective, is a year to ground your intuition (which is also recommended due to the conjunction of Saturn and Neptune this year), practice caution, and be practical with your resources, investments, and shared capitals. Be private and keep your cards close to your chest.

WHAT CAN WE EXPECT?

Let's examine the last two times we slithered along with the earthy snake:

- **October Manifesto** (October 1905): Tsar Nicholas II issues the October Manifesto, granting civil liberties and the creation of the Duma (a legislative assembly) in response to revolutionary pressures.
- **Battle of Tsushima** (May 27-28, 1905): A decisive naval battle where the Japanese fleet defeats the Russian fleet, leading to Japan's victory in the Russo-Japanese War.
- **Special Theory of Relativity** (1905): Albert Einstein publishes his paper "On the Electrodynamics of Moving Bodies," introducing the special theory of relativity and forever changing our understanding of space and time. 1905 was the year we first heard of $E=mc^2$.
- **Expressionism Begins** (1905): A group of four German architecture students who dabbled in painting: Ernst Ludwig Kirchner, Fritz Bleyl,

Karl Schmidt-Rottluff, and Erich Heckel, formed the group Die Brücke (The Bridge) in Dresden, initiating a new art style.

- **"Dune" by Frank Herbert** (1965): Frank Herbert's science fiction masterpiece is published, becoming one of the best-selling science fiction novels of all time and profoundly influencing the genre. Think of the spice-creating giant worms that look like earth snakes.
- **"In Cold Blood" by Truman Capote** (1965): A pioneering work in the true crime genre that examines the murders of the Clutter family in Kansas. Snakes are associated with Scorpio, the sign of murder and investigation.
- **The Beatles Release *Help!*** (1965): The Beatles release their influential album *Help!* and continue to shape the music and cultural landscape of the 1960s. We might also need Help! in 2025.
- **Discovery of Cosmic Microwave Background Radiation** (1965): Penzias and Wilson provide significant support for the Big Bang theory.

Interestingly, the two times the USA experienced a surprise attack on its soil were in the Year of the Snake: September 11, 2001, and December 7, 1941.

PAST YEARS OF THE SNAKE

Here is a list of recent Years of the Snake. See if you can identify major events that happened to you during these years, as the snake might coil back to those periods and deepen your transformation.

- **1953**: Death of Joseph Stalin; Discovery of the structure of DNA by James Watson and Francis Crick, with contributions from Rosalind Franklin and Maurice Wilkins.
- **1977**: Egyptian President Anwar Sadat visits Israel; George Lucas's "Star Wars" premieres.
- **1989**: Tiananmen Square Massacre; Fall of the Berlin Wall; Velvet Revolution.
- **2001**: Completion of the Human Genome Project; USA invasion of Afghanistan.

- **2013**: Typhoon Haiyan devastates parts of Southeast Asia; Human stem cell cloning.

Earth slinking Serpent Years: 2013, 2001, **1989**, 1977, 1965, **1953**, 1941.

The bolded *1989* and *1953*, were not only Serpent year but also shared their numerology with 2025—the transformative 9. In 1989, as mentioned, the Iron Wall began to crumble and in 1953, Joseph Stalin died, Queen Elizabeth II was coronated, the Korean War ended, and the Iranian Coup d'état restored the rule of the Shah. It was also the year the DNA was discovered, and the first human made it to the top of Mount Everest.

PRACTICAL SUGGESTIONS

The lucky hour for the Year of the Snake is said to be 9:00 am—11:00 am, as the Sun warms the Earth, and the snakes and other creepy crawlers come out of their holes. Try to schedule important meetings around that time (just make sure the Moon is not void of course or Mercury retrogrades). If you love plants, surround yourself this year with all types of cactus and orchids, which are associated with the Serpent.

The lucky colors are red, bright yellow, and black, which is interesting considering that fashionistas have declared "Future Dusk," a dark purple/blue, as the color of the year 2025.

2025 COLOR:
FUTURE DUSK

Fashion leaders have declared "Future Dusk" as the color of the year for 2025. Announced by WGSN and Coloro (Coloro 129-35-18), this shade is a dark, moody blend of blue and purple, symbolizing mystery and intrigue—qualities typical for a year whose numerology is 9 and associated with the snake. In the Kabbalistic Tree of Life, the 9th sphere represents shedding, death, and sexuality, all aspects of the snake (Scorpio). For your reference, this book's cover is Future Dusk.

Future Dusk aligns with themes of transition and change and is expected to dominate fashion as well as the year astrologically and kabbalistically. The color offers versatility, serving as a gender-inclusive purple and a contemporary alternative to navy. Considering that Pluto (the planet of Scorpio, symbolized by the snake) will finally enter Aquarius (whose color is purple) for good in 2025, this color is truly energetically correct for the year.

I always contended that, according to Genesis, the oldest profession is not prostitution, but rather fashion design. Remember, the first thing Adam and Eve did after they tasted the fruits of the forbidden Tree of Knowledge was to cover themselves with fig leaves—the birth of haute couture.

LILITH IN SCORPIO
The Mother of Demons Wrapped in Snakes

In Mesopotamian and Jewish mythology, Lilith is often depicted as a demoness or a dark goddess. She is sometimes referred to as Adam's first wife, who, refusing to always be subservient to Adam, finally left him for a sexy demon. Some feminists have adopted her as their heroine, but to be honest, just as we have toxic masculinity, we also have toxic femininity. Thus, in astrology charts, Lilith is associated with the Black Moon, representing the lunar apogee—the point where the Moon is furthest from Earth. In astrology, as well as in psychoanalysis, she symbolizes the archetype of *Paradise Lost*, hidden aspects of the self, suppressed desires, shadow work, and raw, primal instincts.

Lilith Black Moon spends nine months (the gestation period) in each sign, therefore, every 9 years you experience your Lilith Return. From the end of March until the end of December, Lilith transits Scorpio, the sign symbolized by the serpent. This could be dangerous, as Scorpio embodies several attributes similar to Lilith—magic, the occult, possessiveness, stalking, jealousy, and manipulation. Be extra careful with how you express your emotional needs and who you allow into your heart or bed. And be careful not to find yourself a victim of a *Baby-Reindeer-type stalker*.

NEW YEAR'S RESOLUTION

2025, akin to her older sisters, 2023 and 2024, kicks off with a retrograde. Mars in retrograde at the start of the year means you must watch closely every action you take, as the reaction might come swiftly and harshly. Listed below are select auspicious dates to kickstart your New Year's resolutions, aiming to offer you some cosmic support. However, embarking on a new project or resolution during a retrograde is possible only if you've previously pursued the same goal but didn't see it through. Unfortunately, most New Year's resolutions, statistically speaking, tend to flop miserably. To counter this, I have two pieces of advice:

Ensure that you embark on the manifestation journey at the optimal time (refer to the date list below). I strongly encourage you to employ the methodology developed by George T. Doran (1981), neatly summarized by the acronym SMART: Be Specific; Choose a Measurable wish; Assign the resolution to your wants and not what others wish for you; Be Realistic and make your resolution Time-related.

While the New Year celebrations might inspire potential resolutions, below are the most propitious times to initiate the manifestation process.

On my web site www.CosmicNavigator.com you'll find the Wish Maker, a complimentary tool created to aid you in manifesting your wishes using the principles of Kabbalah from my book *A Wish Can Change Your Life*.

DATES TO INITIATE YOUR RESOLUTION

- **December 30, 2024–New Moon in Capricorn**: While it is before the New Year, it is a great Moon to start working on achieving your 2025 long-term goals. Ideal for resolutions that relate to career, professional life, overcoming fears and insecurities, or any aspiration that demands a great deal of discipline and persistence.
- **January 4–Venus exalted conjunct Moon**: The Moon is growing and passing over Venus in her most powerful sign. Great for wishes relating to love, finances, art, and relationships.
- **January 9–Moon exalted conjunct Uranus and trines Sun and Minerva**: A great day for resolutions related to e-commerce, friendships, technology, companies, as well as real estate, parenting, and family.
- **January 13–Full Moon in Cancer**: The Moon in her home sign can help you with resolutions that relate to letting go, detoxing, cleansing, getting rid of ancestral traumas, and healing.
- **January 29–New Moon in Aquarius and Chinese New Year**: An exceptional day to set any resolution, given that billions globally celebrate this fresh start. Like surfing a massive intention wave, you can ride its momentum. With a trine from Jupiter, your wishes can materialize.
- **February 1–Cluster of planets in Pisces**: An opportune time for wishes that relate to meditation, yoga, dance, imagination, art, intuition, and mysticism.
- **March 20–Equinox and the astrological New Year**: Celebrated as the New Year in various cultures (including the Persians' Nowruz, Bahá'í, Kurds, Mayans, Ancient Egyptians, and Babylonians). It's an ideal moment to refresh or initiate your resolution. However, be aware that both Venus and Mercury are retrograde, therefore, you can only start something you tried in the past and failed to complete.

NOW FOR
YOUR TRIBE

Y ou're now primed to set forth on your 2025 odyssey. You've garnered the essential information and the lay of the sky. In the next section, it's advisable to delve into the chapter relating to both your Sun sign as well as rising sign.

Wishing you a year filled with protection (Pluto), calmness (North Node), health (Jupiter), transformation (Earth Snake), creativity (Neptune conjunct Saturn), synchronicities (eclipses in Pisces), magic (Uranus in Gemini), and good health (Jupiter)!

PART IV

YOUR COSMIC NAVIGATION GUIDE & TECH SUPPORT

ARIES AND
ARIES RISING: I AM

Letting Go & Changing Gears

General Trends: This is a powerful year for your clan as Neptune, Saturn, and the North Node transit over your border with Pisces, allowing you to tap into your mystical potential as well as achieve your practical mundane goals. The first and last three months of the year you continue letting go and detoxing from negative people and situations, but from April until September, you will be hosting Saturn for the first time since 1996–1998, and this means things are getting serious with the Lord Karma auditing you but nevertheless grounding your gifts and talents. This is a great year for real-estate, relocation, and starting a family.

JANUARY

On January 3, Venus enters Pisces until February 4, blessing you with abundant access to your imagination, as well as people, gifts, places, and talents from previous lives. This is a great time to access your subconscious, engage in creative visualization, as well as let go of outdated patterns from past relationships. A great time for couple's therapy. She could also present opportunities to improve your finances and self-worth. However, on January 6, your ruler, Mars retrogrades into Cancer until April 18. Mars was already retrograding since December 2024, but as he moves into Cancer, his sign of fall, things can get more challenging, so watch out. Be careful of accidents, falling (unless it is in love) and issues with water, water damages in your home, office, and floods. Conflict can arise with family members.

On January 8, Mercury enters Capricorn until January 28 and brings about new connections and possibility for success in career and your professional life. Serious thought, discipline study, lessons coming from matured and experienced figures, especially bosses and superiors. Slow your thought, speech, and writing, be mindful of every word, take your time and ground your ideas with discipline and strategy to bring them into fruition.

January 13 Full Moon in Cancer and pits home and family versus career. This Full Moon squares your sign and can force you into action you rather not take. Due to the opposition of retro Mars and Pluto, take extra heed of over emotionality and guilt casting with family as well as professional life. This trend continues into January 18 and 19 as Venus conjuncts Saturn where you should watch your finances as well as relationships with coworkers and employees.

As the Sun transits into Aquarius, from January 19 to February, you will feel a better connection to your friends, community, as well as immerse yourself in science, technology and innovation. Don't be afraid to be original and think and act out of the box. In addition, on January 25–26 Venus trines your planet Mars, and love with friends and partners blooms. New relationships and or harmonizing current relationships are probable.

From January 28 until February 14 Mercury will be in Aquarius bringing you in contact with new friends, connections, technology, and innovation. This trends peaks on January 28–29, which is the New Moon in Aquarius and Chinese New Year. Jupiter is blessing this New Moon with wisdom and synchronicity especially in the form of new contracts, writing projects and improved relationships with relatives.

On January 29, the North Node retrogrades away from your sign where he was since July 2023 and plunges into Pisces until August 19, 2026. A time

ARIES AND ARIES RISING: I AM

to say goodbye to the Dragon as he now joins Saturn to help you detox, let go of things you do not need, and connect you to people, talents, and locations you have known in previous lives. The Dragon asks you to connect to yoga, dance, or martial arts while the South Node in Virgo, beacons you to let go of criticism, perfectionism, and overanalytical tendencies. There could be major changes in your workplace, diet, and health.

FEBRUARY

On February 4, Venus enters Aries, your sign, until March 27, while she is not super happy to be hosted by your fiery vibes, you are very pleased to have her over. She can bestow upon you a new look, and you will feel and appear more attractive, artistic, and charming. Watch for impulsiveness in matters of finances.

On February 12 as the Moon is Full in a fellow fire sign (Leo), the love affair with Venus will grow. There could be a romantic partner coming your way and a great deal of creativity. You might feel the pull and push between the need to spend time with your children or romantic partner versus friends or your company.

Right on Valentines, February 14, Mercury enters Pisces until March 3. This adds to your ability to tap into your imagination and subconscious. However, you might feel confused and misunderstood. Make sure to use the words "I feel" or "I imagine" or "I believe," instead of "I think." This trend is enhanced by the Sun's transit into Pisces until March 20's Equinox. Imagination, dance, movement, dreaming, meditation, intuition, mysticism, and empathy are heightened. Just make sure to guard your boundaries and avoid addictions or self-destructive tendencies. The dive into the Collective Unconscious and your past lifetimes reaches its peak on the New Moon in Pisces of February 28. A great day to start something new that involves your imagination, photography, movement, yoga, meditation as well as letting go of things that hinder your growth. There is a tendency to absorb negativity from others. Since Jupiter is squaring the New Moon, conflicts could arise from issues relative to finances and values. Be careful of deceptions and illusions.

MARCH

On March 1-2, Venus begins her stationary and retrograde motion in your sign, Aries, until April 14. Not only she is exile but now she is walking backward in her high heels over burning Aries coals. You might be quick to anger and try your best to avoid conflict or arguments with partners or lovers. It is not the best time to get married, start new relationships (work or life), or get engaged. Exes or lovers from previous lives or this life could make an entrance. Be extra mindful with finances, as people tend to lose money or make bad investments.

On March 3, Mercury enters your sign until March 30. Mercury can be a bit impatient when in Aries and favors practical and concise communication. From March 14 to April 8 Mercury Retrogrades and you should avoid signing documents or starting new projects unless you have tried before and failed. Just be aware that the worst time of the retrograde takes place when Mercury retrogrades into his sign of fall, Pisces, between March 30 and Apil 8. At that moment he joins Saturn and shows you what you need to cut away from or break free from. In addition, it could bring about melancholy, confusion, and disorientation. However, dreams and intuition are enhanced.

On March 14, Pi Day, the Lunar Eclipse in Virgo kicks off the eclipse season. A great time to bring a project at work to an end, as well as focus on diet, service, and combining your analytical and wholistic aspects in life.

On March 20, the Equinox, the Sun moves into your sign until April 19. Happy New Astrological Year! A time to focus on your body, health, physical activity, leadership, your brand and image, as well as leadership. On March 29, the Solar Eclipse in Aries kicks off the eclipse season. The next two weeks are going to quicken and intensify everything in your life and create some tension between you and your partners in work and life. Be mindful of unnecessary aggression and impulsiveness.

From March 30 to April 14, Mercury retrogrades into his sign of fall, therefore, communication could get extra hard as the messenger is not only retro but drowning in subjectivity. With both Venus and Mercury retrograding (March 14-April 7) there could be extra challenges for those of you who are having a birthday to celebrate between those dates. Talk and write from your heart rather than mind. Great for intuition and applying imagination to overcome challenges.

On March 30, Neptune enters your sign until October 22. Last time the god of the ocean was in your sign was 1861–1875. This is one of the most important transits of the year. From 2012 Neptune was helping you dissolve ancient patterns you carry from previous life and now he is ready to infuse you with the superpowers of imagination, intuition, mystical abilities, and dream-walking, if you open your heart and mind and start a meditation practice. Until 2039 you will be hosting the god who granted humanity horses, that was used both for travel and commerce as well as war. A great time to connect to horses as well.

APRIL

From April 5–7, Mars, your ruler, bewitches Venus, inspiring creativity, art, and love even if she's retrograding. It feels like Barbie and Ken falling in love all over again, after all, he was a professional "simply beach" dude, and indeed Mars is in Cancer, a water sign. This aspect can improve relationship at home as well as with family members. Since Venus is also conjunct Saturn, she can help heal and improve relationships with superiors, bosses, or people who are older than you.

On April 9 Mercury finally goes direct and you can start signing documents, make purchases, and initiate new projects. Let Mercury recover a bit as he's still in Pisces, his sign of fall, until April 16 when he returns to his former self in your sign, Aries. Adding to this feeling of completion is the Full Moon in your opposite sign, Libra, taking place on April 13. This is one of the most powerful lunation of the year, marking the story of Exodus—Passover and the Last Supper. This is the day of liberation, coming out of constriction and negativity and marching towards your Promised Land. It is a magical Full Moon where you might connect to your inner Moses, guardian angel, or higher self. There could be a bit of push and pull between you and your partners in work and life.

On April 14 Saturn conjuncts the North Node. Memories from previous lives flood you as well as positive interactions with likeminded people. A great time to join new groups and organizations that share long term goals.

On April 16 Mercury enters your sign until May 10. This is great for everyone but especially for you. You will be able to express yourself clearly and achieve your goals. A good time to write, assert your identity and leadership abilities. This trend is supported by Mars, your planet, entering Leo, a fellow fire sign, on April 18. He will be marching there until June 17. Mars in Leo is perfect for you and your projects, health, and vitality are getting a boost. Great time to connect to romance, love, and your inner child. A great deal of creativity is coming your way. Great for courage, entertainment, hobbies, and sports.

On April 19, it's time to say goodbye to the Sun as he moves into Taurus until May 20. Things are turning sensuous and luxurious, trading conquest for comfort, the yurt with a seven-star hotel. This month you are encouraged to indulge your six senses and connect to Mother Nature. It is a good month to tap into your artistic talents and perhaps discover new ones. Pay extra attention to your values and self-worth. Great month to increase your finances.

Things are turning a bit difficult between April 22–24 as the Sun squares the rulers of Scorpio—Mars and Pluto. This can bring about a great deal of letting go, death, and intense sexuality. Watch your steps these days, things can turn ugly or violent. However, things are changing around April 27, on the exalted New Moon in Taurus. A great time to start a new artistic or financial project. Spend time in nature, connect to your senses and do something that can symbolize rooting yourself.

On April 30, Venus enters Aries until June 6, you are getting another go at hosting the goddess of love and beauty. This is great for your finances, art, and all types of relationships

MAY

On May 10, Mercury moves into Taurus until May 26, and while it could bring about anxiety especially around finances, make sure to not worry about things you have no control over. A good time to communicate and market (as well as sell) your talents, values, and skills. Speak your mind without attachment or inflexibility.

The May 12 Full Moon in Scorpio can add to the general morbidness. You might feel the sting of the Scorpion today but because it is happening on the 22nd (Master Number) degree of Scorpio, you could build something out of the rubble of an older project or relationship. In this lunation you feel the tug of war between your assets and those of your partners. In addition, you will experience a great deal of magic, and synchronicities. Passion is heightened, just make sure you are attracting what you need. Great for research.

On May 20, the Sun enters Gemini until June 21. For the next 30 days, the Sun can help you attract contracts, write, market, sell, and negotiate. A great time for bridge-building and improving relationships with relatives, roommates, neighbors, and people you consider siblings. Find your message, your way of delivering it as well as your audience. On May 20–24, Venus and your planet, Mars, come together and deliver good news in connection to romantic love, partnerships, creativity, arts and finances.

One of the most important aspects for the year and especially for you is taking place between May 25 to September 1. Saturn, the Lord Karma, once in 30 years, returns to your sign. This period is just a taste of what is to come between 2026–2028 when Saturn settles in your sign. Saturn is asking you to investigate your identity, how you deal with your body and health, and attitudes and skills as a leader. You might feel tested, audited, and scrutinized by people who are older or more experienced.

On May 26, Mercury enters Gemini until June 8 and that can truly help you with all forms of business, marketing, writing, and connections. Information, opportunities, connections, and words flow effortlessly. People are ready to listen to your message, a great time for sales. This trend continues and increases on May 27 as the New Moon in Gemini shines on you brightly. A great day to start something new in connection with communication, networking, businesses, marketing, sales, and written projects. This New Moon is blessed by Pluto and Neptune, making it possible for you to link passion and reason, emotions and intellect. There could be new people joining your friend's circle.

JUNE

On June 6, Venus enters Taurus until July 4, and this is exciting news as the goddess of love can lend a helping hand in matters of art, finances, self-worth, and security. You will experience your five senses in a much stronger way. A great time to connect to an artistic project or talent, connect with your gifts, and translate them into income.

On June 8, Mercury enters Cancer until June 26, and since it is easier to remember information that is attached to emotions, try to use "I feel" over "I think," when you express yourself. Great for healing relationships with family members, as well as real estate transactions. Don't be afraid to express your emotions. This trend is enhanced dramatically when Jupiter enters Cancer on June 9 until June 30, 2026. Jupiter is exalted in Cancer and can give a push to everything that relates to your dwelling place, from remodeling to relocating, buying a property, and improving relationship with family members. A good time for parenting and settling down, nesting, and creating a family. However, since Cancer is squaring your sign, be careful of extremes, or reaching too high with your real estate aspirations.

From June 10 until August 23, Saturn conjuncts Neptune (partly in your sign). This could be somewhat challenging if you don't slow down, meditate, drink a lot of water, and be mindful of deceptions. There are no shortcuts to anything you do, so take heed, breathe deep, and don't rush. Saturn (karma) and Neptune (self-destruction) coming together is both a blessing and a curse. While your intuition, ability to meditate, and connect to your dreams are enhanced, so does your self-destructiveness, addictions, and escapism. Tread carefully, watch out for fanaticism or being too attached to your beliefs.

June 11 brings something into completion especially in matters of education, mass media, traveling, justice, law, and businesses with the Full Moon in Sagittarius. A blessed Full Moon in a challenging month. A cycle of learning is coming to completion, and you are ready for a new intellectual challenge. Great for travel, especially by water or to a location close to the water. Mars gives a boost of energy to the mix. The more authentic you are the more magic you can receive for the Moon.

On June 17, Mars enters Virgo until August 6 and can boost your work. Take a leadership role in your professional life and be assertive. A good time to reorganize your projects, workplace, health, and diet. You can make things happen if you stick to a strict routine.

On June 21, the Sun enters Cancer and will stay there until July 22. Happy Solstice! Talk more using "I feel," instead of "I think," and open your heart to your family. A great month to renovate and remodel your home, relocate, move in with someone, buy a new property, or start a family. As you can see with Jupiter already creating opportunities with home and family, the Sun now can give it a big push. This trend peaks around June 25, as the New Moon in Cancer takes everything to the next level. With Jupiter, exalted in Cancer, blessing the union of the Sun and Moon, this is a great time to start new projects. Besides Pluto, there are no planets retrograde, so full swim ahead!

On June 26, Mercury enters Leo until September 3. Since Mercury is retrograding in July, he will be in the feline sign for a while, sometimes roaring, at times meowing. This Mercury transit can be extremely creative, entertaining, and exciting. Great time to mend issues with your kids, lovers, and cocreators. Mercury also gives you a push around June 27–28 as he connects with Saturn and Neptune. This is a good aspect for making long-term plans and bringing some sanity to a mad mad month. Good for marketing, writing, and sales. It is also a great time for prophetic dreams and practical intuition.

JULY

On July 4, Venus enters Gemini and remains there until July 31. These next few weeks bring you in contact with a potential lover or work partner. Art and communication come together, a great time for marketing, sales, design, and making new connections. It is also an opportune time to communicate your needs with partners in work or life. This concept continues even stronger with one of the most pivotal transits of the year. Beginning July 7, Uranus enters Gemini until November 7. The planet of technology is moving to the binary sign of Gemini. Your IQ is augmented, and you can expect a great deal of innovation, new ideas, as well as newfound ways to communicate your message. Try to incorporate Artificial Intelligence in your business and update and upgrade your digital presence, website, and how you do business.

On July 10, the Full Moon in Capricorn can bring something into completion in your career and professional life. You might feel a push and pull between the need to focus on home and career. Mars, your ruler, is sending his troupes to help you answer a call to action in your professional life.

From July 17, Mercury begins his stationary and retrograde motion until August 12. Since it takes place in Leo it is a bit easier on your sign but still, you know the drill—avoid signing documents and starting new projects. Especially watch your relationships and communication with children, lovers, and people with big egos. The discord is the strongest between July 21–24 as Venus Squares Mars and the celestial lovers file for divorce. All types of relationships can be challenged these days, whether personal or professional. Find it in your heart to have compassion toward your significant others and those surrounding you. Don't make rash decisions regarding breakups or unions with partners.

On July 22 the Sun enters Leo, a fellow fire sign, until August 22. This is a great time to fall for love, having children, connecting to your inner child, and engaging in creative, joyful, and heartwarming activities. Generosity, nobility, chivalry, sportsmanship, and enthusiasm are guiding us this month. A great time to connect to a hobby or a new sport. This trend is magnified by the New Moon in Leo on July 24. However, this is not an easy New Moon since it is smack opposite to Pluto and can bring about a confrontation with a powerful figure in your life whose motivations are unclear. With Mercury retrograding in Leo, it is not the best time to start something new, however, you could initiate a project if you already tried it before and failed to complete it.

On the last day of July Venus enters Cancer until August 25. This can help you in your home and family, joining Jupiter in blessing your home, office and family relationships. Venus is putting on her swimming suit and jumps into the waters of Cancer. In the Tarot cards, the two of cups, dubbed "Love," is the best description of this transit.

AUGUST

On August 6, Mars enters Libra until September 22. Your ruler, the warrior, needs you to give him a mission, something to fight for, otherwise he could cause trouble. Be extra careful with your partners in work and in life as conflicts can arise out of nowhere. It is also a time when an enemy or a competitor could raise their head and strike, therefore, best be extra diplomatic and surround yourself with helpful people (and lawyers).

August 9 presents a shining bright Full Moon in Aquarius, which in Biblical times was celebrated as the Day of Love. You might feel a push and pull between the need to spend time with lovers or your children and the demands of your friends or company. On August 12, Mercury finally goes direct in Leo, a fellow fire sign, and communication, business, and life start to realign.

Between August 12–13 Venus conjunct Jupiter, which is an aspect of luck and positivity. Luck, flow in finances, new relationships and maybe a novel love but more than anything, this aspect can help with relationships at home and for relocation.

On August 22, the Sun enters Virgo until September 22. In the next 30 days you should focus on diet, health, routine, work, and service. An ideal time to eliminate impediments to health and productivity. It is also a great time to adopt a pet. This trend peaks on August 23, the New Moon in Virgo. A great time to initiate a new diet, work project, reorganize your home and office, or home-office. A bit of chaos is added by a square to Uranus that can awaken your inner critic and perfectionist. Try to channel these propensities into something productive with work.

On August 25, Venus enters Leo until September 19. The goddess of love in the sign of romance is always good news especially for you as a fellow fire sign. Just be careful of romance outside your existing relationship if you already have one. It is a very creative time with your inner child is active and happy. A great time to reconnect to a hobby you had in your teens. Between August 25–27, Venus trines Saturn and Neptune which is a delightful aspect of art, design, justice, and romance. Long-term plans and relationships are favored.

SEPTEMBER

On September 2, Mercury enters Virgo until September 18. In his sign of exaltation, Mercury is helpful in all aspects of communication, writing, editing, and health. He could specifically be helpful for projects in work that demand precision, micromanagement, organizing, and purification. A wonderful time for detoxing and cleansing.

The intensity increases as we enter eclipse season on September 7 with a Full Moon in Pisces. The Harvest Full Moon and a Lunar Eclipse brings things in work and in your life in general towards closure and resolution. Now's the time to harvest the fruits of whatever you've planted around March/April this year.

From September 18, Mercury enters Libra until October 6. This Mercury craves peace, compromise, harmony and beauty. A great time for healing and openness in your primary relationships as well as harmonizing your workplace. Art and business are coming together. You can revamp your website, redesign your logo, and come up with new ways to brand yourself.

On September 19, Venus switches places with Mercury and enters Virgo until October 13. You might feel over critical about your talents, artistic expression, your partners as well as feel the criticism of others directed toward you. You can gain from being on your own or practicing self-sufficiency. Good time to be frugal, balance the sheets, and detox. This trend is magnified on September 21 Solar Eclipse in Virgo. Just shy of the equinox, this lunation is granted much more power. A great time to balance your diet, start a new work project, and get the energy you need to reach the finish line. There is a wonderful trine between Pluto (power and intimacy), Saturn (focus), Neptune (imagination and intuition), and Uranus (innovation). A powerful surge of energy you can surf to success.

On September 22, as the Sun enters Libra until October 23, you can bask in the positive energies of the Equinox. For the next 30 days, the Sun shines upon your relationships and gives you a strong sense of justice, beauty, and harmony. On the same day, Mars enters Scorpio until November 4. Mars is thrilled to be back in the sign he rules jointly with Pluto, thus propels you into action. A wonderful time to collaborate on big projects that demand shared resources and energy. Passion, intimacy and sexuality are on the rise. Great for physical activities in water or reconnecting to sports you are passionate about. An opportune time for research and investigation, as well as fighting for what you believe in.

OCTOBER

On October 6, Mercury enters Scorpio until October 29, adding to the growing transformative vibes. An ideal period for research, finding lost objects or people, and expressing intimacy. It's a good time to let go, overcome grief, let bygones be bygones, and explore investments and collaborations with likeminded people. On October 7, this idea is furthered by the Full Moon in Aries. This Full Moon, bordering on a lunar eclipse, is a tad challenging even for you. With Chiron's involvement in Aries, it's an occasion for learning, teaching, and shamanistic journeys. While there's an aggressive undertone, it's a good moment to conclude matters and transition.

On October 11, Venus opposes Saturn and Neptune, which is not an easy aspect on your relationships or finances. There is an emotional frustration with partners, especially long-term ones. The challenges in relationships continue with Neptune creating illusions as well as dependency and codependency. There could be a disappointment with someone you placed on a pedestal only to learn they are not what you expected. Be careful of unwarranted expenditure.

Venus enters Libra from October 13 until November 6. The goddess of love and art is back on her turf and can help you reconnect to beauty, design, fashion, diplomacy, justice, and fix our primary relationships. This trend is enhanced even further by the New Moon in Libra of October 21. Dubbed the Moon of Peace, this New Moon is a great time to start a relationship or an art project. However, both Jupiter and Pluto are squaring off with the Sun and Moon, creating uncomfortable situations. Be extra cautious and focus on breathwork and meditation. Slow things down, don't over stress the system.

On October 22, Neptune leaves Aries and reenters Pisces until Jan 27, 2026. Neptune is back to his sign for the last time in 165 years. This is the last chance to start a deep meditation practice, journal your dreams, work with your imagination, and be as creative as possible. A great time to continue the theme of letting go that started in March 2023 and continues until February 2026.

On October 23, the Sun enters Scorpio until November 22. For the next 30 days, you are to focus on being true to your passion. It is a wonderful month of healing, transformation, magic, occult, and assisting others in their talents, finances, and endeavors. This month can help you in all forms of research, investigation, and unearthing the truth. However, be mindful that on October 26, Mars conjuncts Lilith and that spells out some trouble, aggression, accident, gossip and defaming. This is a violent and aggressive aspect. Tread cautiously.

There is a breeze of fresh air from October 29 as Mercury enters Sagittarius until November 19. Being a fellow fire sign, facilitates all forms of communication, especially with in-laws, foreigners and in trade. However, Mercury in his sign of exile might make you feel a bit absent-minded and distracted. A good time for traveling and doing business with foreigners. Stick to the truth and avoid liars and half-truths.

NOVEMBER

On November 4, Mars enters Sagittarius until December 15, which is great news for you, especially if you plan to travel, work with people from abroad, publish or be involved in education. Mars loves Sagittarius, where he can practice riding horses, motorbikes, or anything that allows him to travel fast. A call for adventure, as well as an expedition. Mars wants you to conquer, hunt, and expand your knowledge. It is an Indiana Jones aspect.

On November 5, the Full Moon in Taurus, brings something into completion around finances. Since it is taking place on the 13th degree of Scorpio, it carries a powerful connection to love and oneness (the Gematria value of 13). A talent or gift you have abandoned in the past might resurrect.

On November 6, Venus enters Scorpio until November 30. There could hand you good news about investments or your partner's money as well as inheritance. Be mindful of jealousy and possessives.

On November 8, Uranus returns to Taurus until April 26, 2026. Uranus was in Taurus from 2018 and this is his final visit to Taurus in the next 84 years. Changes can occur around your finances. A good time to be innovative and explore the more unique and strange talents you have. A good time to invest in startups.

From November 9, Mercury begins his retrograde and stationary motion until December 1. Avoid signing documents or starting new projects. This retrograde dances on the cusp or Sagittarius where he is overthinking to Scorpio where he is secretive. Avoid initiating anything unless you tried to do so before and failed to accomplish it.

November 20 is the New Moon in Scorpio. It is a great time to investigate your passions, what you really want out of life, what you wish to transform, investigate, or heal. A good New Moon to initiate projects that need shared resources, talents, or fundings. However, since Mercury is retro, you can only start things you already did in the past and failed to bring to completion. An opportune time to start therapy, a shamanistic journey, or a mystical quest. The New Moon is getting a boost from Saturn, Jupiter, and Neptune, that bless this lunation with structure and focus, imagination and inspiration, and a great deal of learning.

The energy dramatically changes on November 22, as the Sun enters Sagittarius until December 21. For the next 30 days, you have the strongest connection to your higher self or guardian angel. This is a month for teaching, mentoring, learning, speaking your truth, mass media, publishing, and connecting to foreigners, and in-laws.

On November 28 as Venus conjuncts Lilith, be extra careful with all your relationships and partners. A three-sided relationship might form around you. Be beware of stalkers, gossip, enemies, and lawsuits. The energy shifts on November 30 as Venus enters Sagittarius until December 24. Venus is putting on her safari's outfit and ready with her overpacked luggage for a journey. It is a great time for connecting to educators, foreigners, explore investments and possibilities from travel and abroad. A good time to improve relationships with in-laws.

DECEMBER

December 4 is the Full Moon in Gemini, an optimal moment to finalize projects especially as we are getting closer to the year's end. An opportune time to end the year since soon a set of challenging squares mar the flow of energy. On December 10, Mercury goes direct, so it is a good time to start moving things forward. On December 11, Mercury enters Sagittarius until January 1, 2026. A good for traveling and businesses abroad as well as for philosophy.

On December 15, Mars enters Capricorn until January 26, 2026. Mars is exalted and happy to march forward. Make sure you have a mission for him, something you need help conquering and or mastering, especially in your career. It is a good aspect for leadership and initiation. A call for action is coming, make sure not to refuse the call.

December 20 is the New Moon in Sagittarius, which is a rather difficult lunation since Neptune is sending squares along with Saturn. Not the best time to start new projects. Be careful of aggression and anger. A sense of war approaching. In addition, on the same day, Lilith enters Sagittarius for nine months. We are better off with Lilith, Mother of Demons, in the sign of optimism and luck rather than having her where she was most of the year, in deadly Scorpio. There could be discord with students and teachers, as well as foreigners. Take extra care when traveling.

December 21, the Sun enters Capricorn until January 20, 2026. The ensuing month calls for Capricorn-like discipline and focus especially in your career. Strategize for the year ahead, bearing in mind that patience is vital.

On December 24, Venus enters Capricorn until January 17, 2026. This is a great time to add an element of art or design into your career. In addition, relationships with superiors, bosses, or people in your work can improve.

TAURUS AND
TAURUS RISING: I HAVE

All About My People

General Trends: Saturn continues rectifying your standing in your community and focusing you on your tribe, company, and friends. However, from May—August, Saturn asks you to let practice letting go, detoxing, and spending more time on your own. In the first part of the year, you will experience a great deal of expansion around your finances, talents, and self-worth, while the second part of 2025 you could benefit from writing, business opportunities, and new ways to express yourself.

JANUARY

Between January 1–5, Mars is opposite his Scorpio coruler, Pluto, which is not an easy beginning of the year. In addition, Mars is retrograding and can cause havoc in your home and family, therefore, take extra care on the first few days of the year. People around you might experience paranoia, resort to manipulation, conflict and aggression.

On January 3, Venus puts on her swimming suit and dives into Pisces until February 4. This mystical plunge is great news, and you will feel her help especially with your friends, companies, and anything to do with technology and innovation. A surge of opportunities that could improve your finances, relationships as well as artistic gifts manifest. Creative visualization can be extremely potent.

On January 6, Mars retrogrades into Cancer until April 18. Mars, the warrior, doesn't like to transit in compassionate Cancer, his sign of fall, therefore, be vigilant of accidents, falling (unless it is in love) and issues with or around water such as leaks and floods. Conflict can arise with family members as well as neighbors, roommates, and relatives.

On January 8 Mercury enters Capricorn until January 28, and this means serious thought, discipline study, lessons coming from mature and experienced mentors. Slow your thought, speech, and writing, and be mindful of every word. Great for travel, education, as well as trade with foreigners. Speak your truth!

January 13 is the Full Moon in Cancer, where she loves to be. It could get emotional and a bit aggressive with family and loved ones due to the opposition of retro Mars and Pluto. In addition, there could be a push and pull between your relatives and those of your partner. Try to spend time by water.

Between January 18–19, Venus conjuncts Saturn. Finances, values, and your relationships are being scrutinized and audited. I call this aspect "marriage or divorce." You will feel it especially around your friendships and colleagues in your company or organization.

On January 19 the Sun enters Aquarius until February 18. This transit can shine your career and give you opportunities for advancement in your professional life. Friends can be especially helpful to further your worldly goals.

Between January 25–26, as Venus trines Mars, the cosmic lovers can bring a new relationship into your life or help you harmonize partnerships you already have. There could also be new ways to market yourself and your work as well as improve relationships with relatives.

From January 28 until February 14, Mercury transits in Aquarius, and ideas flow fast. New friendships are forming with likeminded people. A great time to make new contacts and reconnect to old friendships.

On January 29 is the New Moon in Aquarius and Chinese New Year. Time to welcome the Year of the Earth Snake. Jupiter is blessing this New Moon with wisdom and synchronicity. A great time to initiate something new in your professional life. A new friend or company might be coming into your life.

On January 29, the North Node retrogrades into Pisces until August 19, 2026, for the first time in 19 years. Right on the New Moon in Aquarius, the North Node aka "Dragon," is retrograding into the sign of mysticism, intuition, and imagination. For the next 18 months we are asked to practice empathy, meditation, any form of trance or movement practice (yoga, dance, or martial arts). The North Node will be blessing your tribe, connecting you to new companies, and bringing new clients, followers, and friends into your life. However, the South Node will be in Virgo asking us to let go of criticism, perfectionism, and overanalytical tendencies.

FEBRUARY

February 3 is a great day for writing, conjuring pragmatic ideas. Jupiter and Mercury are in air signs and that facilitates our communications, storytelling, sales, and connections with friends. They can especially help you connect your career with finances, linking your talents and gifts to your professional life.

On February 4, Venus enters Aries, until March 27. Conflicts and aggression with relationships and partners can arise. Watch impulsiveness with your finances. People and talents from previous lives are coming back. Your imagination is enhanced, as is your intuition. This positive flow is magnified between February 6 and 12, as Mars trines Saturn bringing a weeklong of constructive action, stable effort, and sustained passion. Help could come from a friend who is older than you.

On February 12, the Full Moon in Leo brings energy to both your family and career. You might feel the pull and push between the need to spend time with family and career demands. The square with Uranus can cause disruption and lunacy to this lunation.

On Valentine's Day (February 14), Mercury enters Pisces until March 3. Communications can be a bit challenged while intuition and mediumship are on the rise. Trust your gut feelings rather than your brain. Make sure to use the words "I feel" or "I imagine" or "I believe," instead of "I think." This trend is supported by the Sun entering Pisces from February 18 until March 20's Equinox. Focus on friends and your company. You would feel a stronger connection to imagination, dance, movement, dreaming, meditation, intuition, mysticism, and empathy.

The month ends with the New Moon in Pisces on February 28. A great day to start something new that involves your imagination, photography, movement, yoga and meditation. There is a tendency to absorb negativity from others so watch what you take in. Be careful of overdoing or illusions. A friend or someone in your community can bring something new into your life.

MARCH

Between March 1 to April 14, Venus, your ruler, stands still and then retrogrades in Aries. Avoid getting married, starting new relationships, getting engaged, starting lawsuits, and signing partnerships agreements. Exes or lovers from previous lives or this life might reach out. Be extra mindful with finances, as people tend to lose money or make bad investments. This retro asks you to let go and get rid of old patterns in relationships. This trend is taken to the next level as on March 3, when Mercury joins Venus in Aries and will be there until March 30. Mercury can be a bit impatient when in Aries and favors practical and short and concise communication. A great deal of messages come from your subconscious, intuition, and dreams.

A very intense time takes place between March 11–13, as the Sun conjunct Saturn while Mercury conjunct Venus. Seriousness, focus, discipline and planning can bring tactical or strategical accomplishments. A good time to improve relations with superiors. A relationship with a friend can become more serious.

March 14, Pi Day, we have the first Lunar Eclipse of the year. The Full Moon in precise and analytical Virgo, a fellow earth sign, therefore, it is a great time to bring a project to completion. On the same day, Mercury goes stationary and retrograde until April 18. Since it is happening in Aries this month, be extra careful with anger, impulsiveness, and rush decisions. You will be asked to let go of some projects, substances, or people.

On March 17, the Sun conjuncts North Node. A day to access skills and knowledge from past lifetimes. There could be an encounter with powerful and successful individuals or groups that can further your goals. A new company or organization might reach out, as well as a meeting with a friend that feels familiar from time long gone.

The equinox is on March 20 and the Sun transits into Aries until April 19. Happy New Year! A time to focus on your body, health, leadership, as well as your brand and image. This is a mystical month for you with your imagination and subconscious wide open.

On March 27, Lilith enters Scorpio until December 20. Since it is your opposite sign, this transit can be extra fateful on your partnerships and significant others. Emotional intensity, powerful desires, fascination with the forbidden, shadow work, possessiveness, and jealousy. Power struggles, manipulation, abuse, distrust, and criminality. Stay clear of any form of gossip. A good time to place a heap of salt in the four corners of your bedroom as protection against negativity. Watch out for enemies and lawsuits.

March 29 is the first Solar Eclipse of the year, and she shines upon Aries. Be mindful of unnecessary aggression and impulsiveness. A great time for a detox, letting go, and cutting away from any addictions. There might be a visit to the hospital.

From March 30 to April 15, Mercury is in Pisces. Mercury retrogrades into his sign of fall; thus, communication can be extra hard as the messenger is not only retro but drowning in subjectivity. Talk and write from your heart rather than mind. Great for intuition and applying imagination to overcome challenges. Watch out for issues with friends and colleagues in your company. Governments officials could be extra challenging,

From March 30 to October 22, Neptune enters Aries for the first time in 165 years. Confusion can lead to war, be extra careful of fanaticism or aggression triggered by propaganda of misinformation. Watch your immune system, inflammation, and your head. Once again, be extra careful with your health. You might feel confined or in need of isolation. You will feel very open to other people's suffering. Your intuition and messages from dreams are enhanced.

APRIL

Between April 5–7, the celestial lovers meet again. Venus is Barbie and Mars in water sign Cancer is Ken, the "simply beach" dude. As a Taurus, these are great days for romance, increasing your income using talents you are passionate about, and improving relationships with significant others. This is a great time for marketing and sales even if it is Mercury retrograde.

From April 5 to 10, Venus, your ruler, conjuncts Saturn. While this aspect can introduce you to someone older that could be helpful with finance and developing your talents, this conjunction can also sit heavy over all your relationships. A time to reassess your primary relationships and how you make money. There could be extra responsibilities given to you by your company or a friend in need. However, on April 8, Mercury finally goes direct, and things start moving forward. The best news is that between April 7 to 16 Mercury trines Mars and that could give a kick forward to your projects and business. A new contract awaits you.

April 13 is the Full Moon in Libra. A magical lunation that connects your work with imagination. The Moon could improve your health if you are willing to let go of something in your diet.

April 14, Pi Day, is when Saturn conjuncts the North Node in Pisces. Positive interactions with groups of powerful individuals or people who are older. You are downloading gifts or connections from previous lives. A good day to join new groups and organizations that share your long-term goals. This trend continues between April 16 to May 10 as Mercury transits in Aries, speeding things up but also showing signs of impatience. Mercury connects you to memories and lessons you mastered in previous lives.

From April 18 to June 17 Mars enters Leo bringing about a great deal of courage and a call for adventure. There could be some issues with family members or appliances that need fixing. In addition, Mars might be forcing you into action you rather not take.

On April 19 the Sun enters Taurus, your sign, and will remain there until May 20. Happy birthday! This month you are to indulge your six senses and connecting with Mother Nature. It is a good month to tap into your artistic talents and perhaps discover new ones. Focus on your body, health, leadership, and initiation. This is your time to shine. However, between April 22–24, as the Sun square the rulers of Scorpio—Mars and Pluto, take extra heed especially with your primary relationships. Watch out for enemies and lawsuits.

April 27 is the exalted New Moon in Taurus. A great time to start a new artistic or financial project. Spend time in nature, connect to your senses and do something that can symbolize rooting yourself. This trend continues from April 30 as Venus enters Aries until June 6. There could be a bit more conflict and aggression in your primary relationships. People or talents from previous lives are making an entrance into your life. You might meet someone who feels familiar, a soulmate from a previous life.

MAY

Between May 1 to May 3, Venus conjuncts Neptune and infuses us with romance, creativity, art, improved finances and intuition. This is especially powerful for your clan, once again, memories from previous lives flood you, however, you might be called to let go of a relationship, especially a toxic one.

From May 10 to May 26, Mercury enters your sign, Taurus, which can bring an increased intellectual curiously and an opportunity to rebrand yourself. A good time to communicate and market your talents and gifts. Speak your mind without attachment or rigidity.

May 12 is the Full Moon in Scorpio, and while the Moon is fallen, it is still a great time for shadow work, deal with temptation, and shine light on your primary relationships. Because the Moon falls on the 22nd (Master Number) degree of Scorpio, we can build something out of the rubble of an older project or relationship. In this lunation you feel the tug of war between "mine" and "yours," as well as "I" versus "Us." All your relationships are being placed under the magnifying glass.

Between May 17–18, the Sun conjuncts Uranus and everyone's IQ is getting a temporary elevation. A fantastic day for humor, jumping into the unknown, and embracing the original and innovative. Spend time with friends or in a group. Uranus is still in your sign and will be there on an off until next year. He is shaking your life and causing a bit of instability.

From May 20 to June 21, the Sun enters Gemini, and you need to channel the spirit of intelligence, communication, and bridge-building. This is a great month for business, contracts, improving relationships with relatives, roommates, neighbors, and siblings. Your finances can receive a boost, and your talents shine forth. The peak of this trend takes place between May 20 to 24, as Venus and Mars come together in a harmonious aspect. Romance, love, harmony (the daughter of Venus and Mars), is around you as well as an ability to see people's beautiful sides.

Between May 25 to September 1 Saturn enters Aries. Saturn in Aries wishes to rectify how you deal with your identity, body, leadership, and vitality. There is a focus on memories from past lives, as well as a need to let go and deal with subconscious issues. You might feel at times lonely, isolated, and perchance must visit a hospital or another place of confinement. There is a strong need to start meditating and release whoever and whatever holds you back.

Between May 26 to June 8 Mercury enters Gemini which can bring a great ideas or opportunities to increase your income and tap into new talents. Information, opportunities, connections, and words flow effortlessly. This trends peaks on May 27's New Moon in Gemini. A great day to start something new in connection with communication, networking, businesses, marketing, sales, and written projects. This New Moon is blessed by Pluto and Neptune, making it possible for you to link passion and reason, emotions with intellect. A great deal of intimacy and a possibility for a lover coming into your life. An opportune time for investments and new sources of income.

JUNE

Between June 4 to 8, Venus, Jupiter, Mercury, and Mars are blessing us and each other. Windows of positive opportunities can improve sales, communication, writing, health, education, and art. This is a wonderful aspect that could bless all facets of your life. This flow continues June 6 when Venus enters your sign, Taurus, until July 4. The goddess of love is lending a helping hand in matters of art, finances, relationships, and security. You will experience your five senses much stronger, perhaps getting a glimpse of the sixth one as well. A great time to connect to an artistic project or a talent, reconnect with your gifts and translate them into income. You will feel, look, and attract beauty and harmony.

On June 8, Mercury transits in Cancer until June 26. Great for healing relationships with family members. Don't be afraid to express your emotions. Mercury can mend issues with relatives and neighbors. However, between June 9 to 10 there are many cosmic conflicts between Mercury, Neptune, Saturn, Venus, and Pluto. Watch your body and direction in life. There is deception, lies, theft, and disinformation. Breakups, manipulation, and discord with people of power.

On June 9 Jupiter enters Cancer and will stay there until June 30, 2026. This is a great year for real estate, healing familial relationships, connecting to fortune and abundance, and opening new doors. Be careful of overdoing and over commitments. In addition, Jupiter could increase business opportunities as well as new contacts and contracts. A wonderful time for writing, marketing, writing, and sales.

From June 10 until August 23, Saturn conjuncts with Neptune. While your intuition, ability to meditate, and connect to your dreams are enhanced, so does your self-destructiveness, addictions, and escapism. Tread carefully, watch out for fanaticism or being too attached to your beliefs.

On June 11, the Full Moon is in Sagittarius and could create opposition between your assets and those of other people. Dealing with death and letting go, as well as tension between your values and those of your partner. However, it is a blessed Full Moon in a challenging month. Jupiter, ruler of Sagittarius is exalted, creating what is called Mutual Reception with the

Moon, which is auspicious. A wonderful time to complete a cycle of learning and preparation for something new. Great for travel, especially by water or to a location close to the water. Mars gives a boost of energy to the aspect.

From June 17, Mars enters Virgo until August 6, which could help you get things done. He is the watchmaker, the engineer, the organizer—here to protect and serve. Conflicts can arise if you are too critical of yourself and others. A good time for diets and a new health regiment. Sticking to a routine can yield positive results in all aspects of your life.

From June 21 the Sun transits Cancer until July 22. Happy Solstice! Open your heart to your family, and perhaps you might meet family members from past lives. A great month to renovate and remodel your home, relocate, move in with someone, get a new property, or start a family. This is a great time for writing, sales, and making new connections. The peak of this expansion takes place on June 25's New Moon is in Cancer. A new beginning that involves home and family, real estate, security, and emotional support. With Jupiter, exalted in Cancer, blessing the union of the Sun and Moon, this is a great time to start new projects. Besides Pluto, there are no planets retrograde, so full swim ahead!

From June 26 until September 3, Mercury transits into Leo and opens channels of communication with family members and loved ones. Since Mercury is retrograding in July, he will be in the feline sign for a while. This Mercury transit can be extremely creative, entertaining, and exciting. Good for mending issues with children and romantic partners,

Between June 27 to 28, Mercury trines Saturn and Neptune. This is a good aspect for making long-term plans and bringing some sanity to a mad mad month. Good for marketing, writing, and sales. It is also a great time for prophetic dreams and practical intuition.

JULY

On July 4 Venus conjuncts Uranus and while relationships can be exciting, they can also show an unpredictable side. Pay extra attention to your body, and how you present yourself to other people. There is a need for freedom and exploration of new frontiers especially with your finances, relationships, and self-expression. Embrace the original and unique. Be extra aware there could be volatility in the market.

From July 4 Venus, your ruler, flirts with Gemini until July 30 and the next few weeks money, art, and self-worth are increased. Beauty, creativity, and communication merge together, a great time for marketing, sales, design, and making new connections.

From July 7 to November 8, Uranus leaves your sign and enters Gemini. Uranus was causing a great deal of disruption in your life since 2018, so the fact that he leaves you alone for a few months is a welcomed repose, however for the next 7 years he will be causing changes and unpredictable turns and twists in the way you make money, awakening new talents, and asking you to upgrade the way you deal with your finances.

July 10 is the Full Moon in Capricorn. This lunation can bring opposition between home and career as well as issues with in-laws and relatives. The Moon is exiled in Capricorn and could create a sense of emotionality and longing for a paradise lost. However, Mars is sending his troupes to help you, and with a bit of action, determination, and a clear mission, you can disperse the emotional confusion of the Full Moon and get things done.

From July 17 to August 12, Mercury retrogrades in Leo, making your home, office, and family subjects or maybe the source of misunderstandings. You know the drill. Avoid signing docs and starting new projects. Especially watch your relationships and communication with kids, lovers, and people with big egos.

From July 22 to August 22, Sun enters Leo. Engage in creative, joyful, and heartwarming activities. Generosity, nobility, chivalry, sportsmanship, and enthusiasm are guiding you this month. A great time to connect to a hobby or a new sport. The Sun shines your home and family which can be helpful while Mercury is retrograding in the same area of your chart.

Between July 23–25, the Sun trine Saturn and Neptune creating a wonderful flow and help with vitality, intuition, healing, and the ability to bring some new structure into your lives. This is a glorious aspect, and you can benefit from creative visualizations, meditation, dance and self-expression.

July 24 is the New Moon is in Leo. This is not an easy New Moon since it is smack opposite to Pluto and can bring confrontations with powerful figures in your life whose motivations are unclear. With Mercury retrograding in Leo, it is not the best time to start something new, however, you could initiate a project you already tried before and failed to complete it. Be extra aware that there could be some issues at home or with family members.

From July 31 to August 25, Venus transits in Cancer. Marriage, social events with family members, as well as harmonious flow with family members. There could be financial opportunities coming through new contracts as well as possible lucrative business contacts. Improved relationships with relatives, neighbors, and roommates.

AUGUST

The month starts with a hard aspect on August 1 and 2 between Venus, Saturn and Neptune. Watch out for deception, illusions, and fantasies in your primary relationships as well as financial dealings. Not the best time to start a new relationship. Rapport with people who are older than you can be fraught with discord. Try a new approach to an old problem.

On August 6 Mars enters Libra and stays there until September 22. Not Mars' favorite position unless he can be given the mission to fight or defend peace. Watch your health, injuries, stress, inflammation, and stay away from sharp objects. There could be legal issues you might need to deal with but remember it is a good time to compromise and find peaceful resolutions to conflicts. Especially be mindful of conflict with coworkers. However, between August 7 to 9, Mars trines Uranus bringing about brilliance and originality. Search for innovative and original solutions. Connections with friends can thrive. Action is guided by new approaches, especially in health and work.

Watch it between August 8 to 10 as Mars opposites both Saturn and Neptune. Accidents, mishaps, and physical challenges especially since Mercury is retrograding. Stay away from arguments with superiors. The opposition to Neptune adds more hardships to the already difficult days. Stay away from stormy seas (metaphysically and physically speaking).

August 9 is the Full Moon in Aquarius. You might feel a push and pull between the need to spend time with lovers or your children and the demands of friends or company. There is also tension between home life and career responsibilities.

On August 12, Mercury finally goes direct in Leo. You can now start moving ahead, especially since on August 12 and 13, Venus conjuncts Jupiter, which is one of the best aspects this year. Luck, flow in finances, new relationships and maybe a novel love.

Between August 12 to October 27, Uranus trines Pluto. A powerful aspect that can bring about transformation through technology, science, social movements, and revolutions. Changes in government that can, in the long run, bring more prosperity. Your talents and gifts are in service of your career and there could be a raise or new ideas flowing in your professional life.

From August 22 to September 22 the Sun transits in Virgo. You are asked to focus and refine your diet, health, routine, work, and how you serve. An ideal time to eliminate impediments to health and productivity. As the Sun travels in a fellow Earth sign, this brings you a great deal of healing and vitality. Love is in the air, and improved relationship with children. This is especially true on August 23 when the New Moon is in Virgo. A great time for a new diet, work and health. It is recommended to reorganize your home and office or home office. A bit of chaos is added by a square to Uranus that can awaken the critic and perfectionist in you. Try to channel these propensities into something productive at work.

On August 25, Venus transits in Leo until September 19. The planet of love in the sign of romance is always good news. Just be careful of extra martial affairs if you are already in a committed relationship. It is a very creative time with your inner child fully active and playful. A great time to reconnect to a hobby you had in your teens. Be careful of pointless drama.

SEPTEMBER

On September 1 Saturn returns to Pisces until February 13, 2026. Confusion, floods, conflicts about water or in locations that are close to seas, lakes, and rivers. A time to ground your mystical practices, dreams, and intuition. Saturn brings with him a renewed focus on your friends, community, and responsibility towards humanity.

From September 2 to September 18, Mercury transits into Virgo, which is wonderful for your creativity, romantic love, and connection with children. Sales, ideas, and information flow effortlessly. A great time for editing projects, micromanagement, organizing, and purification. A wonderful time for detoxing and a cleanse.

September 7 is the Full Moon in Pisces—the Harvest Full Moon as well as a Lunar Eclipse. Momentum builds towards closure especially at work and in personal affairs. Now's the time to harvest the fruits of what you have planted in your life in March/April. Mercury provides a touch of reason to an otherwise emotional lunation. There is a push and pull between your romantic love or children and the demands of your friends and community.

From September 18, Mercury transits into Libra until October 6. This Mercury promotes peace, compromise, and beauty. A great time for healing relationships and harmonizing the workplace. Art and business come together. You can revamp your website, redesign your logo, and come up with new ways to brand yourself and your projects. This is especially good for your work and relationships with coworkers.

From September 19, Venus transits Virgo until October 13. You might feel overcritical about your art or your partners as well as feel scrutinized by others. You can gain from being on your own or practicing self-sufficiency. Good time to be frugal, balance your expenses and income, and detox. Venus in your sector of love and creativity is great news and romance and artistic projects.

September 21 is the Solar Eclipse in Virgo. A great time to balance your diet, start a new work project, and get the energy you need to reach the finish line. The Eclipse is helping planets bestow their gifts on you: Pluto (power and intimacy); Saturn (focus); Neptune (imagination and intuition); Uranus (innovation). Things are quickened around romance, children, and your connection to friends.

On September 22, the Sun enters Libra until October 23, marking the Equinox! Over the next 30 days, you need to embody Libra's traits—diplomacy, balance, harmony, compromise and attentiveness towards partners. This transit can result in a promotion or opportunities with work and health.

On September 22, Mars enters Scorpio until November 4. A wonderful time to collaborate on big projects that demand shared energy and resources. Passion, intimacy and sexuality are on the rise. Great for physical activities in water or reconnecting to sports you are passionate about. An opportune time for research and investigation, as well as fighting for what you believe in. This transit can generate conflicts and strife with your primary relationships, so take heed and be patient with your partners. This is especially important between September 23–25, as Mars squares Pluto. Aggression and manipulative folks are around you. Take extra heed in general. Actions can be easily misconstrued.

OCTOBER

On October 6 Mercury transits into Scorpio until October 29. An ideal period for research, finding lost objects or people, and expressing intimacy. It's a good time to move on, let bygones be bygones, bury the zombies in your life, while exploring investments and collaborations with other people's assets and talents. Since the Sun transits the sector of your chart that governs relationships and marriage, this is a great time to heal and attract positive partners in work and life.

October 7 is the Full Moon in Aries. This Full Moon, bordering on a lunar eclipse, is a tad challenging. With Chiron's involvement, it's an occasion for learning, teaching, and shamanistic journeys. While there's an aggressive undertone, it's a good moment to conclude matters and move on. There could be conflicts with partners in life or work. Take some time off work, a nice retreat would be optimal, take long walks in nature.

Between October 11 to 14, Venus is opposite Saturn and Neptune. This can be hard on your relationships and or finances. There is an emotional frustration with partners, especially long-term ones. Illusions as well as dependency and codependency and some disappointment with someone close to you. However, you can use this aspect to connect mysticism and art. There could be discord and strife with friends or people in your company, also your digital friends might act out.

From October 13 to November 6, Venus returns to her other sign, Libra and can help you connect to beauty, diplomacy, justice, relationship, and harmony. This is especially strong between October 14–15 as Venus trine Uranus and Pluto. Venus receives much praise from Pluto (intimacy, sexuality, power) and Uranus (innovation, technology, friendships). This is another good aspect that carries us upward with Venus (finances, relationships) leading the way. This is a powerful time for igniting, transforming, balancing, and solidifying partnerships in work and personal life.

The New Moon in Libra takes place October 21. Dubbed the "Moon of Peace," the Libra New Moon is a great time to start a relationship or an art project. However, both Jupiter and Pluto are squaring off with the Sun and Moon, creating uncomfortable situations. Be extra cautious and focus on breathwork and meditation. This Moon enhances your work and improves your health. A great time to fix your diet.

On October 22, Neptune returns for the last time to his sign, Pisces, until January 27, 2026. A great time to start meditation practice, dreams, imagination, channeling, mediumship, poetry, and art. Join groups that engage in mystical work, you also might meet people that you knew in previous lives.

On October 23, the Sun enters Scorpio until November 22. Focus on being true to your passion. It is a month of healing, transformation, magic, occult, and assisting others in their talents, finances, and endeavors. Your partnerships are shining, and it is a great time to attract and harmonize your primary relationships. Good time to overcome legal challenges or issues with enemies.

Around October 26 Mars conjuncts Lilith, please be extra careful today as the Mother of Demons hired an assassin. This is a violent and aggressive aspect. Tread cautiously.

On October 29, Mercury enters Sagittarius until November 19. You might feel a bit absent-minded and distracted. A good time for traveling and doing business with foreigners. Stick to the truth and avoid liars and half-truths. This is great for investments, dealing with shared resources and inheritance.

NOVEMBER

Between November 3 to 5 Mars opposes Uranus, therefore, be extra careful of accidents and mishaps involving aggression, impatience, speed or sharp objects. You might experience erratic behavior that doesn't make sense as well as gadgets and machines breaking or malfunctioning. The robot is out of control.

From November 4 to December 15, Mars enters Sagittarius. A call for adventure, as well as an expedition. Your Mars wants you to conquer, hunt, and expend your knowledge. Your focus should be shifting to working with other people's talents and finances. A great time to reconnect to your passion, sexuality, and intimacy.

November 5 is the Full Moon in Taurus. This is your Full Moon! An opportune time to bring something into completion. Since the lunation is on the 13th degree of Scorpio, it carries a powerful connection to love. Spend time in nature and indulge your five senses. A great time to rebrand and reinvent yourself.

On November 6, Venus enters Scorpio until November 30. This transit can make you feel lonely or unwanted, possessive as well as jealous. However, it is a good time to focus on your partner's money and talents rather than yours. Look into your investments as there might be a need to readjust. There is a good opportunity to meet with potential partners in work and life. A wonderful time for romance.

From November 8 to April 26, 2026, Uranus returns for the last time to Taurus. Yes, you must host the mad professor for another half-year. Changes in finances, fluctuations in cryptocurrency, new ways of expressing artistic talents. Watch your diet and health. Humor is the remedy for any disruption.

From November 9 to December 1 Mercury is stationary and retrograde. Avoid signing documents or starting new projects. This retrograde dances on the cusp of Sagittarius where he is overthinking to Scorpio where he is secretive. Avoid signing documents, starting new projects, and initiating anything unless you tried to do so before and failed to accomplish it. Issues could come up with partners in work or life. Watch out for investments that don't make sense or are too good to be true.

On November 19, Mercury enters Scorpio until December 10. Mercury returns to Scorpio as he retrogrades back into the underworld. Good for investigations and finding lost objects and people. This is especially challenging in your primary relationships. Be kind and patient.

On November 20, we have the New Moon in Scorpio. A great time to investigate your passions, what you really want in life, what you wish to transform, and start today. A good New Moon to initiate projects that need shared resources, talents, or funding. However, since Mercury is retro, you can only start things you already did in the past and failed to bring to completion. An opportune time to initiate healing, therapy, a shamanistic journey, especially with or around your primary relationships. The New Moon is getting a boost from Saturn, Jupiter, and Neptune, which bless this lunation with structure and focus, imagination and inspiration, and a great deal of open-mindedness.

On November 22, the Sun transits in Sagittarius until December 21. Sagittarius is the time of the year when we have the strongest connection to our higher self or guardian angel. This is a month for teaching, mentoring, learning, speaking your truth, mass media, publishing, and connecting to foreigners, and in-laws. The Sun shines on shared resources and grants you the ability to produce, promote, and enhance your partners' talents and finances. Intimacy, sexuality, and the occult are the focus this month.

November 23 is an interesting day when the Sun trines Neptune; Mercury trines Jupiter and Saturn; Jupiter trines Saturn. This day can further your goals in almost all aspects of your life.

On November 28 Venus conjuncts Lilith. Be extra careful with all your relationships and partners in work or in personal life. A three-sided relationship might form around you. Be beware of stalkers, gossip, enemies, and lawsuits.

From November 30 until December 24 Venus transits in Sagittarius. It is a great time for connecting to educators, foreigners, explore investments and possibilities from travel and abroad. A good time to improve relationships with in-laws. This is a great time for investments.

DECEMBER

December 4 is the Full Moon in Gemini. An optimal moment to finalize projects. Since this is the year's last Full Moon, it is a good time to complete what you wish to accomplish this year. This lunation can manifest as a push and pull between your money and talents and those of your partner. Focus on collaborations.

On December 11, Mercury enters Sagittarius until January 1, 2026. In exile, Mercury is unhappy. However, it is good for traveling and businesses abroad as well as for philosophy. A great time to bury the zombies in your life, half-dead relationships, projects, or friendships.

From December 15, Mars transits in Capricorn until January 26, 2026. Make sure you give him a mission—something you need help conquering and or mastering. It is a good aspect for leadership and initiation. A call for action is coming, make sure not to refuse the call. A great time for business with foreigners or multinational corporations. If you can focus on travel and or education, Mercury could best help you.

December 20 is the New Moon in Sagittarius. A difficult New Moon with Neptune and Saturn sending squares all over the place. Not the best time to start new projects. Be careful of aggression and anger. A sense of war approaching. Lay low and be vigilant.

From December 20, Lilith enters Sagittarius for nine months. There could be discord with students and teachers, as well as foreigners. Take extra care when traveling. While it is great Lilith moved away from your sector of relationships, she did enter the part of your chart associated with death, intimacy, sexuality, and the occult. Be extra careful the next 9 months who you bring into your life.

On December 21 the Sun enters Capricorn and will stay there until January 20, 2026. Happy Solstice! The ensuing month calls for Capricorn-like discipline and focus. Strategize for 2026, bearing in mind that patience is vital. A great month for travel, teaching, and learning. This trend continues between December 24 to January 17, 2026, as Venus transits in Capricorn. This transit of Venus can help you improve relationships with people who are older, long-term partnerships, as well as bosses and superiors. A time to connect art and design to your professional life. A great time to heal relationship with in-laws. Also, good energy around justice.

GEMINI AND
GEMINI RISING: I THINK

Reaching the Top of the Mountain

♊

General Trends: You are continuing your journey up the sacred mountain of your career and need to focus on your professional life and worldly achievements. With Jupiter in your sign until June, you have all the help you need to reach the summit, and in the second part of the year Jupiter helps you monetize these professional successes. In 2025 you can access your talents as well as increase your self-worth. With the North Node in your career, you need to let go of family expectation and even compromise your home life in favor of career and responsibility toward your community's welfare.

JANUARY

Between January 1–5, Mars is opposite his Scorpio coruler, Pluto, which is not a promising beginning of the year. In addition, Mars is retrograde therefore, take extra care on the first few days of the year. There is an opposition between your will and that of your community, company, or friends. People around you might experience paranoia, resort to manipulation, conflict and aggression. Misunderstanding with relatives, in-laws, and neighbors. Your words might be taken out of context.

On January 3, Venus puts on her swimming suit and dives into Pisces until February 4. Opportunities to improve your finances, relationships as well as artistic gifts manifest. This is especially beneficial for your career and relationship with superiors.

On January 6, Mars retrogrades into Cancer until April 18. Be extra vigilant of accidents, falling (unless it is in love), and issues with or around water such as leaks and floods. Conflict can arise with family members. A good time to go back to a project you were passionate about in the past and failed to manifest.

On January 8 Mercury enters Capricorn until January 28, a time to focus on serious subjects that demand strategy and planning and discipline. Lessons come from mature and experienced figures. Slow your thought, speech, and writing, and be mindful of every word. Great for furthering your career goals and forging long-term plans. A great time to focus on investments and business opportunities that demand shared resources.

January 13 is the Full Moon in Cancer. It could get emotional and a bit aggressive with family members and loved ones due to the opposition of the retrograding Mars. Take heed of over emotionality and guilt casting. You might feel a push and pull between your money and your partner's—mine versus ours. This trend is magnified between January 18–19, as Venus conjuncts Saturn. Finances, values, and your relationships are being scrutinized and audited. This is an aspect of "marriage or divorce." Whatever is going on in your personal and professional relationships are galvanized and crystallized, for good or bad.

On January 19 the Sun enters Aquarius until February 18. A time to spend with friends, community, as well as immerse yourself in science, technology, and innovation. This is a great time for traveling and furthering your education.

Between January 25–26, as Venus trines Mars, the cosmic lovers can bring a new relationship into your life or help you harmonize partnerships you already have. There could be a promotion, raise or good news in your professional life. This trend is enhanced between January 28 to February 14, as Mercury transits through Aquarius. Ideas, humor, and ingenuity are abounded as well as new friendships forming with likeminded people. This will be especially noticed in your professional life. The New Moon in Aquarius and Chinese New Year take place on January 28/29. Time to welcome to the Year of the Earth Snake. Jupiter is blessing this New Moon with wisdom and synchronicity. A great time to start a study group. A new friend or group from whom you can learn a great deal is making an entrance into your life.

On January 29, the North Node retrogrades into Pisces until August 19, 2026, for the first time in 19 years. For the next 18 months you are asked to practice empathy, meditation, and all forms of trance and movement (yoga, dance, or martial arts). This is especially beneficial for your career and achieving your goal. However, the South Node will be in Virgo asking us to let go of criticism, perfectionism, and overanalytical tendencies, as well as family expectations.

FEBRUARY

On February 3 Mercury, your ruler, and Jupiter link philosophy and logic. A great day for writing and conjuring pragmatic ideas. The two planets are in air signs and that facilitates our communications, storytelling, sales, and connections with friends.

On February 4, Venus enters Aries, until March 27. Conflicts and aggression with relationships and partners can arise. Watch impulsiveness with your finances. However, Venus can bring you in contact with new friends and colleagues and improve your ability to connect art and design with technology. This is especially strong between February 6–12, when Mars trines Saturn bringing a weeklong of constructive action, stable effort, and sustained passion. This aspect can give you the endurance to complete a marathon or two. An opportune time for your career and finances.

February 12 is the Full Moon in Leo, and you might feel the pull and push between the gravitational forces of your children or romantic partner versus demands of friends or your company. Be extra careful if you are traveling or if you have to undergo tests or exams (better study harder). The square with Uranus can cause disruption and an extra dose of lunacy to this lunation.

On Valentine's Day (February 14), Mercury enters Pisces until March 3. Communications can be a bit challenged while intuition and mediumship are heightened. Trust your gut feeling rather than your brain. Make sure to use the words "I feel" or "I imagine" or "I believe," instead of "I think." However, you can experience new opportunities in your career. This trend is supported by the Sun entering Pisces from February 18 until March 20's Equinox. Your career and professional life are getting a boost. Use imagination, dance, movement, dreaming, meditation, intuition, mysticism, and empathy to further your mundane goals.

The month ends with the New Moon in Pisces on February 28. A great day to start something new in your career and professional life especially if it involves your imagination, photography, movement, yoga and meditation. There is a tendency to absorb negativity from others so watch what you take in. Be careful of overdoing or illusions.

MARCH

Between March 1 to April 14, Venus stands still and then retrogrades into Aries, her sign of exile. Avoid getting married, starting new relationships, getting engaged, starting lawsuits, signing partnerships agreements. Exes or lovers from previous lives or this life might make an appearance. Be extra mindful with finances, as people tend to lose money or make bad investments during Venus retrograde. Pay extra attention to issues with friends and people in your community. There could be clashes in values within your friend groups.

On March 3, Mercury enters Aries and stays there until March 30. Mercury can be a bit impatient when in Aries and favors practical, short, and concise communication. Your planet now travels through the sector of your chart relating to technology, the future, and friendships. Expect interesting messages coming from friends and people in your community, while being aware that Venus is retrograde in the same area in your chart.

Between March 11–13, Sun conjunct Saturn while Mercury conjunct Venus. Seriousness, focus, discipline and planning can bring tactical or strategical accomplishments. A good time to improve relations with superiors. A great time for team sports or physical activity involving large groups of people.

March 14, Pi Day, is the first Lunar Eclipse of the year—Full Moon in Virgo. A great time to bring a project to an end, as well as focus on diet, service, and combining your analytical and wholistic aspects in life. You might be forced into an action you rather not take with family or real estate.

March 14–April 8 Mercury is stationary and then retrograde. Since it is happening in Aries, be extra careful with anger, impulsiveness, and rush decisions. A few of your friendships could become harder to handle. There could also be issues with government officials. This aspect is intensified on March 17, as the Sun conjuncts North Node and you could have an encounter with powerful and successful individuals or groups that can further your goals.

March 20 is the Equinox and the Sun transits into Aries until April 19. Happy New Year! A time to focus on your body, health, leadership, as well as your brand and image. Your friendships improve and possibly a new affiliation to a club or an organization.

From March 27 Lilith enters Scorpio until December 20. Emotional intensity, powerful desires, fascination with the forbidden, shadow work, possessiveness, and jealousy. Power struggles, manipulation, abuse, distrust, and criminality. Stay clear of any form of gossip. A good time to place a heap of salt in the four corners of your bedroom as protection against negativity. Issues could arise with coworkers, employees and clients. Give extra care to your diet and health in the next nine months.

On March 29, we have the first Solar Eclipse of the year, and she shines upon Aries. Be mindful of unnecessary aggression and impulsiveness. Things are moving fast within your company or friend groups. A possibility of meeting a new friend.

From March 30 to April 15, Mercury is in Pisces. Mercury retrogrades into his sign of fall; communication can be extra hard as the messenger is not only retrograde but drowning in subjectivity. Talk and write from your heart rather than mind. Great for intuition and applying imagination to overcome challenges. Misunderstanding and miscommunication can be more evident in your career, father figures, and superiors.

From March 30 to October 22, Neptune enters Aries for the first time in 165 years. Confusion can lead to war, be extra careful of fanaticism or aggression triggered by propaganda of misinformation. Watch your immune system, inflammation, and your head. Be mindful of deceptions and illusions with friends, government officials, and corporations. A great time to join a group that involves mystical activities, dance, movement, poetry, martial arts, and or meditation.

APRIL

Between April 5–7, the celestial lovers meet again. Venus is Barbie and Mars, in water sign Cancer, is Ken, the "simply beach" dude. These are great days for romance, increasing your income from talents you are passionate about, and better relationships with significant others as well as brothers and sisters in arms. Mars and Venus are linking your finances with career opting to help you connect your values and gifts in a practical way in your career. This is supported by Venus and Saturn coming together between April 5 to 10. While this aspect can introduce you to someone older that could be helpful with finance and developing your talents, this conjunction can also sit heavy over all your relationships. A person who is older or more experienced than you can be helpful to your advancement in career.

On April 8 Mercury, your ruler, finally goes direct and you can start signing documents and initiating new projects. Between April 7–16 Mercury trine Mars and that could give a kick forward to your projects and business dealings.

April 13 is the Full Moon in Libra. This is the day of liberation, coming out of constriction and negativity and marching towards your Promised Land. This lunation can be helpful in your romantic relationship as well as your connection to creativity as well as your inner child. A day later, on April 14, Saturn conjuncts the North Node in Pisces and brings a powerful boost to your career and dealing with superiors. Positive interactions with groups of powerful individuals or people who are older. A good period for joining new groups and organizations that share your long-term goals.

From April 16 to May 10 Mercury transits in Aries, speeding things up but also showing signs of impatience. Once again, your friends, and connection to groups or government can be helped by Mercury. However, words can easily be weaponized so be extra careful.

From April 18 to June 17 Mars enters Leo bringing about a great deal of courage and a call for adventure. Great for entertainment, sports, creativity, and reconnecting to lovers. You might feel passion towards a new business or a writing project. Be mindful of unnecessary conflicts with relatives and neighbors.

On April 19 the Sun enters Taurus and will remain there until May 20. This month you are to indulge your six senses and connect to Mother Nature. It is a good month to tap into your artistic talents and perhaps discover new ones. Spend time on your own, meditating, reading, or going on retreats. The mystic in you is activated.

April 27 is the exalted New Moon in Taurus. A great time to start a new artistic or financial project. This is your mystical moon and could enhance your intuition as well as bring memories from previous lives.

On April 30, Venus enters Aries until June 6. There could be a bit more conflict and aggression in your primary relationships. In her sign of exile, Venus might be somewhat snappy and can cause hasty decisions and actions with finances and love. A good time to connect with friends or join new groups.

MAY

Between May 1 to May 3, Venus conjuncts Neptune and infuses us with romance, creativity, art, improved finances and intuition. This conjunction can be utilized better if you spend time with friends or a community of likeminded people.

From May 10 to May 26, Mercury enters Taurus, which can bring a sense of worry and anxiety. However, it is a good time to communicate and market your talents and gifts. Your intuition as well as memories from previous lives are flowing. A great time for breakthroughs in therapy as your subconscious is wide open.

May 12 is the Full Moon in Scorpio, and while the Moon is fallen, it is still a great time for shadow work, dealing with temptation, and discovering the light within you. Because the Moon falls on the 22nd (Master Number) degree of Scorpio, you can build something out of the rubble of an older project or relationship. In this lunation you feel the tug of war between "mine" and "yours." You might have a feeling of wanting to be alone, isolate yourself, and break free from work commitments. Spending time in or around water can help ease some of the lunation's morbidity.

Between May 17–18, the Sun conjuncts Uranus and everyone's IQ is getting a temporary elevation. A fantastic day for humor, jumping into the unknown, and embracing the original and innovative. Spend time with friends or in a group. Uranus is close to moving into your sign and you can feel this ominous change coming about, the quiet before the storm.

From May 20 to June 21, the Sun enters Gemini, and your tribe is awakening. All aspects of your life are now in the spotlight. This is a great month for business, contracts, improving relationships with relatives, roommates, neighbors, and people you consider siblings. A time to reinvent yourself and rebrand your image.

Between May 20 to 24, Venus trines Mars again. Romance, love, harmony (the daughter of Venus and Mars), is around you as well as an ability to see people's beauty. Great time for making money from things you are passionate about. You might discover a new talent or artistic gift which you could bring into your professional life.

On May 25, Saturn transits into Aries and will be there until September 1. Saturn in Aries wishes to rectify how we deal with our identity, body, anger, and vitality. While career pressures are lifted for a few months, there could be issues emerging with your friends, company, or dealings with governments and authorities.

Between May 26 to June 8 Mercury enters Gemini. Information, opportunities, connections, and words flow effortlessly. Great for a marketing campaign and becoming a messenger, an angel to someone. This trend continues May 27, as the Sun and Moon conjunct—New Moon in Gemini. A great day to start something new in connection with communication, networking, businesses, marketing, sales, and written projects. This New Moon offers a new way to express yourself, try wearing something new. You are also blessed by Pluto and Neptune, making it possible for you to link passion and reason, emotions and intellect. A great deal of intimacy and a possibility for a lover coming into your life.

JUNE

Between June 4 to 8, Venus, Jupiter, Mercury, and Mars are blessing us and each other. Windows of positive opportunities can improve sales, communication, writing, health, education, and art.

On June 6 Venus enters Taurus until July 4. The goddess of love is lending a helping hand in matters of art, finances, relationships, and security. You will experience your five senses in a much stronger way, perhaps getting a glimpse of the sixth one as well. A great time to connect to an artistic project or a talent, reconnect with your gifts, and monetize them. There also could be gifts or talents you developed in previous lives that are returning, as well as people you have known in the past.

On June 8, Mercury transits Cancer until June 26. Great for healing relationships with family members. Don't be afraid to express your emotions. This is an opportune time for making new contacts that can help your finances. However, be mindful between June 9 to 10 as a bundle of challenging aspects come together. There is deception, lies, theft, and disinformation. Monkey mind is out of the cage, causing us to jump from one subject or project to the other. Breakups, manipulation, and discord with people of power.

On June 9 Jupiter enters Cancer and will stay there until June 30, 2026. This is great news for your finances, uncovering new talents and gifts, and increasing your self-worth. Jupiter leaves your sign where he was for a year and will now move to your neighboring sign, but he doesn't abandon you, he will gift you with awards, recognition, and improved self-image. This is a great year for real estate, healing familial relationships, connecting to fortune and abundance, and opening new doors. Be careful of overdoing and over commitments.

From June 10 until August 23, Saturn conjuncts with Neptune. While your intuition, ability to meditate, and connect to your dreams are enhanced, so does your self-destructiveness, addictions, and escapism. Tread carefully, watch out for fanaticism or being too attached to your beliefs. Be careful with deception coming from friends or corporations as well as government officials.

June 11 is the Full Moon in Sagittarius. A blessed Full Moon in a challenging month. A wonderful time to complete a cycle of learning and preparation for something new. Great for travel, especially by water or to a location close to the water. Mars gives a boost of energy to the aspect. This Full Moon creates tension with your partners in work or life.

From June 17, Mars enters Virgo until August 6. Mars in Virgo gets things done. He is the watchmaker, the engineer, the organizer—here to protect and serve. Conflicts can arise if you are too critical of yourself and others. A good time for diets and a new health regiment. You can make things happen if you stick to a strict routine. An opportune time for remodeling your home and or office. Be mindful that there could be conflicts arising with family members.

From June 21 the Sun transits Cancer until July 22. Happy Solstice! Open your heart to your family, and perhaps you might meet family members from past lives. Another good time to focus on your home, real estate, relocate, move in with someone, get a new property, or start a family. This month you might get a raise or an award. This is especially prominent around the New Moon in Cancer, June 25. The Moon provides a new beginning that involves home and family, real estate, security, and emotional support. With Jupiter, exalted in Cancer, blessing the union of the Sun and Moon, this is a great time to start new projects. Besides Pluto, there are no planets retrograde, so full swim ahead!

From June 26 until September 3, Mercury is in Leo. This Mercury transit can be extremely creative, entertaining, and exciting. A great time for new contracts, making new connections and creative writing, especially between June 27 to 28, when Mercury trines Saturn and Neptune. Good for marketing, writing, and sales. It is also a great time for prophetic dreams and practical intuition.

JULY

On July 4 Venus conjuncts Uranus and while relationships can be exciting, they can also show an unpredictable side. There is a need for freedom and exploration of new frontiers with your finances, relationships, and artistic expression. Embrace the original and unique. Be extra aware there could be volatility in the market.

From July 4 Venus flirts with you, Gemini, until July 30 and the next few weeks can bring you in contact with a potential lover or partner at work. Art and communication come together, a great time for marketing, sales, design, and making new connections. As Venus graces your sign, you connect to the artist within you and to beauty in general. You look and feel better and able to attract opportunities.

From July 7 to November 8, Uranus enters your sign, Gemini for the first time in 84 years. Your IQ is augmented. This can create a great deal of unpredictable situations as Uranus is the Great Awakener and he is waking all aspects of your life. Please refer to the introduction of the book to learn what this monumental transit means.

July 10 is the Full Moon in Capricorn. This lunation can bring about an opposition between home and career. The Moon is exiled in Capricorn and can create a sense of abandonment, emotionality, and longing for a paradise lost. However, Mars is sending his troupes to help you, and with a bit of action, determination, and a clear mission, you can disperse the emotional confusion of the Full Moon and get things done. There could be conflict between your money and your partner's.

From July 17 to August 12, Mercury is retrograde in Leo. Avoid signing documents and starting new projects. Especially watch your relationships and communication with kids, lovers, and people with big egos. Since Mercury is retrograding in the area of your chart related to communication, take extra care from miscommunications and misunderstandings.

From July 22 to August 22, the Sun enters Leo. Engage in creative, joyful, and heartwarming activities. Generosity, nobility, chivalry, sportsmanship, and enthusiasm are guiding you this month. A great time to connect to a hobby or a new sport. This transit can help your business, marketing, and writing.

Between July 23–25, the Sun trine Saturn and Neptune creating a wonderful flow and help with vitality, intuition, healing, and the ability to bring some new structure into our lives. This is a glorious aspect, and you can benefit from creative visualizations, meditation, dance, and self-expression.

July 24 is the New Moon in Leo. This is not an easy New Moon since it is smack opposite to Pluto and can bring about a confrontation with a powerful figure in your life whose motivations are unclear. With Mercury retrograding in Leo, it is not the best time to start something new, however, you could initiate a project you already tried before and failed to complete in the past. Watch what you say, write, post, or tweet.

From July 31 to August 25, Venus transits in Cancer. Marriage, social events with family members, as well as harmonious flow with family members. Expect a boost in your income and self-worth.

AUGUST

The month starts with a hard aspect on August 1 and 2 between Venus, Saturn and Neptune. Watch out for deception, illusions, and fantasies in your primary relationships as well as financial dealings. Rapport with people who are older than you can be fraught with discord. Try a new approach to an old problem.

On August 6 Mars enters Libra and stays there until September 22. There could be legal issues but also a good time for compromise and finding resolutions to conflicts. Nevertheless, it is an opportune time to get back into shape, create, indulge your inner child, and spend time with your kids. Between August 7 to 9, Mars trines Uranus bringing about brilliance and originality. Search for innovative and unique solutions. Connections with friends can thrive.

Watch it between August 8 to 10 as Mars opposites both Saturn and Neptune. Accidents, mishaps, and physical challenges especially since Mercury is retrograding. Stay away from arguments with superiors. The opposition with Neptune adds more hardships to an already difficult day. Stay away from stormy seas (metaphysically and physically speaking). There is a push and pull between the need to spend time with children and friends and commitment to your company and friends.

August 9 is the Full Moon in Aquarius. This is a Moon of love and romance, a great time to travel, education, and writing.

On August 12, Mercury finally goes direct in Leo. Things are flowing especially since on August 12 and 13, Venus conjuncts Jupiter, which is one of the best aspects this year. Luck, improved finances, relationships and maybe a new love. Great for publishing, marketing, sales, and making new connections as well as signing contracts.

Between August 12 to October 27, Uranus trines Pluto. A powerful aspect that can bring about transformation through technology, science, social movements, and revolutions. This is really good news for you Gemini, this wonderful aspect is a big boost for your career.

From August 22 to September 22 the Sun transits in Virgo. You are asked to focus and refine your diet, health, routine, work, and how you serve others. An ideal time to eliminate impediments to health and productivity. A month to focus on your home, family, and maybe find a way to work from home. This is especially true on August 23 when the New Moon is in Virgo. A great time for a new diet, taking a new direction at work and improve relationships with clients and coworkers. It is recommended to reorganize your home and office or home office. A bit of chaos is added by a square to Uranus that can awaken the critic and perfectionist in you. Try to channel these propensities into something productive at work.

On August 25, Venus transits in Leo until September 19. A great time for romance, just be careful of extra martial affairs. It is a very creative time with your inner child active and playful. A great time to reconnect to a hobby you had in your teens. Be careful of pointless drama. Venus can inspire your communications and ability to forge new connections with people that can be helpful in all aspects of life.

SEPTEMBER

On September 1 Saturn returns to Pisces until February 13, 2026. Confusion, floods, conflicts about water or in locations that are close to seas, lakes, and rivers. A time to ground your mystical practices, dreams, and intuition. Saturn returns to the top of your chart giving you discipline and focus on your career. Use this last journey of Saturn in the sector of your chart related to professional life to manifest your worldly goals.

From September 2 to September 18, Mercury transits into Virgo. Sales, ideas, and information flow effortlessly. A great time for editing projects that need precision, micromanagement, organizing, and purification. An opportune time to heal relationships with family members as well as for real estate.

September 7 is the Full Moon in Pisces. The Harvest Full Moon and Lunar Eclipse combo. Momentum builds towards closure especially with work and personal affairs. Now's the time to harvest the fruits of your labor from March/April. Mercury provides a touch of reason to an otherwise very emotional lunation. You might feel a push and pull between home and career.

From September 18, Mercury transits into Libra until October 6. This Mercury wants peace, compromise, and beauty. A great time for healing relationships and harmonizing the workplace. Art needs to be practical. You can revamp your website, redesign your logo, and come up with new ways to brand yourself and your projects. A great time for creativity, romance, and connecting with your children.

From September 19, Venus transits in Virgo until October 13. Venus is coming to visit you in your home, a great time to beautify your dwelling place and office. However, you might feel over critical about your art and talents as well as feel the criticism of others. You can gain from being on your own or practicing self-sufficiency. Good time to be frugal, balance your expenses and income, and detox. This trend is enhanced on September 21 as you experience the Solar Eclipse in Virgo. A time to balance your diet, start a new work project, and get the energy you need to reach the finish line. The Eclipse pushes events forward allowing all the planets involved to bestow their gifts upon you: Pluto (power and intimacy); Saturn (focus); Neptune (imagination and intuition); Uranus (innovation).

On September 22, the Sun enters Libra until October 23, marking the Equinox! As one of the four sacred days in the astrological calendar, commemorate it by celebrating relationships, justice, beauty, and art. Over the next 30 days, you should embody Libra traits—diplomacy, balance, and being attentive to others. A creative surge is coming your way.

On September 22, Mars enters Scorpio until November 4. A wonderful time to collaborate on big projects that demand a lot of energy and resources. Passion, intimacy and sexuality are on the rise. Great for physical activities in water or reconnecting to sports you are passionate about. An opportune time for research and investigation, as well as fighting for what you believe in. This transit can help you in your work and getting your health on track. However, between September 23–25, tread cautiously as Mars squares Pluto. Aggression and manipulative folks are around you. Take extra heed in general. Your actions can be easily misconstrued.

OCTOBER

On October 6 Mercury transits into Scorpio until October 29, which could help you with your routine, aligning your work with your passion, and maybe adopting a pet. A great time for pushing your business and making new connections. It's also a good time to move on, let bygones be bygones, bury the zombies in your life, and explore investments and collaborations with other people's assets and talents. Mercury can be your private investigator and expose hidden information.

October 7 is the Full Moon in Aries which can help complete a project in your organization as well as introduce you to new contacts and potential friendships. This Full Moon, bordering on a lunar eclipse, is a tad challenging. With Chiron's involvement, it's an occasion for learning, teaching, and shamanistic journeys. While there's an aggressive undertone, it's a good moment to conclude matters and move on. There could be conflicts with partners in life or work. You might also experience a push and pull between your need to be with your lover or children and the duty thrust upon you by friends or company.

Between October 11 to 14, Venus is opposite Saturn and Neptune. This can be hard on your relationships and or finances. There is an emotional frustration with partners, especially long-term ones. Illusions as well as dependency and codependency and some disappointment with someone close to you. However, you can use this aspect to connect mysticism with art.

From October 13 to November 6, Venus returns to her sign, Libra, and can help you connect to beauty, diplomacy, justice, relationship, and harmony. This is great for love, creativity, and improving relationships with your kids. This is especially strong between October 14–15 as Venus trine Uranus and Pluto. Venus receives much praise from Pluto (intimacy, sexuality, power) and Uranus (innovation, technology, friendships). This aspect carries you upward with Venus (finances, relationships) leading the way. This is a powerful time for igniting, transforming, balancing and solidifying partnerships in work and personal life.

The New Moon in Libra takes place October 21. Dubbed the "Moon of Peace," the Libra New Moon is a great time to start a relationship or an art project. However, both Jupiter and Pluto are squaring off with the Sun and Moon, creating uncomfortable situations. Be extra cautious and focus on breathwork and meditation. The lunation can bring about a new creative project, romantic love, or a child into your life.

On October 22, Neptune returns for the last time to his sign, Pisces, until January 27, 2026. A great time to start a meditation practice. Dreams, imagination, channeling, mediumship, poetry, and art are enhanced, as well as your intuition. Use this last Neptune visit to your career to explore how you could infuse your professional life with imagination and empathy.

On October 23, the Sun enters Scorpio until November 22. Focus on being true to your passion. It is a month of healing, transformation, magic, occult, and assisting others in their talents, finances, and endeavors. The place you can feel the strongest influence of the Sun is in your work, health, diet, and service of others. A great time to rework your routine.

Between October 24 to 26 Mercury trines Jupiter and Saturn. This aspect creates a triangle of protection in the time you need it most. An older individual can come to your aid. Long-term projects and or endeavors involving foreigners or education can be extra successful.

Around October 26 Mars conjuncts Lilith, please be extra careful today as the Mother of Demons hired an assassin. This is a violent and aggressive aspect. Tread cautiously, especially with your work and health.

On October 29, Mercury enters Sagittarius until November 19. You might feel a bit absent-minded and distracted. A good time for traveling and doing business with foreigners. Stick to the truth and avoid liars and half-truths. Great for education and publishing. A good time to improve your communication with partners in work or life.

NOVEMBER

From November 3 to 5 Mars opposes Uranus, therefore, be extra careful of accidents and mishaps involving aggression, impatience, speed or sharp objects. You might experience erratic behavior that doesn't make sense as well as gadgets and machines breaking or malfunctioning.

From November 4 to December 15, Mars enters Sagittarius. A call for adventure, as well as an expedition. Your Mars wants you to conquer, hunt, and expend your knowledge. This transit can bring about renewed passion in your relationships, but the spark can also cause conflicts. It is a time to be patient and understanding with all your partnerships.

November 5 is the Full Moon in Taurus. An opportune time to bring something into completion. Since the lunation is on the 13th degree of Scorpio, it carries a powerful connection to love. Spend time in nature and indulge your five senses. There could be tension between your duties at work and the need to spend time alone and break free from responsibilities. Balance those two needs and give each their due attention. However, from November 6, Venus enters Scorpio until November 30, and that is a great time to push forward with your work and professional life. An opportune time to add art and creativity to your workplace. A new partner might come to or through your work. It is also a good time to focus on your partner's money and talents rather than your own.

From November 8 to April 26, 2026, Uranus returns for the last time to Taurus. Changes in finances, fluctuations in cryptocurrency, new ways of expressing artistic talents. You might need to let go of something or someone in your life.

From November 9 to December 1 Mercury is stationary and retrograde. Avoid signing documents or starting new projects. This retrograde dances on the cusp of Sagittarius where he is overthinking to Scorpio where he is secretive. Avoid signing documents, starting new projects, and initiating anything unless you tried to do so before and failed to accomplish it. Watch out for misunderstandings and issues with partners in work and life. From November 19, Mercury enters Scorpio until December 10, and the retrograde issues can appear in your work or with health. Nevertheless, it is a good period for investigations and finding lost objects and reigniting past projects that failed.

November 20 is the New Moon in Scorpio. A great time to investigate your passions, what you really want in life, what you wish to transform, and start today? A good New Moon to initiate projects that need shared resources, talents, or funding. However, since Mercury is retrograde, you can only start things you already did in the past and failed to bring to completion. An opportune time to initiate healing, therapy, a shamanistic journey, or an investigation. The New Moon is getting a boost from Saturn, Jupiter, and Neptune, which bless this lunation with structure and focus, imagination and inspiration, and a great deal of open-mindedness.

On November 22, the Sun transits in Sagittarius until December 21. This is a month for teaching, mentoring, learning, speaking your truth, mass media, publishing, and connecting to foreigners, and in-laws. The next 30 days could bring you closer to someone who has the potential of being your partner in work or life. Balance is the key to achieving your goals.

November 23 is an interesting day when the Sun trines Neptune; Mercury trines Jupiter and Saturn; Jupiter trines Saturn. This day can further your goals in almost all aspects of your life.

On November 28 Venus conjuncts Lilith. Be extra careful with all your relationships and partners in work or in personal life. A three-sided relationship might form around you. Be beware of stalkers, gossip, enemies, and lawsuits. There could be intrigues and manipulations in your workplace.

From November 30 until December 24 Venus transits in Sagittarius. It is a great time for connecting to educators, foreigners, explore investments and possibilities from travel and abroad. A good time to improve relationships with in-laws. This is a wonderful time for healing and attracting relationships.

DECEMBER

December 4 is the Full Moon in Gemini. An optimal moment to finalize projects. As this is the year's last Full Moon. There could be tension between you and your partner. On December 10, Mercury goes direct and on December 11 he enters Sagittarius until January 1, 2026, where he can help your communication with your significant others.

From December 15, Mars transits in Capricorn until January 26, 2026. Make sure you give him a mission—something you need help conquering and or mastering. It is a good aspect for leadership and initiation. A call for action is coming, make sure not to refuse the call. A good time to focus on investments and shared resources. Mars can also help you get rid of things you don't want to bring into 2026.

December 20 is the New Moon in Sagittarius. Not the best time to start new projects. Be careful of aggression and anger. A sense of war approaching. On the same day, Lilith enters Sagittarius for nine months and can bring discord to your primary relationships. Take extra care when traveling.

On December 21 the Sun enters Capricorn and will stay there until January 20, 2026. Happy Solstice! The ensuing month calls for Capricorn-like discipline and focus. Strategize for 2026, bearing in mind that patience is vital.

From December 24 Venus transits in Capricorn until January 17, 2026. This transit of Venus can help you improve relationships with people who are older, long-term partnerships, as well as bosses and superiors. A time to connect art and design to your professional life. A great time for investments, dealing with inheritance, and profiting from shared resources.

CANCER AND
CANCER RISING: I FEEL

Championing Truth in an Age of Deception

♋

General Trends: Your focus on the truth, morality, learning, teaching, and searching for wisdom continues this year. You are asked to leave your comfort zone and embark on an adventure, traveling physically or intellectually. However, between May to August you are to implement all that you have learned from 2023 and practically use it in your career. In the first part of the year, you are asked to practice letting go as well as connecting to your mystical and imaginative side. However, from June, Jupiter, the giver of gifts, is entering your sign and begins a yearlong of wonderful expansion, showering you with opportunities and success.

JANUARY

Between January 1 and 5, Mars is opposite his Scorpio coruler, Pluto, which is not a promising beginning of the year. In addition, Mars is retrograde therefore, take extra care. There is an opposition between your will and that of your community, company, or friends. People around you might experience paranoia, resort to manipulation, conflict and aggression. There is also a feeling of things dying, and a need to let go. A time to practice detachment.

On January 3, Venus puts on her swimming suit and dives into Pisces until February 4. This mystical plunge is great news for you as you are a fellow water sign and will benefit from this transit. Opportunities to improve your finances, relationships as well as artistic gifts. Creative visualization can be extremely potent.

On January 6, Mars retrogrades into Cancer, your sign, until April 18. Be vigilant of accidents, falling (unless it is in love), and issues with or around water such as leaks and floods. Conflict can arise with family members. However, you will feel passionate and energized and could accomplish feats while Mars is in your sign.

On January 8 Mercury enters Capricorn until January 28, and this means serious thought, disciplined study, as well as lessons coming from mature and experienced figures. Slow your thought, speech, and writing, and be mindful of every word you utter. Great for furthering your career goals and forging long-term plans. This is a good time to heal or attract relationships.

January 13 is the Full Moon in Cancer, where she loves to be. It could get emotional and a bit aggressive with family and loved ones due to the opposition of retro Mars and Pluto. Take heed of over emotionality and guilt casting. There could be a push and pull between you and your partner so use Mercury's transit to focus on open communications in your primary relationships.

Between January 18–19, Venus conjuncts Saturn. Finances, values, and your relationships are being scrutinized and audited. Whatever is going on in your personal and professional relationships are galvanized and crystallized, for good or bad.

On January 19 the Sun enters Aquarius until February 18. A time to spend with friends, community, as well as immerse yourself in science, technology, and innovation. This is a good time to benefit from shared resources and investments. A month to connect to your passion, intimacy and sexuality.

Between January 25–26, as Venus trines Mars, the cosmic lovers can bring a new relationship into your life or help you harmonize partnerships you already have.

From January 28 until February 14, Mercury transits in Aquarius, and ideas flow fast as well as new friendships forming with likeminded people. A great time to make new contacts and reconnect to old friendships. January 29 is also the New Moon in Aquarius and Chinese New Year. Time to welcome to the Year of the Earth Snake. Jupiter is blessing this New Moon with wisdom and synchronicity. A great time to start a study group.

On January 29, the North Node retrogrades into Pisces until August 19, 2026, for the first time in 19 years. Right on the New Moon in Aquarius, the North Node aka "Dragon," is retrograding into the sign of mysticism, intuition, and imagination. For the next 18 months you are asked to practice empathy, meditation, any form of trance or movement practice (yoga, dance, or martial arts). A wonderful time to study, attain another degree, and travel abroad. However, the South Node will be in Virgo asking us to let go of criticism, perfectionism, and overanalytical tendencies.

FEBRUARY

On February 3 Mercury and Jupiter aligning your two hemispheres. A great day for writing and conjuring pragmatic ideas. A day later, February 4, Venus enters Aries, until March 27 and will bless your career as well as relationships with bosses or superiors. However, there could be conflicts and aggression with relationships. Watch out for impulsive financial decisions.

Between February 6–12, Mars trines Saturn bringing a weeklong of constructive action, stable effort, and sustained passion. This aspect can give you the endurance to complete a marathon or two. Since Mars is in your sign, this position can give you a sense of power and purpose. A great time for travel and education.

February 12 is the Full Moon in Leo, and you might feel the pull and push between the need to spend time with your children or romantic partner and the demands posed by friends or your company. The square with Uranus can cause disruption and lunacy to this lunation. There could be a need to balance your talents and money with that of your partner in work or life.

On Valentine's Day (February 14), Mercury enters Pisces until March 3. Communications can be a bit challenged while intuition and mediumship are on the rise. Trust your gut feelings rather than your brain. Make sure to use the words "I feel" or "I imagine" or "I believe," instead of "I think." This is a great time for publishing and education. This trend is supported by the Sun entering Pisces from February 18 until March 20's Equinox. Imagination, dance, movement, dreaming, meditation, intuition, mysticism, and empathy are heightened. Just make sure to guard your boundaries and avoid addictions or self-destructive tendencies. A wonderful time to connect to wisdom, truth, and education, the themes that you need to focus on this year.

The month ends with the New Moon in Pisces on February 28. A great day to start something new that involves your imagination, photography, movement, yoga and meditation. There is a tendency to absorb negativity from others so watch what you take in. Be careful of overdoing or illusions. An opportune time to start a new cycle of study.

MARCH

From March 1 to April 14 Venus stands still and then retrogrades in Aries, her sign of exile, which is especially challenging for you being a water sign. You must be extra mindful in your career and your relationships with people in your professional life. Avoid getting married, starting new relationships, getting engaged, starting lawsuits, and signing partnerships agreements. However, exes or lovers from previous lives or this life might return. Be extra mindful with finances, as people tend to lose money or make bad investments.

On March 3, Mercury enters Aries until March 30. This can actually help you deal with the misunderstanding that Venus brings about in your professional life. Mercury can be a bit impatient when in Aries and favors practical and short and concise communication.

Between March 11–13, Sun conjunct Saturn while Mercury conjunct Venus. Seriousness, focus, discipline, and strategy can bring tactical or strategical accomplishments. A good time to improve relations with superiors. There could be offers or opportunities for professional education or travel for work.

March 14, Pi Day, we have the first Lunar Eclipse of the year. The Full Moon is in mathematical and analytical Virgo. This can help your communication skills, writing, sales, and marketing. A great time to bring a project to an end, as well as focus on diet, service, and combining your analytical and wholistic aspects in life.

March 14–April 8 Mercury stationary and retrograde. Since it is happening in Aries this month, be extra careful with anger, impulsiveness, and rush decisions. You are now having two retrogrades in your career, so it is best to delay important projects until after April 9.

On March 17, the Sun conjuncts North Node. A day to access skills and knowledge from past lifetimes. There could be an encounter with powerful and successful individuals or groups that can further your goals. A major revelation is taking place, truth exposed, wisdom unearthed, and a teacher from a previous life coming into your life. A global or multicultural organization might reach out.

On March 20 we have the Equinox and the Sun's transits into Aries until April 19. Happy New Year! A time to focus on your body, health, leadership, as well as your brand and image. The Sun can help clear the fog in your career and the next month can help you further your goals.

On March 27, Lilith enters Scorpio until December 20. Emotional intensity, powerful desires, fascination with the forbidden, shadow work, possessiveness, and jealousy. Power struggles, manipulation, abuse, distrust, and criminality. Stay clear of any form of gossip. A good time to place a heap of salt in the four corners of your bedroom as protection against negativity. Be aware of secret love affairs, intrigues, and romantic blunders. Your children might be going through a rough patch.

March 29 is the first Solar Eclipse of the year, and she shines upon Aries. Be mindful of unnecessary aggression and impulsiveness. Something is unveiled in your career. Watch your relationships with coworkers or superiors.

From March 30 to April 15, Mercury is in Pisces. Mercury retrogrades into his sign of fall, thus, communication can be extra hard as the messenger is not only retro but drowning in subjectivity. Talk and write from your heart rather than your mind. Great for intuition and applying imagination to overcome challenges. Compared with other signs, you can benefit from this transit especially if you are studying and or teaching. Traveling can flow easier the next few weeks as well as dealing with foreigners.

From March 30 to October 22, Neptune enters Aries for the first time in 165 years. Confusion can lead to war, be extra careful of fanaticism or aggression triggered by propaganda of misinformation. Watch your immune system, inflammation, and your head. This can be especially important for your career. Intuition and your famous mediumship abilities can help you in your professional life. Try to use your imagination to find creative solutions to problems in your career.

APRIL

Between April 5–7, the celestial lovers meet again. Venus is Barbie and Mars in water sign Cancer is Ken, the "simply beach" dude. These are great days for romance, increasing your income from talents you are passionate about, and better relationships with significant others as well as brothers and sisters in arms. A wonderful aspect for your Cancer! At the same time, from April 5 to 10, Venus conjuncts Saturn. While this aspect can introduce you to someone older that could be helpful with finance and developing your talents, this conjunction can also sit heavy over all your relationships. A time to reassess your primary relationships and how you make money.

On April 8 Mercury finally goes direct so you can start signing documents and initiate new projects. Between April 7–16 Mercury and Mars could provide a push to your projects and life in general.

April 13 is the Full Moon in Libra. This is the day of liberation, coming out of constriction and negativity. It is a magical Full Moon where you might connect to your inner Moses, guardian angel, or higher self. You might feel a push and pull between home and career.

April 14 is a dramatic day when Saturn conjuncts the North Node in Pisces. Positive interactions with groups of powerful individuals or people who are older. You are downloading skills or connections from previous lives. Good for joining new groups and organizations that share long-term goals.

From April 16 to May 10 Mercury transits back into Aries, speeding things up but also showing signs of impatience. Words can easily be weaponized so be extra careful. Communication in your career improves especially your dealings with superiors and clients.

From April 18 to June 17 Mars enters Leo bringing about a great deal of courage and call for adventure. Great for entertainment, sports, creativity, and reconnecting to your inner child. Mars could energize your income and help you fight for what you believe in.

On April 19 the Sun enters Taurus and will remain there until May 20. This month you are to indulge your six senses and connect to Mother Nature. It is a good month to tap into your artistic talents and perhaps discover new ones. This is great news for you especially in connections with friends, your company, and dealing with government officials.

Between April 22–24, as the Sun square the rulers of Scorpio—Mars and Pluto, take extra heed. This can bring about a great deal of letting go, death, and intense sexuality. Watch your steps these days, things can turn ugly or violent. Be extra careful with investments, stock market or any other risky endeavor.

April 27 is the exalted New Moon in Taurus. A great time to start a new artistic or financial project. Spend time in nature and do something that could symbolize rooting yourself. A new friendship is coming your way or maybe a promotion in your company. From April Venus enters Aries until June 6. This can energize your career. Try to add an artistic element to your professional life. Great for connecting to new clients and coworkers.

MAY

Between May 1 to May 3, Venus conjuncts Neptune and infuses you with romance, creativity, art, improved finances, and intuition. You will experience this transit the strongest in your career and professional life. Try to use this aspect to bring in more art, imagination, intuition and flow into your mundane activities.

From May 10 to May 26, Mercury enters Taurus, which can bring a sense of worry and anxiety. However, it is a good time to communicate and market your talents and gifts. Speak your mind without attachment or inflexibility. A good time to make new friends and find your "angels" as in messengers that could further your goal and ambitions.

May 12 is the Full Moon in Scorpio, and while the Moon is fallen, it is still a great time for shadow work, dealing with temptation and discovering the light in you. Because the Moon falls on the 22nd (Master Number) degree of Scorpio, we can build something out of the rubble of an older project or relationship. In this lunation you feel the tug of war between "mine" and "yours." There could be a push and pull between your need to focus on your romantic love or children and your company or friends.

Between May 17–18, the Sun conjuncts Uranus and everyone's IQ is getting a temporary elevation. A fantastic day for humor, jumping into the unknown, and embracing the original and innovative. Spend time with friends or in a group.

From May 20 to June 21, the Sun enters Gemini, and you are channeling the spirit of intelligence, communication, and bridge-building. This is a great month for business, contracts, improving relationships with relatives, roommates, neighbors, and people you consider siblings who didn't share a womb. The Sun shines the sector of your chart relating to past lives, imagination, and intuition. A wonderful time to let go of things that hinder your growth and connect to skills and people from previous lives.

Between May 20 to 24, Venus trines Mars once again. Romance, love, harmony (the daughter of Venus and Mars), is around you as well as an ability to see people's beautiful side. Great time for making money from things you are passionate about.

Between May 25 to September 1 Saturn enters Aries. Saturn in Aries wishes to rectify how you deal with your identity, body, anger, and vitality. Your career and relationship with your bosses are being scrutinized. A good time to make drastic changes in your professional life and change directions if you are not happy with your current job. There could be issues with superiors or father figures.

Between May 26 to June 8 Mercury enters Gemini. Mercury is back to his domicile, and he is happy to unpack and work for you extra hours. Information, opportunities, connections, and words flow effortlessly. You might receive valuable messages in the form of vision, psychic hits, and dreams. These messages increase May 27, the New Moon in Gemini. It is also a great day to start something new in connection with communication, networking, businesses, marketing, sales, and written projects. This New Moon is blessed by Pluto and Neptune, making it possible for you to link passion and reason, emotions and intellect. A great deal of intimacy and a possibility for a lover coming into your life.

JUNE

Between June 4 to 8, Venus, Jupiter, Mercury, and Mars are blessing us and each other. Windows of positive opportunities can improve sales, communication, writing, health, education, and art. While this takes place Venus transits into Taurus from June 6 until July 4. The goddess of love is blessing any activity involving art, finances, relationships, and attaining a sense of security. You will experience your five senses in a much stronger way than regularly, perhaps getting a glimpse of the sixth one as well. A great time to connect to artistic projects especially if you can do it with a group or digitally.

On June 8, Mercury transits into Cancer, your sign, until June 26. Great for healing relationships with family members. Don't be afraid to express your emotions. This is a great time to promote yourself and speak your truth. You are now the center of the conversation. A good time to rebrand yourself. Try a new haircut, new clothes, new style.

Between June 9 to 10 Mercury squares Neptune and Saturn and Venus squares Pluto. A bundle of challenging aspects come together. There is deception, lies, theft, and disinformation. Monkey mind is out of the cage, causing you to jump from one subject or project to the other. Breakups, manipulation, and discord with people of power.

On June 9 the most important transit of the year for you takes place as Jupiter enters Cancer, your sign, and will stay there until June 30, 2026. Once in 12 years you are getting the kiss of the gods. All aspects of your life can be blessed. Just be careful not to spread yourself too thin or overindulge. There is a danger of gaining weight, so it is better to use this aspect to start a new physical activity. This transit is also good for real estate, healing familial relationships, connecting to fortune and abundance, and opening new doors.

On June 11, the Full Moon is in Sagittarius. A blessed Full Moon in a challenging month. A wonderful time to complete a cycle of learning and preparation for something new. Great for travel, especially by water or to a location close to the water. Mars gives a boost of energy to the aspect. Watch your health and diet.

From June 17, Mars enters Virgo until August 6. Mars in Virgo gets things done. He is the watchmaker, the engineer, the organizer—here to protect and serve. Conflicts can arise if you are too critical of yourself and others. A good time for diets and a new health regiment. You can make things happen if you stick to a strict routine. An opportune period for business, marketing and sales. However, be careful of conflicts with relatives, neighbors or roommates.

From June 21 the Sun transits Cancer until July 22. Happy Solstice! Open your heart to your family, and perhaps you might meet family members from past lives. A great month to renovate and remodel your home, relocate, move in with someone, get a new property, or start a family. With Jupiter and the Sun's blessing you can surf to success. This is especially powerful on June 25—the New Moon is in Cancer. The lunation provides a new beginning that involves home and family, real estate, security, and emotional support.

From June 26 until September 3, Mercury is in Leo. This Mercury transit can be extremely creative, entertaining, and exciting. A great time to energize your finances, take control, ask for a raise and connect to your self-worth.

Between June 27 to 28, Mercury trines Saturn and Neptune. This is a good aspect for making long-term plans and bringing some sanity to a mad mad month. Good for marketing, writing, and sales. It is also a great time for prophetic dreams and practical intuition.

JULY

On July 4 Venus conjuncts Uranus and while relationships can be exciting, they can also show an unpredictable side. There is a need for freedom and exploration of new frontiers with your finances, relationships, and artistic expression. Embrace the original and unique. Be extra aware there could be volatility in the market.

From July 4 Venus flirts with Gemini until July 30 and the next few weeks art and communication come together, a great time for marketing, sales, design, and making new connections. People, talents, gifts from previous lives are coming back into your life. This is magnified by Uranus' transit into Gemini between July 7 to November 8. Unpredictable changes, visits to hospitals (not always because of your health issues) as well as recalling memories from previous lives. There could be a spiritual awakening!

On July 10 the Full Moon in Capricorn brings tension between your home life and career responsibilities as well as between you and your partner (in work or life). The Moon is exiled in Capricorn and can create a sense of emotionality and longing for a paradise lost. However, Mars is sending his troupes to help you, and with a bit of action, determination, and a clear mission, you can disperse the emotional confusion of the Full Moon and get things done.

From July 17 to August 12, Mercury is retrograde in Leo. Avoid signing documents and starting new projects. Especially watch your relationships and communication with kids, lovers, and people with big egos. This retrograde can create misunderstandings and glitches around finances, so take heed, unexpected expenses can come up.

From July 22 to August 22, the Sun enters Leo. Engage in creative, joyful, and heartwarming activities. Generosity, nobility, chivalry, sportsmanship, and enthusiasm are guiding you this month. A great time to connect to a hobby or a new sport. In the last 10 days of this transit, you will experience an improvement in finances and self-worth.

Between July 23–25, the Sun trine Saturn and Neptune creating a wonderful flow and help with vitality, intuition, healing, and the ability to bring some new structure into our lives. This is a glorious aspect, and you can benefit from creative visualizations, meditation, dance and self-expression.

July 24 is the New Moon in Leo. This is not an easy New Moon since it is smack opposite to Pluto and can bring about a confrontation with a powerful figure in your life whose motivations are unclear. With Mercury retrograding in Leo, it is not the best time to start something new, however, you could initiate a project you already tried before and failed to complete.

From July 31 to August 25, Venus transits in Cancer. Marriage, social events with family members, as well as harmonious flow with family members. This is great news for you, and it can help you look and feel better about yourself and life. A great time for a rebrand, trying a new image, and presenting yourself differently.

AUGUST

The month starts with a hard aspect on August 1 and 2 between Venus, Saturn and Neptune. Watch out for deception, illusions, and fantasies in your primary relationships as well as financial dealings. Not the best time to start a new relationship. Rapport with people who are older than you can be fraught with discord. Try a new approach to an old problem.

On August 6 Mars enters Libra and stays there until September 22. There could be legal issues but also a good time for compromise and finding resolutions to conflicts. Be extra cautious in your relationships with family members. However, between August 7 to 9, Mars trines Uranus bringing about brilliance and originality. Search for innovative and original solutions. Connections with friends can thrive.

Watch it between August 8 to 10 as Mars opposites both Saturn and Neptune. Accidents, mishaps, and physical challenges especially since Mercury is retrograding. Stay away from arguments with your superiors. Stay calm and try to do less. The opposition with Neptune adds more hardships to already difficult few days. Stay away from stormy seas (metaphysically and physically speaking).

August 9 is the Full Moon in Aquarius. You might feel a push and pull between the need to spend time with lovers or your children and demands coming from your friends or company. Shared resources could also be on the spotlight for you, as well as the duality of "mine" versus "ours." Intimacy and sexuality are heightened.

On August 12, Mercury finally goes direct in Leo. You can now start plowing ahead, especially since on August 12 and 13 Venus conjuncts Jupiter, which is one of the best aspects this year. Luck, flow in finances, new relationships and maybe a novel love. Funds that were held back are returning your way.

Between August 12 to October 27, Uranus trines Pluto. A powerful aspect that can bring about transformation through technology, science, social movements, and revolutions. Changes in government that can, in the long run, bring more prosperity.

From August 22 to September 22 the Sun transits in Virgo. You are asked to focus and refine your diet, health, routine, work, and how you serve. An ideal time to eliminate impediments to health and productivity. This is a great transit for marketing, sales, and writing.

August 23 is the New Moon in Virgo. A great time for a new diet, work project, or service. It is recommended to reorganize your home and office or home office. A bit of chaos is added by a square to Uranus that can awaken the critic and perfectionist in you. Try to channel these propensities into something productive at work.

On August 25, Venus transits in Leo until September 19. The planet of love in the sign of romance is always good news. Just be careful of extra martial affairs. It is a very creative time with your inner child active and playful. A great time to reconnect to a hobby you had in your teens. Link your values with your talents to find new ways of making money.

SEPTEMBER

On September 1 Saturn returns to Pisces until February 13, 2026. While it might be hard for others, for your clan it is good news. A time for renewed sense of discipline especially around education and truth finding, justice, and authenticity. A time to ground your mystical practices, dreams, and intuition.

From September 2 to September 18, Mercury transits into Virgo. Sales, ideas, writing, and information flow effortlessly. A great time for editing projects that need precision, micromanagement, organizing, and purification. A wonderful time for detoxing and a cleanse.

September 7 is the Full Moon in Pisces. The Harvest Full Moon is also a Lunar Eclipse. Momentum builds towards closure especially with work and personal affairs. Now's the time to harvest the fruits of your labor you have planted or started back in March/April. Mercury provides a touch of reason to an otherwise emotional lunation. This Full Moon flows well with you and can combine writing with publishing, as well as shine your talents as a teacher and student.

From September 18, Mercury transits into Libra until October 6. This Mercury wants peace, compromise, and beauty. A great time for healing relationships and harmonizing family life. A good time for real estate.

From September 19, Venus transits in Virgo until October 13. You might feel over critical about your art or your partners as well as feel the criticism of others directed at you. However, there are opportunities for new contracts, business leads, and a wonderful time to mend issues with relatives.

September 21 is the Solar Eclipse in Virgo. A great time to balance your diet, start a new work project, and get the energy you need to reach the finish line. The Eclipse is giving a bit push allowing the planets involved to bestow their gifts on you: Pluto (power and intimacy); Saturn (focus); Neptune (imagination and intuition); Uranus (innovation).

On September 22, the Sun enters Libra until October 23, marking the Equinox! As one of the four sacred days in the astrological calendar, commemorate it by celebrating relationships, justice, beauty, and art. Over the next 30 days, you should embody Libra traits—diplomacy, balance, and being attentive to your partners. For you Cancer this is wonderful times since the Sun shines over your home and family which are the bedrock of your sign.

On September 22, Mars enters Scorpio until November 4. A wonderful time to collaborate on big projects that demand a lot of energy and resources. Passion, intimacy and sexuality are on the rise. Great for physical activities in water or reconnecting to sports you are passionate about. An opportune time for research and investigation, as well as fighting for what you believe in. An opportune time for creativity and reconnecting to your children or creative projects. However, between September 23–25, tread cautiously as Mars squares Pluto. Aggression and manipulative folks are around you. Take extra heed in general. Actions can be easily misconstrued.

OCTOBER

On October 6 Mercury transits into Scorpio until October 29. An ideal period for research, finding lost objects or people, and expressing intimacy. Mercury is known as the psychopomp—the guide of souls to the realm of the dead. It's a good time to move on, let bygones be bygones, bury the zombies in your life, and explore investments and collaborations with other people's assets and talents. If you have any issues with romantic lovers or your children, this transit is an opportune time for healing and reconnecting.

October 7 is the Full Moon in Aries. This Full Moon, bordering on a lunar eclipse, is a tad challenging. With Chiron's involvement, it's an occasion for learning, teaching, and shamanistic journeys. While there's an aggressive undertone, it's a good moment to conclude matters and move on. There could be conflict or an opposition between home and career.

Between October 11 to 14, Venus is opposite Saturn and Neptune. This can be hard on your relationships and or finances. There is an emotional frustration with partners. Dependency and codependency and some disappointment with someone close to you. However, you can use this aspect to connect mysticism with art, become a medium, and channel information.

From October 13 to November 6, Venus returns to her sign, Libra, and can help you connect to beauty, diplomacy, justice, relationship, and harmony. Home remodeling or beautifying your dwelling place and office is recommended. This is especially strong between October 14–15 as Venus trine Uranus and Pluto. Venus receives much praise from Pluto (intimacy, sexuality, power) and Uranus (innovation, technology, friendships). This aspect carries you upward with Venus (finances, relationships) leading the way. Great for relocation as well as building bridges between family members. This positive vibe in home and real estate are magnified on the New Moon in Libra, which takes place October 21. Dubbed the "Moon of Peace," the Libra New Moon is a great time to start a relationship or an art project. However, both Jupiter and Pluto are squaring with the Sun and Moon, creating uncomfortable situations. Be extra cautious and focus on breathwork and meditation.

On October 22, Neptune returns for the last time to his sign, Pisces, until January 27, 2026. A great time to start meditation practice as well as keep a dream journal, activate your imagination, connect to poetry, and art or any form of movement.

On October 23, the Sun enters Scorpio until November 22. Focus on being true to your passion. It is a month of healing, transformation, magic, occult, and assisting others in their talents, finances, and endeavors. Love, romance, creativity, sports and hobbies are especially recommended this month.

Around October 26 Mars conjuncts Lilith, please be extra careful today as the Mother of Demons hired an assassin. This is a violent and aggressive aspect. Tread cautiously. Be careful of extra martial affairs or falling in love with the wrong person. There could be issues with your children, so pay more attention to them.

On October 29, Mercury enters Sagittarius until November 19. You might feel a bit absent-minded and distracted. Traveling is recommended as well as conducting business with foreigners. A great time for taking your work to the next level as well as your diet and health.

NOVEMBER

From November 3 to 5 Mars opposes Uranus, therefore, be extra careful of accidents and mishaps involving aggression, impatience, speed or sharp objects. You might experience erratic behavior that doesn't make sense as well as gadgets and machines breaking or malfunctioning. The robot is out of control. Be extra careful with your health, injuries, accidents especially around your workplace.

From November 4 to December 15, Mars enters Sagittarius. A call for adventure, as well as a possible expedition. Mars wants you to conquer, hunt, and expand your knowledge. It is an Indiana Jones aspect. Mars can infuse your work with passion and enthusiasm, beaconing you to take on a leadership role, promotion, and take the initiative. Watch out for injuries, inflammation, and infections.

On November 5 the Full Moon is exalted in Taurus. An opportune time to bring something into completion. Since the lunation is on the 13th degree of Scorpio, it carries a powerful connection to love. Spend time in nature and indulge your five senses. You might feel a conflict between the need to spend time with friends and the demands of your lover or children.

On November 6, Venus enters Scorpio until November 30. The goddess of love can bring you closer to a lover or a new creative project. It is a good time to focus on your partner's money and talents rather than your own. Look into your investments as there might be a need to make some adjustments.

From November 8 to April 26, 2026, Uranus returns for the last time to Taurus. Changes in finances, fluctuations in cryptocurrency, new ways of expressing artistic talents. This transit can cause disruption with friends or your company. A great time to upgrade and update your gadgets and computers, get invested in new technologies.

From November 9 to December 1 Mercury is stationary and retrograde. Avoid signing documents or starting new projects. This retrograde dances on the cusp of Sagittarius where he is overthinking to Scorpio where he is secretive. Most of the miscommunications can be around health and work.

On November 19, Mercury retrogrades into Scorpio until December 10. Mercury returns to Scorpio as he retrogrades back into the underworld. Good for investigations and finding lost objects and people. This retrograde in Scorpio is a bit easier for you but can inflict problems with romantic lovers, children, as well as your creative projects.

November 20 is the New Moon in Scorpio. A great time to investigate your passions, what you really want in life, what you wish to transform, and start today. A beneficial New Moon to initiate projects that need shared resources, talents, or funding. However, since Mercury is retro, you can only start things you already did in the past and failed to bring to completion. An opportune time to initiate healing, therapy, a shamanistic journey, or an investigation. The New Moon is getting a boost from Saturn, Jupiter, and Neptune, which bless this lunation with structure and focus, imagination and inspiration, and a great deal of open-mindedness.

On November 22, the Sun transits in Sagittarius until December 21. Sagittarius is the time of the year when you have the strongest connection to our higher self or guardian angel. This is a month for teaching, mentoring, learning, speaking your truth, mass media, publishing, and connecting to foreigners, and in-laws. The Sun can shine on your work and help you heal. On November 23 the Sun trines Neptune; Mercury trines Jupiter and Saturn; Jupiter trines Saturn. This day can further your goals in almost all aspects of your life.

On November 28 Venus conjuncts Lilith. Be extra careful with all your relationships and partners in work or in personal life. A three-sided relationship might form around you. Be beware of stalkers, gossip, enemies, and lawsuits. Intrigue in love, issues with your kids, sports injuries, in other words, take heed.

From November 30 until December 24 Venus transits in Sagittarius. It is a great time for connecting to educators, foreigners, explore investments and possibilities from travel and abroad. A good time to improve relationships with in-laws. Venus can bring a creative element into your workplace as well as improve your connection with clients and coworkers.

DECEMBER

December 4 is the Full Moon in Gemini which is an optimal time to finalize projects in work. As this is the year's last Full Moon. A great time for volunteering, charity, and altruistic work.

On December 10, Mercury finally goes direct, and you can start signing documents and initiating projects. It is a good time for traveling and businesses abroad as well as for philosophy. Mercury can now help you push forward work projects that were stagnated.

From December 15, Mars transits in Capricorn until January 26, 2026. Make sure you give him a mission—something you need help conquering and or mastering. It is a good aspect for leadership and initiation. This transit can be challenging on your primary relationships and create unnecessary conflicts with partners in work and life.

December 20 is the New Moon in Sagittarius, a good time to start a new project at work or start a new health regimen. However, it is a difficult New Moon with Neptune and Saturn sending squares all over the place. Not the best time to start new projects. Be careful of aggression and anger. A sense of war approaching.

From December 20, Lilith enters Sagittarius for nine months. There could be discord with students and teachers, as well as foreigners. Take extra care when traveling. For the next nine months you should be extra careful in your relationships with people you meet through your work. In addition, be mindful of addictions.

On December 21 the Sun enters Capricorn and will stay there until January 20, 2026. Happy Solstice! The ensuing month calls for Capricorn-like discipline and focus. Strategize the year ahead, bearing in mind that patience is vital. The Sun shines on your primary relationships. A good time to find a partner either in work or life. This trend is magnified by Venus entering Capricorn between December 24 until January 17, 2026. This transit of Venus can help you improve relationships with people who are older, long-term partnerships, as well as bosses and superiors. A time to connect art and design to your professional life.

LEO AND
LEO RISING: I WILL

Open Soul Surgery

♌

General Trends: The lessons regarding your passion, intimacy, sexuality, continue this year as well as your journey of reclaiming your power. It is a year of death and transformation, with a strong urge to visit your shadow and retrieve your true potential. However, from May to August you will experience a resurrection and spread your wings, able to soar to higher ground, and have the chance to start educating yourself, travel to exotic lands and discover your wisdom. The North Node can help you tap into shared resources and investments. In the first part of the year, you are experiencing an expansion with friends and community and in the second part of 2025 you will dive into the collective unconscious and experience a surge of intuition, tapping into your imagination and memories from previous lives.

JANUARY

Between January 1–5, Mars is opposite his Scorpio coruler, Pluto, which is not a promising beginning of the year. In addition, Mars is retrograde in your sign, therefore, take extra care on the first few days of the year. There is an opposition between your will and that of your community, company, or friends. People around you might experience paranoia, resort to manipulation, conflict and aggression. Since Mars is retrograding in your sign until end of February, take extra care in all aspects of your life but especially with your health.

On January 3, Venus puts on her swimming suit and dives into Pisces until February 4. Opportunities to improve your finances, relationships as well as artistic gifts manifest. Creative visualization can be extremely potent. A great time for investments and working with shared resources. A great time to connect to an intimate partner.

On January 6, Mars retrogrades into Cancer until April 18, which means he is leaving you alone for a bit. Conflict can arise with family members. Be extra vigilant and watch out for hidden enemies or people who try to sabotage you from behind the scenes. Be aware of self-destructive tendencies.

On January 8 Mercury enters Capricorn until January 28, and this means serious thought, discipline study, lessons coming from mature and experienced figures. Slow your thought, speech, and writing, and be mindful of every word. Great for furthering your career goals and forging long-term plans. Mercury can help you in your work and health. Marketing, sales, and negotiations are facilitated by Mercury.

January 13 is the Full Moon in Cancer, where she loves to be. It could get emotional and a bit aggressive with family and loved ones due to the opposition of the retrograding Mars. Take heed of over emotionality and guilt casting. Watch your health. It is also a good time for a detox.

On January 19 the Sun enters Aquarius until February 18. A time to spend with friends, community, as well as immerse yourself in science, technology, and innovation. The Sun's transit in your opposite sign places your primary relationships in the spotlight. It is a good time to forge new partnerships and win lawsuits as well as overcome adversities.

Between January 25–26, the cosmic lovers, Mars and Venus are bringing a new relationship into your life or helping harmonize partnerships you already have.

From January 28 until February 14, Mercury transits in Aquarius, and ideas flow fast as well as new friendships forming with likeminded people. A great time to make new contacts and reconnect to old friendships. This transit can help with your communications with partners in work or life. January 29 is the New Moon in Aquarius and Chinese New Year. A great time to start a study group. A new partnership, friend or community is formed around you. On the same day, January 29, the North Node retrogrades into Pisces until August 19, 2026, for the first time in 19 years. Right on the New Moon in Aquarius, the North Node aka "Dragon," is retrograding into the sign of mysticism, intuition, and imagination. For the next 18 months you are asked to practice empathy, meditation, or any form of trance or movement (yoga, dance, or martial arts). This is especially good for your investments as well as benefiting from joint artistic and financial affairs. A time to connect to the occult, healing and shamanism. However, the South Node will be in Virgo asking you to let go of criticism, perfectionism, and overanalytical tendencies.

FEBRUARY

On February 4, Venus enters Aries, until March 27. Conflicts can manifest with relationships and partners. Watch impulsiveness with your finances. As a fellow fire sign this is not a bad transit, especially if you plan to travel or connect to education. Justice is on your side.

Between February 6–12, Mars trines Saturn bringing a weeklong of constructive action, stable effort, and sustained passion. This aspect can give you the endurance to complete a marathon or two. February 12 is the Full Moon in Leo, and you might feel the pull and push between the gravitational forces of your children or romantic partner versus friends or your company. This lunation is asking you to balance your needs and those of your partner.

On Valentine's Day (February 14), Mercury enters Pisces until March 3. Communications can be a bit challenged while intuition and mediumship are on the rise. Trust your gut feeling rather than your brain. Make sure to use the words "I feel" or "I imagine" or "I believe," instead of "I think."

A great time for research, investigation and communicating your intimacy needs. You might even have a connection to the dead or spirits. This trend is supported by the Sun entering Pisces from February 18 until March 20's Equinox. Imagination, dance, movement, dreaming, meditation, intuition, mysticism, and empathy are heightened. Just make sure to guard your boundaries and avoid addictions or self-destructive tendencies.

The month ends with the New Moon in Pisces on February 28. A great day to start something new that involves your imagination, photography, movement, yoga, and meditation. There is a tendency to absorb negativity from others. A great time to start a process of letting go, detoxing, quitting something that is hindering you.

MARCH

March 1–April 14 Venus stands still and then retrogrades in Aries, her sign of exile. Avoid getting married, starting new relationships, getting engaged, starting lawsuits, signing partnerships agreements. As a Leo this retro is not as difficult and can help you reconnect to something you wanted to learn in the past and failed (a language maybe). However, exes or lovers from previous lives or this life might return. Be extra mindful with finances, as people tend to lose money or make bad investments.

On March 3, Mercury enters Aries until March 30. Mercury can be a bit impatient when in Aries and favors practical and short and concise communication. Teaching, learning, and traveling is blessed by Mercury.

Between March 11–13, Sun conjunct Saturn while Mercury conjunct Venus. Seriousness, focus, discipline and planning can bring tactical or strategical accomplishments. A good time to improve relations with superiors. It is time to bury the zombies (half-dead) in your life so that you can regenerate after the equinox on March 20.

March 14, Pi Day, we have the first Lunar Eclipse of the year. The Full Moon in mathematical and analytical Virgo. A great time to bring a project to an end, as well as focus on diet, service, and combining your analytical and wholistic aspects in life. Something is quickening in your life in connection with finances, talents, awards, and self-worth.

March 14–April 8 Mercury stationary and retrograde. Be extra careful with anger, impulsiveness, and rush decisions. Relationships with in-laws or foreigners may be harder on this retrograde.

On March 17, the Sun conjuncts North Node. A day to access skills and knowledge from past lifetimes. There could be an encounter with powerful and successful individuals or groups that can further your goals.

March 20 is the Equinox and the Sun's transits into Aries until April 19, which is great news for you. Happy New Year! A time to focus on your body, health, leadership, as well as your brand and image. There could be a new culture you feel an affinity to or a call to study something new.

On March 27, Lilith enters Scorpio until December 20. Emotional intensity, powerful desires, fascination with the forbidden, shadow work, possessiveness, and jealousy. Power struggles, manipulation, abuse, distrust, and criminality. Stay clear of any form of gossip. A good time to place a heap of salt in the four corners of your bedroom as protection against negativity. This is especially hard for you, so take heed. A family member might act in a mean or destructive ways forcing you into an action you rather not take.

March 29 is the first Solar Eclipse of the year, and she shines upon Aries. Be mindful of unnecessary aggression and impulsiveness. A good time to forge a message and find the way to deliver it.

From March 30 to April 15, Mercury transits in Pisces. Mercury retrogrades into his sign of fall, thus, communication can be extra hard as the messenger is not only retro but drowning in subjectivity. Talk and write from your heart rather than mind. Great for intuition and applying imagination to overcome challenges. Take heed not to fall prey to Ponzi schemes or bad investments or to start a sexual relationship with someone you can tell is bad news.

From March 30 to October 22, Neptune enters Aries for the first time in 165 years. Confusion can lead to war, be extra careful of fanaticism or aggression triggered by propaganda of misinformation. Watch your immune system, inflammation, and your head. Mystical studies as well as traveling to sacred places are recommended.

APRIL

Between April 5–7, the celestial lovers meet again. Venus is Barbie and Mars in water sign Cancer is Ken, the "simply beach" dude. These are great days for romance, increasing your income from talents you are passionate about, and better relationships with significant others as well as brothers and sisters in arms. The lovers create a link between career and investments.

From April 5 to 10, Venus conjuncts Saturn. While this aspect can introduce you to someone older that could be helpful with finance and developing your talents, this conjunction can also sit heavy over all your relationships. A time to reassess your primary relationships and how you make money. A great time for couple's therapy and or diving deeper into your passion and intimacy. The healer in you is activated.

On April 8 Mercury finally goes direct so you can start signing documents and initiate new projects. Between April 7–16 Mercury trine Mars and that could give a kick forward to your projects and business. This is especially beneficial for travel and publishing.

April 13 is the Full Moon in Libra. This is the day of liberation, coming out of constriction and negativity and marching towards your Promised Land. It is a magical Full Moon where you might connect to your inner Moses, guardian angel, or higher self. Speak your truth, this is a lunation of connecting to wisdom and being able to share it.

April 14 is a dramatic day when Saturn conjuncts the North Node in Pisces. Positive interactions with groups of powerful individuals or people who are older. You are downloading gifts or connections from previous lives. Good for joining new groups and organizations that have long term goals. The world of the occult is calling you. Explore the mysteries of life, investigate, research, and connect to the enchanter in you.

From April 16 to May 10 Mercury transits in Aries, speeding things up but also showing signs of impatience. Words can easily be weaponized so be extra careful. This is a great transit for you, communication flows much better than before. Great for publishing and mass media.

From April 18 to June 17 Mars enters Leo bringing about a great deal of courage and a call for adventure. Great for entertainment, sports, creativity,

and reconnecting to your inner child. At last Mars comes to visit your domain. Your physical strength and mental clarity are elevated.

On April 19 the Sun enters Taurus and will remain there until May 20. This month you are to indulge your six senses and connect to Mother Nature. It is a good month to tap into your artistic talents and perhaps discover new ones. A month to focus on your career and professional life. Be flexible as there could be a tendency to be too rigid.

April 27 is the exalted New Moon in Taurus. A great time to start a new artistic or financial project. Spend time in nature, connect to your senses and do something that can symbolize rooting yourself. This is a wonderful time to initiate something new in your career and professional life. This trend continues from April 30 as Venus enters Aries until June 6. There could be a bit more conflict and aggression in your primary relationships. In her sign of exile, Venus might be somewhat snappy and can cause hasty decisions and actions with finances and love. Relationship with educators, foreigners and in-laws improve.

MAY

Between May 1 to May 3, Venus conjuncts Neptune and infuses us with romance, creativity, art, improved finances and intuition.

From May 10 to May 26, Mercury enters Taurus, which can bring a sense of worry and anxiety. However, it is a good time to communicate and market your talents and gifts. Speak your mind without attachment or inflexibility. All types of communication flow better in your career as well as better rapport with your superiors.

May 12 is the Full Moon in Scorpio, and while the Moon is fallen, it is still a great time for shadow work, dealing with temptation and discovering the light in you. Because the Moon sits on the 22nd (Master Number) degree of Scorpio, we can build something out of the rubble of an older project or relationship. In this lunation you feel the tug of war between "mine" and "yours." There is a push and pull between home and career, try to balance your personal and professional life.

Between May 17–18, the Sun conjuncts Uranus and everyone's IQ is getting a temporary elevation. A fantastic day for humor, jumping into the unknown, and embracing the original and innovative. Spend time with friends or in a group. A time to update and upgrade your career and look for ways to innovate and modernize your workplace and workflow.

From May 20 to June 21, the Sun enters Gemini, and you are channeling the spirit of intelligence, communication, and bridge-building. This is a great month for business, contracts, improving relationships with relatives, roommates, neighbors, and people you consider siblings who didn't share a womb. A month you could explore new companies, groups, and make new friends.

Between May 20 to 24, Venus trines Mars once again. Romance, love, harmony (the daughter of Venus and Mars), is around you as well as an ability to see people's beautiful side. Great time for making money from things you are passionate about.

Between May 25 to September 1 Saturn enters Aries. Saturn in Aries wishes to rectify how we deal with our identity, body, anger, and vitality. This is great for you being a fellow fire sign. Shared resources are going to flow better than before but take more heed when traveling. A good time for long term studies like a language or a degree.

Between May 26 to June 8 Mercury enters Gemini. Mercury is back in his domicile, and he is happy to unpack and connect you to new businesses and ideas. Information, opportunities, connections, and words flow effortlessly.

The May 27 New Moon in Gemini is a great day to start something new in connection with communication, networking, businesses, marketing, sales, and written projects. This New Moon is blessed by Pluto and Neptune, making it possible for you to link passion and reason, emotions and intellect. A great deal of intimacy and a possibility for a lover coming into your life. Great time to make new friends and join groups or clubs.

JUNE

Between June 4 to 8, Venus, Jupiter, Mercury, and Mars are blessing us and each other. Windows of positive opportunities can improve sales, communication, writing, health, education, and art.

On June 6 Venus enters Taurus until July 4. The goddess of love is lending a helping hand in matters of art, finances, relationships, and security. You will experience your five senses in a much stronger way than regularly, perhaps getting a glimpse of the sixth one as well. A great time to connect to an artistic project or a talent, reconnect with your gifts and translate them into income. This is an opportune time to look for partners to further your career and add an artistic element into your professional life.

On June 8, Mercury transits Cancer until June 26. Great for healing relationships with family members. Don't be afraid to express your emotions. An opportune period to focus on your imagination, get messages from dreams and meditation. A wonderful time for therapy, your subconscious is wide open.

Between June 9 to 10 we have Mercury squares Neptune and Saturn and Venus squares Pluto. A bundle of challenging aspects come together. There is deception, lies, theft, and disinformation. Monkey mind is out of the cage, causing us to jump from one subject or project to the other. Breakups, manipulation, and discord with people of power.

On June 9 Jupiter enters Cancer and will stay there until June 30, 2026. This is a great year for real estate, healing familial relationships, connecting to fortune and abundance, and opening new doors. Be careful of overdoing and over commitments. This is an interesting transit for you since Jupiter can enhance your imagination, tap you into memories and talents from previous lives and make you a moder day mystic. Make sure you take time off and spend quality time in isolation.

From June 10 until August 23, Saturn conjuncts with Neptune. While your intuition, ability to meditate, and connect to your dreams are enhanced, so does your self-destructiveness, addictions, and escapism. Tread carefully, watch out for fanaticism or being too attached to your beliefs.

June 11 is the Full Moon in Sagittarius. Jupiter, ruler of Sagittarius is exalted, creating what is called Mutual Reception with the Moon, which is auspicious. A wonderful time to complete a cycle of learning and preparation for something new. Great for travel, especially by water or to a location close to the water. Mars gives a boost of energy to the aspect. There could be love in the air.

From June 17, Mars enters Virgo until August 6. Mars in Virgo gets things done. He is the watchmaker, the engineer, the organizer—here to protect and serve. Conflicts can arise if you are too critical of yourself and others. A good time for diets and a new health regiment. You can make things happen if you stick to a strict routine. This is a great time to increase your income or get a raise.

From June 21 the Sun transits Cancer until July 22. Happy Solstice! Open your heart to your family, and perhaps you might meet family members from past lives. This is a powerful time to let go and cut away from whatever hinders your growth, be it toxic relationships, certain substances, or negative attitude.

June 25 is the New Moon is Cancer, providing a new beginning that involves home and family, real estate, security, and emotional support. With Jupiter, exalted in Cancer, blessing the union of the Sun and Moon, this is a great time to start new projects. Besides Pluto, there are no planets retrograde, so full swim ahead! A revelation, a formidable "aha!" moment, and messages from dreams.

From June 26 until September 3, Mercury is in Leo. Since Mercury is retrograding in July, he will be in your sign for a while. This Mercury transit can be extremely creative, entertaining, and exciting. Mercury is making you roar! Writing, business, contracts and contacts come your way.

Between June 27 to 28, Mercury trines Saturn and Neptune. This is a good aspect for making long-term plans and bringing some sanity to a mad mad month. Good for marketing, writing, and sales. It is also a great time for prophetic dreams and practical intuition.

JULY

On July 4 Venus conjuncts Uranus and while relationships can be exciting, they can also show an unpredictable side. There is a need for freedom and exploration of new frontiers with your finances, relationships, and artistic expression. Embrace the original and unique. Be extra aware there could be volatility in the market.

From July 4 Venus flirts with Gemini until July 30 and the next few weeks can bring you in contact with a potential lover or partner at work. Art and communication come together, a great time for marketing, sales, design, and making new connections. Artistic groups or artistic friends might walk into your life.

From July 7 to November 8, Uranus enters Gemini, and your IQ is augmented. However, intelligence and IQ does not mean wisdom or kindness, so take heed not to become a heartless cyborg. Encounters with unusual and ingenious people. There could be disruption with your companies or organization.

July 10 is the Full Moon in Capricorn. This lunation can bring about a bit of opposition between home and career. The Moon is exiled in Capricorn and can create a sense of emotionality and longing for a paradise lost. However, Mars is sending his troupes to help you, and with a bit of action, determination, and a clear mission, you can disperse the emotional confusion of the Full Moon and get things done. Be extra careful with your health and relationship with coworkers.

From July 17 to August 12, Mercury is retrograde in Leo. Be extra careful Leo! Avoid signing docs and starting new projects. Especially watch your relationships and communication with kids, lovers, and people with big egos. While there could be chaotic situations in your life, there is also more magic and synchronicities.

From July 22 to August 22, Sun enters Leo. Engage in creative, joyful, and heartwarming activities. Generosity, nobility, chivalry, sportsmanship, and enthusiasm are guiding us this month. A great time to connect to a hobby or a new sport. A great month for healing and rebranding yourself. Happy birthday!

Between July 23–25, the Sun trine Saturn and Neptune creating a wonderful flow and help with vitality, intuition, healing, and the ability to bring some new structure into our lives. This is a glorious aspect, and you can benefit from creative visualizations, meditation, dance and self-expression.

On July 24 the New Moon is in Leo. This is not an easy New Moon since it is smack opposite to Pluto and can bring about a confrontation with a powerful figure in your life whose motivations are unclear. With Mercury retrograding in Leo, it is not the best time to start something new, however, you could initiate a project you already tried before and failed to complete. A powerful new beginning for you regardless of the retrograde.

From July 31 to August 25, Venus transits in Cancer. Marriage, social events with family members, as well as harmonious flow with family members. Mystical encounters as well as heightened imagination. Talents and people from past lives can come back into your life.

AUGUST

The month starts with a hard aspect between August 1 to 2 between Venus, Saturn and Neptune. Watch out for deception, illusions, and fantasies in your primary relationships as well as financial dealings. Not the best time to start a new relationship. Rapport with people who are older than you can be fraught with discord. Try a new approach to an old problem.

On August 6 Mars enters Libra and stays there until September 22. There could be some legal issues but also a good time for compromise and finding resolutions to conflicts. On the other hand, Mars can help you assert yourself in business dealing, with your communication, and negotiation. Between August 7 to 9, Mars trines Uranus bringing about brilliance and originality. Search for innovative and original solutions. Connections with friends can thrive. Action is guided by new approaches.

Watch out between August 8 to 10 as Mars opposites both Saturn and Neptune. Accidents, mishaps, and physical challenges especially since Mercury is retrograding. Stay away from arguments with superiors. Chill out as much as possible, less is more. Stay away from stormy seas (metaphysically and physically speaking).

August 9 is the Full Moon in Aquarius. You might feel a push and pull between the need to spend time with lovers or your children and your friends or company. This lunation can create an opposition between you and your partners in work and life. However, it is a good time to shine upon issues you might have with your significant others and resolve them.

On August 12, Mercury finally goes direct in your sign, Leo. You can now start plowing ahead, especially since on August 12 and 13, Venus conjuncts Jupiter, which is one of the best aspects this year. Luck, flow in finances, new relationships and maybe a novel love.

Between August 12 to October 27, Uranus trines Pluto. A powerful aspect that can bring about transformation through technology, science, social movements, and revolutions. Changes in government that can, in the long run, bring more prosperity.

From August 22 to September 22 the Sun transits in Virgo. This is great for your finances, reconnecting to your talents and getting a raise or award for your hard work. An ideal time to eliminate impediments to health and productivity. This is especially true on August 23—New Moon in Virgo. A great time for a new diet, work project, or service. A bit of chaos is added by a square to Uranus that can awaken the critic and perfectionist in you. Try to channel these propensities into something productive at work.

On August 25, Venus transits in Leo until September 19. The planet of love in the sign of romance is always good news. You are going to look and feel good, attracting a great deal of opportunities. Be careful of extra marital affairs. A great time to reconnect to a hobby you had in your teens. Be careful of pointless drama.

SEPTEMBER

On September 1 Saturn returns to Pisces until February 13, 2026. Confusion, floods, conflicts over water or in locations that are close to seas, lakes, and rivers. A time to ground your mystical practices, dreams, and intuition. A good time for research, connecting to your passion and reexamining how you work with shared resources. There could be a death and a letting go, symbolically or literally.

From September 2 to September 18, Mercury transits into Virgo. Sales, ideas, and information flow effortlessly. A great time for editing projects that need precision, micromanagement, organizing, and purification. This transit can bring a great deal of clarity and opportunity in your financial realm. Time to balance the sheets and organize your life.

On September 7 we have the Full Moon in Pisces. The Harvest Full Moon and Lunar Eclipse. Momentum builds towards closure especially with work and personal affairs. Now's the time to harvest the fruits of whatever you planted in your life around March/April. Mercury provides a touch of reason to an otherwise very emotional lunation. You might experience an opposition between your need to focus on your talents and money and those of your partner.

From September 18, Mercury transits into Libra until October 6. This Mercury wants peace, compromise, and beauty. A great time for healing relationships and harmonizing the workplace. Art and business are coming together. You can revamp your website, redesign your logo, and come up with new ways to brand yourself and your projects. A great transit for writing, business, signing contracts, and marketing.

From September 19, Venus transits Virgo until October 13. You might feel over critical about your art or your partners as well as feel the criticism of others. You can gain from being solo or practicing self-sufficiency. Good time to be frugal, balance your expenses and income, and detox. This is your month of improving and solidifying your finances, connecting to artistic talents, and feeling good about yourself.

September 21 is the Solar Eclipse in Virgo. A great time to balance your diet, start a new work project, and get the energy you need to reach the finish line. The Eclipse is giving you a push forward, allowing the planets involved to bestow their gifts on you: Pluto (power and intimacy); Saturn (focus); Neptune (imagination and intuition); Uranus (innovation). Things are quickening around investments and shared resources.

On September 22, the Sun enters Libra until October 23, marking the Equinox! As one of the four sacred days of the astrological calendar, commemorate it by celebrating relationships, justice, beauty, and art. Over the next 30 days, you are asked to embody Libra's traits—diplomacy, balance, and attentiveness to partners. A great time for business partnership as well as being connected to people who can help your causes.

On September 22, Mars enters Scorpio until November 4. A wonderful time to collaborate on big projects that demand abundant energy and resources. Passion, intimacy and sexuality are on the rise. Great for physical activities in water or reconnecting to sports you are passionate about. An opportune time for research and investigation, as well as fighting for what you believe in. A good time for renovation and remodeling your home or office. Be careful of unnecessary conflicts with family members.

Between September 23–25, tread cautiously as Mars squares Pluto. Aggression and manipulative folks are around you. Take extra heed in general. Actions can be easily misconstrued.

OCTOBER

On October 6 Mercury transits into Scorpio until October 29. An ideal period for research, finding lost objects or people, and expressing intimacy. It's a good time to move on, let bygones be bygones, bury the zombies in your life, and explore investments and collaborations with other people's assets and talents. Mercury can be your private investigator and expose hidden information. A great time for healing within the homestead as well as family businesses or real estate.

October 7 is the Full Moon in Aries. This Full Moon, bordering on a lunar eclipse, is a tad challenging. With Chiron's involvement, it's an occasion for learning, teaching, and shamanistic journeys. While there's an aggressive undertone, it's a good moment to conclude matters and move on. There could be conflicts with partners in life or work. A good time for travel, education, and meeting a mentor.

Between October 11 to 14, Venus is opposite Saturn and Neptune. This can be hard on your relationships and or finances. There is an emotional frustration with partners, especially long-term ones. Illusions as well as dependency and codependency and a disappointment with someone close to you. However, you can use this aspect to connect mysticism and art.

From October 13 to November 6, Venus returns to her sign, Libra, and can help you connect to beauty, diplomacy, justice, relationship, and harmony. A great time for connecting to business partners and fixing relationships with relatives, siblings, and neighbors. This is especially strong between October 14–15 as Venus trine Uranus and Pluto. Venus receives much praise from Pluto (intimacy, sexuality, power) and Uranus (innovation, technology, friendships). This is another wonderful aspect that carries you upward with Venus (finances, relationships) leading the way. This is a powerful time for igniting, transforming, balancing and solidifying partnerships in work and personal life.

The New Moon in Libra takes place October 21. Dubbed the "Moon of Peace," the Libra New Moon is a great time to start a relationship or an art project. A good time for making new connections with clients and business contacts. However, both Jupiter and Pluto are squaring off with the Sun and Moon, creating uncomfortable situations. Be extra cautious and focus on breathwork and meditation.

On October 22, Neptune returns for the last time to his sign, Pisces, until January 27, 2026. A great time to start meditation practice that can be facilitated by the ruler of mysticism. Dreams, imagination, channeling, mediumship, poetry, and art are enhanced, as well as your intuition. Be extra careful with your investments.

On October 23, the Sun enters Scorpio until November 22. Focus on being true to your passion. It is a month of healing, transformation, magic, occult, and assisting others in their talents, finances, and endeavors. A monthlong dedicated to healing and growth within your family as well as a good time to remodel, relocate, and fix your office.

Around October 26 Mars conjuncts Lilith, please be extra careful today as the Mother of Demons hired an assassin. This is a violent and aggressive aspect. Tread cautiously.

On October 29, Mercury enters Sagittarius until November 19. You might feel a bit absent-minded and distracted. A good time for traveling and doing business with foreigners. Stick to the truth and avoid liars and half-truths. Great for education and publishing.

NOVEMBER

From November 4 to December 15, Mars enters Sagittarius. A call for adventure, as well as an expedition. Your Mars wants you to conquer, hunt, and expend your knowledge. It is an Indiana Jones aspect. This is a great time for romantic love, sports, spending time with children and having fun.

November 5 is the Full Moon exalted in Taurus. An opportune time to bring something into completion. Since the lunation is on the 13th degree of Scorpio, it carries a powerful connection to love. Spend time in nature and indulge your five senses. Something in your career is coming to a completion, but there could be some push and pull between family and career.

On November 6, Venus enters Scorpio until November 30. This transit can make you feel alone or unwanted, possessive as well as jealous. However, it is a good time to focus on your partner's money and talents rather than your own. Look into your investments as there might be a need to make some adjustments. However, it is a good time to focus on decorating your home or office.

From November 8 to April 26, 2026, Uranus returns for the last time to Taurus. Changes in finances, fluctuations in cryptocurrency, new ways of expressing artistic talents. The final march of Uranus in your career, therefore, a time to update and upgrade your professional life and workflow. Bring the future to the here and now!

From November 9 to December 1 Mercury is stationary and retrograde. Avoid signing documents or starting new projects. Refrain from signing documents, starting new projects, and initiating anything unless you tried to do so before and failed to accomplish it. There could be issues in your creative projects or with your kids.

On November 19, Mercury enters Scorpio until December 10. Mercury returns to Scorpio as he retrogrades back into the underworld. Good for investigations and finding lost objects and people.

November 20 is the New Moon in Scorpio. A great time to investigate your passions, what you really want in life, what you wish to transform, and start fulfilling these aspects of your life today. A good New Moon to initiate projects that need shared resources, talents, or funding. However, since

Mercury is retro, you can only start things you already did in the past and failed to bring to completion. An opportune time to initiate healing, therapy, a shamanistic journey, or an investigation. The New Moon is getting a boost from Saturn, Jupiter, and Neptune, which bless this lunation with structure and focus, imagination and inspiration, and a great deal of open-mindedness.

On November 22, the Sun transits in Sagittarius until December 21. Sagittarius is the time of the year when we have the strongest connection to our higher self or guardian angel. This is a month for teaching, mentoring, learning, speaking your truth, mass media, publishing, connecting to foreigners, and in-laws. A month to focus on love, happiness, your children and inner child.

On November 28 Venus conjuncts Lilith. Be extra careful with all your relationships and partners in work or in personal life. A three-sided relationship might form around you. Be beware of stalkers, gossip, enemies, and lawsuits. This can especially be tough on your family.

From November 30 until December 24 Venus transits in Sagittarius. It is a great time for connecting to educators, foreigners, explore investments and possibilities from travel and abroad. A good time to improve relationships with in-laws. Venus is activating your love and creativity. A great time to have a baby!

DECEMBER

December 4 is the Full Moon in Gemini. An optimal moment to finalize projects. As this is the year's last Full Moon. A time for new friendships, clients, or connection to a new company.

On December 10, Mercury finally goes direct, a good time for traveling and conducting businesses abroad as well as for teaching and learning.

From December 15, Mars transits in Capricorn until January 26, 2026. Make sure you give him a mission—something you need help conquering and or mastering. It is a good aspect for leadership and initiation. A call for action is coming, make sure not to refuse the call. Mars can now help you get a promotion or revamp your work. Be cautious of conflicts with coworkers or employees.

December 20 is the New Moon in Sagittarius. A difficult New Moon with Neptune and Saturn sending squares all over the place. Not the best time to start new projects. Be careful of aggression and anger. A sense of war approaching. Lay low and be vigilant. A great time to fall in love romantically or with a physical activity or a hobby.

From December 20, Lilith enters Sagittarius for nine months. There could be discord with students and teachers, as well as foreigners. Take extra care when traveling. Be super careful with extra martial affairs or falling for the wrong person.

On December 21 the Sun enters Capricorn and will stay there until January 20, 2026. Happy Solstice! The ensuing month calls for Capricorn-like discipline and focus. Strategize the year ahead, bearing in mind that patience is vital. While it is true that we are in holiday season, it is a great time to get clarity about your work and health. Especially from December 24 when Venus transits in Capricorn until January 17, 2026, and blesses your work, service activities, and health. This transit of Venus can help you improve relationships with people who are older, long-term partnerships, as well as bosses and superiors. A time to connect art and design to your professional life.

VIRGO AND VIRGO RISING: I SERVE

Mirrors, Relationships, and Balance

Major Trends: This year you continue focusing on your relationships and partnerships. Many of you will get divorced, some will find a partner and get married, a few might do both. With the South Node and eclipses falling in your sign, you are asked to be less of a Virgo—stay away from your typical perfectionism and analytical aspects of your sign and learn to accept yours as well as other people's flaws and round the corners. Expect opportunities in the first part of the year furthering your career and in the second part of 2025, you could benefit from connecting to new groups of friends, increased flow of clients, and connection with technology.

JANUARY

Between January 1–5, Mars is opposite his Scorpio coruler, Pluto, which is not a promising beginning of the year. In addition, Mars is retrograde therefore, take extra care on the first few days of the year. You might experience PTSD from previous lives or ancestral traumas; therefore, it is a good time for resting, healing, and sharing your feelings with people who can support you.

On January 3, Venus puts on her swimming suit and dives into Pisces until February 4. Opportunities to improve your finances, relationships as well as artistic gifts manifest. Creative visualization can be extremely potent. A great time to find or harmonize your relationships.

On January 6, Mars retrogrades into Cancer until April 18. Be vigilant of accidents, falling (unless it is in love) and issues with or around water such as leaks and floods. Conflict can arise with family members. There could be unnecessary conflicts with friends or people in your company.

On January 8 Mercury enters Capricorn until January 28, and this means serious thought, disciplined study, and lessons received from mature and experienced people. Slow your thought, speech, and writing, and be mindful of every word. Great for furthering your career goals and forging long-term plans. A good time to communicate with children as well as focusing on creative writing projects.

January 13 is the Full Moon in Cancer, where she loves to be. It could get emotional and a bit aggressive with family and loved ones due to the opposition of retrograding Mars. Take heed of over emotionality and guilt casting. There could be a push and pull between your need to spend time with your children or lover and responsibilities towards your friends or company.

Between January 18–19, Venus conjuncts Saturn. Finances, values, and your relationships are being scrutinized and audited. This is not necessarily a bad aspect as Venus is exalted and Saturn can ground your talents as well as help you use your gifts in a practical way. Whatever is going on in your personal and professional relationships are galvanized and crystallized, for good or bad.

On January 19 the Sun enters Aquarius until February 18. A time to spend with friends, community, as well as immerse yourself in science, technology, and innovation. A month to focus on your work, health and diet.

Between January 25–26, as Venus trines Mars, the cosmic lovers can bring a new relationship into your life or help you harmonize partnerships you already have.

From January 28 until February 14, Mercury transits in Aquarius, and ideas flow fast as well as new friendships with likeminded people. A great time to make new contacts and reconnect to old friendships. This can be beneficial for your work as well as your health. January 29 is also the New Moon in Aquarius and Chinese New Year. Time to welcome to the Year of the Earth Snake. Jupiter is blessing this New Moon with wisdom and synchronicity. A great time to start a study group. A new friend or group from whom you can learn a great deal is making an entrance into your life. A great time for a new work project and or a new diet regimen.

On January 29, the North Node retrogrades into Pisces until August 19, 2026, for the first time in 19 years. Right on the New Moon in Aquarius, the North Node aka "Dragon," is retrograding into the sign of mysticism, intuition, and imagination. For the next 18 months you are asked to practice empathy, meditation, any form of trance or movement practice (yoga, dance, or martial arts). However, the South Node will be in Virgo asking us to let go of criticism, perfectionism, and overanalytical tendencies. This is great news for all your romantic relationships and partners in work. The Dragon can also provide protection against enemies and competitors.

FEBRUARY

On February 4, Venus enters Aries, until March 27. Conflicts and aggression with relationships and partners can arise. Watch impulsiveness with your finances. However, this Venus transit can increase your passion and intimacy as well as help your partners increase their income. Good for investments.

February 12 is the Full Moon in Leo, and you might feel the pull and push between the gravitational forces of your children or romantic partner versus friends or your company. The square with Uranus can cause disruption and lunacy to this lunation. A time to let go, detox, cut something out of your diet that can improve your energy level.

On Valentine's Day (February 14), Mercury enters Pisces until March 3. Communications can be a bit challenged while intuition and mediumship are on the rise. Trust your gut feeling rather than your brain. Make sure to use the words "I feel" or "I imagine" or "I believe," instead of "I think." This trend is supported by the Sun entering Pisces from February 18 until March 20's Equinox. Imagination, dance, movement, dreaming, meditation, intuition, mysticism, and empathy are heightened. Just make sure to guard your boundaries and avoid addictions or self-destructive tendencies. The best time in the year to mend relationships, attract a partner, and balance your life.

The month ends with the New Moon in Pisces on February 28. A great day to start something new that involves your imagination, photography, movement, yoga and meditation. There is a tendency to absorb negativity from others so watch what you take in. Be careful of overdoing or illusions. A wonderful time to start a new relationship in work or life.

MARCH
March 1–April 14 Venus stands still and then retrogrades in Aries, her sign of exile. Avoid getting married, starting new relationships, getting engaged, starting lawsuits, signing partnerships agreements. Be extra careful while managing shared resources as well as investments. In addition, exes or lovers from previous lives or this life might return, be selective who you welcome back.

On March 3, Mercury enters Aries until March 30. Mercury can be a bit impatient when in Aries and favors practical, short and concise communication. A good time for therapy, shamanism, dealing with death, letting go, and peeling off layers that keep you from your true potential.

Between March 11–13, Sun conjunct Saturn while Mercury conjunct Venus. Seriousness, focus, discipline and planning can bring tactical or strategical accomplishments. A good time to improve relations with superiors.

March 14, Pi Day, we have the first Lunar Eclipse of the year. The Full Moon in mathematical and analytical Virgo, this is your eclipse initiation. A great time to bring a project to an end, as well as focus on diet, service, and combining your analytical and wholistic aspects in life. There could be a bit of a conflict between "I" and "Us", or "Me" and "You."

March 14–April 8 Mercury stationary and retrograde. Since it is happening in Aries this month, be extra careful with anger, impulsiveness, and hasty decisions. Be extra cautious as Mercury retrograde affects you more than other signs.

On March 17, the Sun conjuncts North Node. A day to access skills and knowledge from past lifetimes. There could be an encounter with powerful and successful individuals or groups that can further your goals.

On March 20 we have the Equinox and the Sun's transits into Aries until April 19. Happy New Year! A time to focus on your body, health, leadership, as well as your brand and image. This is a month to focus on intimacy, passion, sexuality and working with other people's money and talents. A good time for research, diving deep into the occult and shamanism.

On March 27, Lilith enters Scorpio until December 20. Emotional intensity, powerful desires, fascination with the forbidden, shadow work, possessiveness, and jealousy. Power struggles, manipulation, abuse, distrust, and criminality. Stay clear of any form of gossip. A good time to place a heap of salt in the four corners of your bedroom as protection against negativity. Lilith can cause havoc with or to your relatives, neighbors, roommates, and siblings. Be extra cautious what contracts you sign.

March 29 is the first Solar Eclipse of the year, and she shines upon Aries. Be mindful of unnecessary aggression and impulsiveness.

From March 30 to April 15, Mercury is in Pisces. Mercury retrogrades into his sign of fall; thus, communication can be extra hard as the messenger is not only retro but drowning in subjectivity. Talk and write from your heart rather than mind. Great for intuition and applying imagination to overcome challenges. Mercury can help heal your relationships as well as improve your connection with partners in work.

From March 30 to October 22, Neptune enters Aries for the first time in 165 years. Confusion can lead to war, be extra careful of fanaticism or aggression triggered by propaganda of misinformation. Watch your immune system, inflammation, and your head. Be extra careful of Ponzi schemes, questionable sexual partners, and where you invest your passion and money.

APRIL

Between April 5–7, the celestial lovers meet again. Venus is Barbie and Mars in water sign Cancer is Ken, the "simply beach" dude. These are great days for romance, increasing your income from talents you are passionate about, and better relationships with significant others as well as brothers and sisters in arms. A friend might become a lover or vis versa.

From April 5 to 10, Venus conjuncts Saturn. While this aspect can introduce you to someone older that could be helpful with finance and developing your talents, this conjunction can also sit heavy over all your relationships. A time to reassess your primary relationships and how you make money.

On April 8 Mercury finally goes direct, therefore, you can start signing documents and starting new projects. Between April 7–16 Mercury trine Mars and that could kick forward to your projects and business. Mercury's direct motion could help heal your relationships and open new channels of communication with partners.

April 13 is the Full Moon in Libra. This is the day of liberation, coming out of constriction, and negativity and marching towards your Promised Land. It is a magical Full Moon where you might connect to your inner Moses, guardian angel, or higher self. There could be tension between your need to focus on your money and talents versus those of your partner.

April 14 is a dramatic day when Saturn conjuncts the North Node in Pisces. Positive interactions with groups of powerful individuals or people who are older. You are downloading some gifts or connections from previous lives. Good for joining new groups and organizations that share long-term goals. A person you know from a past life, most likely older or matured, is coming back into your life. Could even be a potential partner.

From April 16 to May 10 Mercury transits in Aries, speeding things up but also showing signs of impatience. Words can easily be weaponized so be extra careful. A great time for research, investments, and working with other people's money and talents.

From April 18 to June 17 Mars enters Leo bringing about a great deal of courage and a call for adventure. Great for entertainment, sports, creativity,

and reconnecting to your inner child. You might experience echoes of traumas from previous lifetimes that have to do with war and violence.

On April 19 the Sun enters Taurus and will remain there until May 20. This month you are to indulge your six senses and connect to Mother Nature. It is a good month to tap into your artistic talents and perhaps discover new ones. A month for travel and education.

April 27 is the exalted New Moon in Taurus. A great time to start a new artistic or financial project. Spend time in nature, connect to your senses and do something that can symbolize rooting yourself. A wonderful time to start learning something new.

On April 30 Venus enters Aries until June 6. There could be a bit more conflict and aggression in your primary relationships. In her sign of exile, Venus might be somewhat snappy and can cause hasty decisions and actions with finances and love. Intimacy, sexuality and passion are all around you. Great for investments.

MAY

Between May 1 to May 3, Venus conjuncts Neptune and infuses you with romance, creativity, art, improved finances, and intuition.

From May 10 to May 26, Mercury enters Taurus, which can bring a sense of worry and anxiety. However, it is a good time to communicate and market your talents and gifts. Speak your mind without attachment or inflexibility. A great time for business travel and speaking your truth.

May 12 is the Full Moon in Scorpio, and while the Moon is fallen, it is still a great time for shadow work, dealing with temptation, and discovering the light in you. Because the Moon falls on the 22nd (Master Number) degree of Scorpio, we can build something out of the rubble of an older project or relationship. In this lunation you feel the tug of war between "mine" and "yours." A time to end one business opportunity or writing project and begin a new one.

From May 20 to June 21, the Sun enters Gemini, and you are channeling the spirit of intelligence, communication, and bridge-building. This is a great month for business, contracts, improving relationships with relatives, roommates, neighbors, and people you consider siblings. This transit can help you in your career and professional life.

Between May 20 to 24, Venus trines Mars once again. Romance, love, harmony (the daughter of Venus and Mars), is around you as well as an ability to see people's beautiful side. Great time for making money from things you are passionate about.

Between May 25 to September 1 Saturn enters Aries. Saturn in Aries wishes to rectify how we deal with our identity, body, anger, and vitality. A time for you to focus on your passion and how you express your power and sexuality. You might have to deal with death and letting go, symbolically or literally.

Between May 26 to June 8 Mercury enters Gemini. Mercury is back to his domicile, and he is happy to unpack and help you achieve your goals. Information, opportunities, connections, and words flow effortlessly. A wonderful time to bring the future into your career—innovation as well as new ways of doing things.

The May 27 New Moon in Gemini is a great day to start something new in connection with communication, networking, businesses, marketing, sales, and written projects. This New Moon is blessed by Pluto and Neptune, making it possible for you to link passion and reason, emotions and intellect. A great deal of intimacy and a possibility for a lover coming into your life. Something new is opening up in your career. A great time to initiate new projects.

JUNE

Between June 4 to 8, Venus, Jupiter, Mercury, and Mars are blessing you and each other. Windows of positive opportunities can improve sales, communication, writing, health, education, and art.

On June 6 Venus enters Taurus until July 4. A wonderful time for exotic love, traveling together with a partner, maybe meeting someone special abroad, and healing relationships with in-laws. It is the best time this year to master a musical instrument or learn a new art. The goddess of love is lending a helping hand in matters of art, finances, relationships, and security. You will experience your five senses in a much stronger way than regularly, perhaps getting a glimpse of the sixth one as well.

On June 8, Mercury transits Cancer until June 26. Great for healing relationships with family members. Don't be afraid to express your emotions. An opportune time to meet new friends and improve your connections with colleagues.

Between June 9 to 10 we have Mercury squares Neptune and Saturn and Venus squares Pluto. A bundle of challenging aspects come together. There is deception, lies, theft, and disinformation. Monkey mind is out of the cage, causing us to jump from one subject or project to the other. Breakups, manipulation, and discord with people of power.

On June 9 Jupiter enters Cancer and will stay there until June 30, 2026. This is a great year for real estate, healing familial relationships, connecting to fortune and abundance, and opening new doors. Be careful of overdoing and over commitments. This transit can help advance your interest within your company, attract new friends and clients, as well as connect to technology and innovations.

From June 10 until August 23, Saturn conjuncts with Neptune. While your intuition, ability to meditate, and connect to your dreams are enhanced, so does your self-destructiveness, addictions, and escapism. Tread carefully, watch out for fanaticism or being too attached to your beliefs.

On June 11, the Full Moon is in Sagittarius. A blessed Full Moon in a challenging month. A wonderful time to complete a cycle of learning and preparing for something new to come into your life at home or career. Great for travel, especially by water or to a location close to the water. Mars gives a boost of energy to the aspect.

From June 17, Mars enters Virgo until August 6. Mars in Virgo gets things done. He is the watchmaker, the engineer, the organizer—here to protect and serve. Conflicts can arise if you are too critical of yourself and others. A good time for diets and a new health regiment. You can make things happen if you stick to a strict routine. Mars in your sign can help you regain your vitality, connect to a new physical activity, and practice your leadership skills. This is the time to focus on your passion, body, and self-assertion.

From June 21 the Sun transits Cancer until July 22. Happy Solstice! Open your heart to your family, and perhaps you might meet family members from past lives. This trend peaks on June 25, as the New Moon in Cancer provides a new beginning that involves home and family, real estate, security, and emotional support. A new project that involves friends or a large group of people. A great time to update and upgrade your workflow.

From June 26 until September 3, Mercury is in Leo. This Mercury transit can be extremely creative, entertaining, and exciting. Since Mercury is activating your imagination and connection to your subconscious, it is a wonderful time for healing and tapping into gifts from previous lives.

JULY

On July 4 Venus conjuncts Uranus and while relationships can be exciting, they can also show an unpredictable side. There is a need for freedom and exploration of new frontiers with your finances, relationships, and artistic expression. Embrace the original and unique. Be extra aware there could be volatility in the market.

From July 4 Venus flirts with Gemini until July 30 and the next few weeks can bring you in contact with a potential lover or partner at work. Art and communication come together, a great time for marketing, sales, design, and making new connections. Try to incorporate art in your professional life, some new design, creative marketing and maybe forming new partnerships in career.

From July 7 to November 8, Uranus enters Gemini, and your IQ is augmented. However, intelligence and IQ does not mean wisdom or kindness, so take heed not to become a heartless cyborg. Uranus is making a visit to your career and implores you to awaken and try new things, take calculative risks and connect to technology and innovation.

July 10 is the Full Moon in Capricorn. This lunation can bring about a bit of opposition between home and career. The Moon is exiled in Capricorn and can create a sense of emotionality and longing for a paradise lost. However, as a fellow Earth sign, it is not a bad transit, and Mars could infuse you with passion and love to a project or a person.

From July 17 to August 12, Mercury is retrograde in Leo. Avoid signing documents and starting new projects. Especially watch your relationships and communication with kids, lovers, and people with big egos. Memories from past life are flooding you and people you have known in previous lives could return.

From July 22 to August 22, Sun enters Leo. The trend of retreating from life and wanting to reflect and isolate increases in the next 30 days. A great time to detox, let go, and rest. This is especially strong between July 23-25, as the Sun trine Saturn and Neptune creating a wonderful flow and help with vitality, intuition, healing, and the ability to bring some new structure into our lives. This is a glorious aspect, and you can benefit from creative visualizations, meditation, dance and self-expression.

July 24 is the New Moon in Leo. This is not an easy New Moon since it is smack opposite to Pluto and can bring about a confrontation with a powerful figure in your life whose motivations are unclear. With Mercury retrograding in Leo, it is not the best time to start something new, however, you could initiate a project you already tried before and failed to complete.

From July 31 to August 25, Venus transits in Cancer. Marriage, social events with family members, as well as harmonious flow with family members. Artistic projects that involve other people are recommended.

AUGUST

The month starts with a hard aspect on August 1 and 2 between Venus, Saturn and Neptune. Watch out for deception, illusions, and fantasies in your primary relationships as well as financial dealings. Not the best time to start a new relationship. Rapport with people who are older than you can be fraught with discord. Try a new approach to an old problem.

On August 6 Mars enters Libra and stays there until September 22. While it is not Mars' favorite position, he can still bring about a great deal of energy into your ability to increase your income. Not a bad time to ask for a raise or promotion. In addition, between August 7 to 9, Mars trines Uranus bringing about brilliance and originality. Search for innovative and original solutions. Connections with friends can thrive. Action is guided by new approaches.

Watch it between August 8 to 10 as Mars opposites both Saturn and Neptune. Accidents, mishaps, and physical challenges especially since Mercury is retrograding. Stay away from arguments with superiors. Stay calm and try to do less. The opposition with Neptune adds more hardships to the already difficult few days. Stay away from stormy seas (metaphysically and physically speaking).

August 9 is the Full Moon in Aquarius. You might feel a push and pull between the need to spend time with lovers or your children and the demands of your friends or company. The Moon brings tension between the need to rest and the call for service and work.

On August 12, Mercury finally goes direct in Leo. You can now start plowing ahead, especially since on August 12 and 13, Venus conjuncts Jupiter, which is one of the best aspects this year. Luck, flow in finances, new relationships and maybe a novel love.

Between August 12 to October 27, Uranus trines Pluto. A powerful aspect that can bring about transformation through technology, science, social movements, and revolutions. Changes in government that can, in the long run, bring more prosperity.

From August 22 to September 22 the Sun transits in Virgo. Happy birthday! A time to focus on your body, asserting yourself and your will, and rebranding. This is especially true on August 23 when the New Moon lands in Virgo. A great time for a new diet, work project, or service. It is recommended to reorganize your life, start a new routine, and focus on your leadership skills. A bit of chaos is added by a square to Uranus that can awaken the critic and perfectionist in you. Try to channel these propensities into something productive at work.

On August 25, Venus transits in Leo until September 19. The planet of love in the sign of romance is always good news. Just be careful of extra marital affairs. It is a very creative time with your inner child, active and playful. A great time to reconnect to a hobby you had in your teens. Be careful of pointless drama. However, this is an ideal time for couple's therapy.

SEPTEMBER

On September 1 Saturn returns to Pisces until February 13, 2026. Since March 2023 you had to deal with Saturn rectifying and focusing your relationships and now you will have a few more months to galvanize and crystalize your relationship and partnerships in work or in life. Watch out for enemies and lawsuits.

From September 2 to September 18, Mercury transits into Virgo. Your ruler returns to you and brings with him a great deal of gifts and business opportunities. Sales, ideas, writing, and information flow effortlessly. A great time for editing projects that need precision, micromanagement, organizing, and purification. A wonderful time for detoxing and a cleanse.

September 7 is the Full Moon in Pisces. The Harvest Full Moon and Lunar Eclipse combo. Momentum builds towards closure especially with work and personal affairs. Now's the time to harvest the fruits of your labor from March/April. Mercury provides a touch of reason to an otherwise very emotional lunation. There could be tension between you and your partners in work and life. You are reaping whatever you have sown in your primary relationships over the last few years.

From September 18, Mercury transits into Libra until October 6. This Mercury wants peace, compromise, and beauty. A great time for healing relationships and harmonizing the workplace. Art and business are coming together. You can revamp your website, redesign your logo, and come up with new ways to brand yourself and your projects. Mercury can help you with your finances, access your talents, and maybe even get a raise.

From September 19, Venus transits Virgo until October 13. You might feel over critical about your art or your partners as well as feel the criticism of others. You can gain from being solo or practicing self-sufficiency. Good time to be frugal, balance your expenses and income, and detox. A wonderful time to reconnect to your body, appearances, image, and brand. You look and feel great!

On September 21 the Solar Eclipse is in Virgo, things are quickened between you and your primary relationships. A great time to balance your diet, start a new work project, and get the energy you need to reach the finish line. The Eclipse creates a powerful aspect allowing the planets involved to bestow their gifts on you: Pluto (power and intimacy); Saturn (focus); Neptune (imagination and intuition); Uranus (innovation).

On September 22, the Sun enters Libra until October 23, marking the Equinox! As one of the four sacred days in the astrological calendar, commemorate it by celebrating relationships, justice, beauty, and art. Over the next 30 days, you should embody Libra traits—diplomacy, balance, and attentiveness to partners. It is a powerful time to increase your income, shine your talents, and elevate your self-worth.

On September 22, Mars enters Scorpio until November 4. A wonderful time to collaborate on big projects that demand shared energy and resources. Passion, intimacy and sexuality are on the rise. Great for physical activities in water or reconnecting to sports you are passionate about. An opportune time for research and investigation, as well as fighting for what you believe in. Watch out for needless conflicts with siblings, relatives, neighbors and roommates.

Between September 23–25, tread cautiously as Mars squares Pluto. Aggression and manipulative folks are around you. Take extra heed in general. Actions can be easily misconstrued. Especially be aware of your communication with coworkers and employees.

OCTOBER

On October 6 Mercury transits into Scorpio until October 29. An ideal period for research, finding lost objects or people, and expressing intimacy. It's a good time to move on, let bygones be bygones, bury the zombies in your life, and explore investments and collaborations with other people's assets and talents. Mercury can be your private investigator and expose hidden information. A great time for new contracts and making new connections. The best time of the year for writing and marketing.

October 7 is the Full Moon in Aries. With Chiron's involvement, it's an occasion for learning, teaching, and shamanistic journeys. While there's an aggressive undertone, it's a good moment to conclude matters and move on. There could be conflicts with partners in life or work.

Between October 11 to 14, Venus is opposite Saturn and Neptune. This can be hard on your relationships and or finances. There is an emotional frustration with partners, especially long-term ones. Illusions as well as dependency and codependency and some disappointment with someone close to you.

From October 13 to November 6, Venus returns to her sign, Libra, and can help us connect to beauty, diplomacy, justice, relationship, and harmony. This is an opportune time for increasing income and connecting to hidden artistic talents. This is especially strong between October 14–15 as Venus links with Uranus and Pluto. Venus receives much praise from Pluto (intimacy, sexuality, power) and Uranus (innovation, technology, friendships). This is a powerful time for igniting, transforming, balancing and solidifying partnerships in work and personal life.

The New Moon in Libra takes place October 21. Dubbed the "Moon of Peace," the Libra New Moon is a great time to start a relationship or an art project. However, both Jupiter and Pluto are squaring off with the Sun and Moon, creating uncomfortable situations. Be extra cautious and focus on breathwork and meditation. Nevertheless, it is a good time to give a push to your finances, developing a new talent, and improving your self-esteem.

On October 22, Neptune returns for the last time to his sign, Pisces, until January 27, 2026. A great time to start meditation practice that can be facilitated by the ruler of mysticism. Dreams, imagination, channeling, mediumship, poetry, and art are enhanced, as well as your intuition. Watch for illusions and deceptions in the context of your relationships.

On October 23, the Sun enters Scorpio until November 22. Focus on being true to your passion. It is a month of healing, transformation, magic, occult, and assisting others in their talents, finances, and endeavors. A good month for writing, sales, and marketing.

Around October 26 Mars conjuncts Lilith, please be extra careful today as the Mother of Demons hired an assassin. This is a violent and aggressive aspect. Tread cautiously. Be extra careful with what you post, write, tweet, like or say. Relatives can act out as well as issues with neighbors can arise.

On October 29, Mercury enters Sagittarius until November 19. You might feel a bit absent-minded and distracted. A good time for traveling and doing business with foreigners. Stick to the truth and avoid liars and half-truths. Great for education and publishing. You should do your best to connect to family, real estate, get a job that allows you to work from home, and develop gifts or positive traits that run in your family.

NOVEMBER

From November 4 to December 15, Mars enters Sagittarius. A call for adventure, as well as an expedition. Your Mars wants you to conquer, hunt, and expend your knowledge. It is an Indiana Jones aspect. A good time for renovation, remodeling, and relocation. Conflicts could arise among family members or at home.

November 5 is the Full Moon in Taurus. An opportune time to bring something into completion. Since the lunation is on the 13th degree of Scorpio, it carries a powerful connection to love. Spend time in nature and indulge your five senses. Be extra careful if you are traveling as there could be some unexpected twists and turns.

On November 6, Venus enters Scorpio until November 30. This transit can make you feel alone or unwanted, possessive as well as jealous. However, it is a good time to focus on your partner's money and talents rather than your own. Look into your investments as there might be a need to make some adjustments. A good time for marketing and sales, especially if you are passionate about your business. An opportune time to heal relationships with relatives and siblings.

From November 8 to April 26, 2026, Uranus returns for the last time to Taurus. Changes in finances, fluctuations in cryptocurrency, new ways of expressing artistic talents. Since 2018 Uranus has been awakening your need to study and teach, travel, and connect to the truth. Now is his last hurrah. Be extra careful when traveling since there could be unpredictable elements to your trips.

From November 9 to December 1 Mercury is stationary and retrograde. Avoid signing documents or starting new projects. This retrograde dances on the cusp of Sagittarius where he is overthinking to Scorpio where he is secretive. This is a bit challenging for you as your ruler is creating setbacks in your sphere of communication and business.

The New Moon in Scorpio takes place on November 20. A great time to investigate your passions, what you really want in life, what you wish to transform, and start today. A good New Moon to initiate projects that need shared resources, talents, or funding. However, since Mercury is retro, you can only start things you already did in the past and failed to bring to completion. An opportune time to initiate healing, therapy, a shamanistic journey, or an investigation. The New Moon is getting a boost from Saturn, Jupiter, and Neptune, which bless this lunation with structure and focus, imagination and inspiration, and a great deal of open-mindedness.

On November 22, the Sun transits in Sagittarius until December 21. Sagittarius is the time of the year when you have the strongest connection to your higher self or guardian angel. This is a month for teaching, mentoring, learning, speaking your truth, mass media, publishing, and connecting to foreigners, and in-laws. A good month to focus on your home and family.

November 23 is an interesting day when the Sun trines Neptune; Mercury trines Jupiter and Saturn; Jupiter trines Saturn. This day can further your goals in almost all aspects of your life.

On November 28 Venus conjuncts Lilith. Be extra careful with all your relationships and partners in work or in personal life. A three-sided relationship might form around you. Be beware of stalkers, gossip, enemies, and lawsuits. Watch out for issues with relatives or neighbors.

From November 30 until December 24 Venus transits in Sagittarius. It is a great time for connecting to educators, foreigners, explore investments and possibilities from travel and abroad. A wonderful time to beautify your dwelling place and or office.

DECEMBER

December 4 is the Full Moon in Gemini. An optimal moment to finalize projects. As this is the year's last Full Moon. There could be conflicts arising from the need to focus on home and responsibilities presented by your career.

On December 10, Mercury finally goes direct. It is good for traveling and businesses abroad as well as for education. Great news for you as your ruler can now push forward all aspects of communications and business.

From December 15, Mars transits in Capricorn until January 26, 2026. Make sure you give him a mission—something you need help conquering and or mastering. It is a good aspect for leadership and initiation. A call for action is coming, make sure not to refuse the call. Mars can push you toward a new physical activity or hobby that relates to sharp objects. However, there could be issues with unruly kids or lovers.

December 20 is the New Moon in Sagittarius. A difficult New Moon with Neptune and Saturn sending squares all over the place. Not the best time to start new projects. Be careful of aggression and anger. A sense of war approaching. Especially be careful with issues that relate to home or family members.

From December 20, Lilith enters Sagittarius for nine months. There could be discord with students and teachers, as well as foreigners. Take extra care when traveling. This is not an easy nine months with family life. There could be a member of the family going through a rough patch or you could be misunderstood by your family.

On December 21 the Sun enters Capricorn and will stay there until January 20, 2026. Happy Solstice! The ensuing month calls for Capricorn-like discipline and focus. Strategize the year ahead, bearing in mind that patience is vital. A great month for love, happiness, connecting to your inner kid as well as your children. A very creative surge of energy is coming your way.

From December 24 Venus transits in Capricorn until January 17, 2026. This transit of Venus can help you improve relationships with people who are older, long-term partnerships, as well as bosses and superiors. This is a very creative time and a potential for falling in love.

LIBRA AND
LIBRA RISING: I BALANCE

In Service of Humanity

General Trends: Saturn continues teaching you valuable lessons in your work, health and diet, however, between May to September, he would like you to look deeper into your significant relationships and reexamine all your partnerships in work or in life. In the first part of the year you will experience expansion in the sphere of traveling and education while in the second part of 2025, expect a raise, promotion, and flow in your career and professional life. The South Node who was creating havoc for you from July 2023 is no longer in your sign, which means you will be feeling much better this year.

JANUARY

Between January 1–5, Mars is opposite his Scorpio coruler, Pluto, which is not a promising beginning of the year. In addition, Mars is retrograde therefore, take extra care on the first few days of the year. There is an opposition between your will and that of your community, company, or friends. People around you might experience paranoia, resort to manipulation, conflict and aggression.

On January 3, Venus, your ruler, puts on her swimming suit and dives into Pisces until February 4. Opportunities to improve your finances, relationships as well as artistic gifts manifest. A great time to meet new interesting people in your workplace or add an artistic element to your professional life.

On January 6, Mars retrogrades into Cancer until April 18. This can be a bit tough on you, especially in your career. You might feel sluggish or a bit depleted of energy. Conflict can arise with family members as well as superiors.

On January 8 Mercury enters Capricorn until January 28, and this means serious thought, discipline study, and lessons coming from mature and experienced figures. A time to communicate with family members. Not bad for real estate transactions. However, it is recommended to slow your thought, speech, and writing. Great for furthering your career goals and forging long-term plans.

January 13 is the Full Moon in Cancer, where she loves to be. It could get emotional and a bit aggressive with family and loved ones due to the opposition of retrograding Mars and Pluto. Take heed of over emotionality and guilt casting. There could be tension between home and career. Balance your scales while being practical.

Between January 18–19, Venus conjuncts Saturn. Finances, your values, and your relationships are being scrutinized and audited. This is not necessarily a bad aspect as Venus is exalted and Saturn can ground your talents as well as help you use your gifts in a practical way. Whatever is going on in your personal and professional relationships are galvanized and crystallized, for good or bad.

On January 19 the Sun enters Aquarius until February 18. A time to spend with friends, community, as well as immerse yourself in science, technology, and innovation. Having the Sun in a fellow air sign is good for you and he can shine on your children, romance, creative projects, and even connect you to fun and happiness. This trend peaks between January

25–26, as Venus trines Mars, the cosmic lovers can bring a new relationship into your life or help you harmonize partnerships you already have.

From January 28 until February 14, Mercury transits in Aquarius, and ideas flow fast as well as the ability to forge new friendships. It is a great transit for creative writing and improving communications with lovers and or your children. January 29 is also the New Moon in Aquarius and Chinese New Year. Jupiter is blessing this New Moon with wisdom and synchronicity. A great time to start a study group. A great time to start a new love or creative project.

On January 29, the North Node retrogrades into Pisces until August 19, 2026, for the first time in 19 years. Right on the New Moon in Aquarius, the North Node aka "Dragon," is retrograding into the sign of mysticism, intuition, and imagination. For the next 18 months you are asked to practice empathy, meditation, any form of trance movement practice (yoga, dance, or martial arts). However, the South Node will be in Virgo asking us to let go of criticism, perfectionism, and overanalytical tendencies. This is a wonderful time to connect to your work, health, diet, and service.

FEBRUARY

On February 4, Venus enters Aries, until March 27. Your planet is blessing the sector of your chart associated with relationship, justice, and design. Time to be active and assertive in your primary relationships and express your needs.

Between February 6–12, Mars trines Saturn bringing a weeklong of constructive action, stable effort, and sustained passion. This aspect can give you the endurance to complete a marathon or two.

On February 12 the Full Moon is in Leo, and you might feel the pull and push between the gravitational forces of your children or romantic partner versus friends or your company. The square with Uranus can cause disruption and lunacy to this lunation.

On Valentine's Day (February 14), Mercury enters Pisces until March 3. Communications can be a bit challenged while intuition and mediumship are on the rise. Trust your gut feeling more than your brain. Make sure to use the words "I feel" or "I imagine" or "I believe," instead of "I think." However, Mercury can bring good tidings to your workplace as well as reconnect you to your diet and health. This trend is supported by the Sun entering Pisces from February 18 until March 20's Equinox. Imagination, dance, movement, dreaming, meditation, intuition, mysticism, and empathy are heightened. Just make sure to guard your boundaries and avoid addictions or self-destructive tendencies. A good time for a promotion at work. Be careful not to medicate yourself on food or shopping sprees.

The month ends with the New Moon in Pisces on February 28. A great day to start something new in your work, health, service, and diet. A wonderful time to connect to your imagination, photography, movement, yoga and meditation. There is a tendency to absorb negativity from others especially in your workplace.

MARCH

March 1–April 14 Venus stands still and then retrogrades in Aries, her sign of exile. Avoid getting married, starting new relationships, getting engaged, starting lawsuits, and signing partnerships agreements. Exes or lovers from previous lives or this life might return. Be extra mindful with finances and how you interact with your partners in work or life. Venus could also expose whoever is trying to sabotage you.

On March 3, Mercury enters Aries until March 30 and can be a bit impatient. Mercury in Aries favors practical, short, and concise communication. Mercury stays a long time in the sector of your chart that relates to significant others. While he can help with communication with your partners, he can also create some miscommunications when he starts his retrograde motion on March 14.

Between March 11–13, the Sun conjuncts Saturn while Mercury conjuncts Venus. Seriousness, focus, discipline and planning can bring tactical or strategical accomplishments. A good time to improve relations with superiors.

March 14, Pi Day is the first Lunar Eclipse of the year. The Full Moon in mathematical and analytical Virgo. A great time to bring a project to an end, as well as focus on diet, service, and combining your analytical and wholistic approaches to life. Take some time to rest today.

March 14–April 8 Mercury is stationary and retrograde. Since it is happening in Aries be extra careful with how you express your anger, impulsiveness, and avoid making rush decisions. Be extra vigilant of misunderstandings with partners in work or life.

On March 17, the Sun conjuncts North Node. A day to access skills and knowledge from past lifetimes. There could be an encounter with powerful and successful individuals or groups that can further your goals. A good time for a general checkup and tending to your diet and health. A person older or more experienced than you can provide help and clarity in your work and/or health.

March 20 is the Equinox and the Sun's transits into Aries until April 19. Happy New Year! A time to focus on your body, health, leadership, as well as your brand and image. In the next 30 days the Sun shines upon your relationships. New potential partners are walking into your life.

On March 27, Lilith enters Scorpio until December 20. Emotional intensity, powerful desires, fascination with the forbidden aspects of life, shadow work, possessiveness, and jealousy. There could also be power struggles, manipulation, abuse, distrust, and criminality. Stay clear of any form of gossip. A good time to place a heap of salt in the four corners of your bedroom as protection against negativity. Be extra careful with financial dealings. You might have someone around you that is trying to lower your self-esteem.

On March 29, we have the first Solar Eclipse of the year, and she shines upon Aries. Be mindful of unnecessary aggression and impulsiveness. A good time to start something new with a partner especially if you already tried it before and failed to accomplish.

From March 30 to April 15, Mercury is in Pisces. Mercury retrogrades into his sign of fall, thus, communication can be extra hard as the messenger is not only retro but drowning in subjectivity. Talk and write from your heart rather than mind. Great for intuition and applying imagination to overcome challenges. A great time for gaining clarity about your work and service you provide.

From March 30 to October 22, Neptune enters Aries for the first time in 165 years. Confusion can lead to war, be extra careful of fanaticism or aggression triggered by propaganda of misinformation. Watch your immune system, inflammation, and your head. Be mindful of extra marital affairs and welcoming escapists or addicts who lack boundaries into your life.

APRIL

Between April 5–7, the celestial lovers meet again. Venus is Barbie and Mars in water sign Cancer is Ken, the "simply beach" dude. These are great days for romance, increasing your income from talents you are passionate about, and better relationships with significant others as well as brothers and sisters in arms.

From April 5 to 10, Venus, your gal, conjuncts Saturn. While this aspect can introduce you to someone older that could be helpful with finance and developing your talents, this conjunction can also sit heavy over all your relationships. A time to reassess your primary relationships and how you make money.

On April 8 Mercury finally goes direct and you can start signing documents and initiating new projects. Between April 7–16 Mercury trine Mars and that could give a kick forward to your projects and business.

April 13 is the Full Moon in Libra. This is the day of liberation, coming out of constriction and negativity and marching towards your Promised Land. It is a magical Full Moon where you might connect to your inner Moses, guardian angel, or higher self. Focus on balancing your needs with those of your partner.

April 14 is a dramatic day when Saturn conjuncts the North Node in Pisces. Positive interactions with groups of powerful individuals or people who are older. You are downloading gifts or connections from previous lives. Good for joining new groups and organizations that share similar long-term goals.

From April 16 to May 10 Mercury transits in Aries, speeding things up but also showing signs of impatience. Words can easily be weaponized so be extra careful. This transit of Mercury promises healing and peacemaking with your partners in work and life.

From April 18 to June 17 Mars enters Leo bringing about a great deal of courage and a call for adventure. Great for entertainment, sports, creativity, and reconnecting to your inner child. While there could be conflict with some colleagues or friends, you might find younger men easier to relate to. A good time for advancement in your company.

On April 19 the Sun enters Taurus and will remain there until May 20. A good month to focus on your intimacy, sexuality, passion, as well as your partner's money and assets. In addition, the Sun's transit can connect you to the six senses. It is a good month to tap into your artistic talents and perhaps discover new ones.

April 27 is the exalted New Moon in Taurus. A great time to start a new artistic or financial project. An auspicious day for investments and starting a process of letting go and burying the dead. Spend time in nature. This trend continues April 30 as Venus enters Aries until June 6. This is a wonderful time for finding a partner as well as harmonizing your current relationships.

MAY

Between May 1 to May 3, Venus conjuncts Neptune and infuses us with romance, creativity, art, improved finances and intuition. Do something artistic with your partner or use creative visualization to attract one.

From May 10 to May 26, Mercury enters Taurus, which can bring a sense of worry and anxiety. However, Mercury can help you with investments, helping your partners make money or tapping into their talents.

May 12 is the Full Moon in Scorpio, and while the Moon is fallen, it is still a great time for shadow work, therapy, and wizardry. Because the Moon falls on the 22nd (Master Number) degree of Scorpio, we can build something out of the rubble of an older project or relationship. In this lunation you feel the tug of war between "mine" and "yours."

Between May 17–18, the Sun conjuncts Uranus and everyone's IQ is getting a temporary elevation. A fantastic day for humor, jumping into the unknown, and embracing the original and innovative. Spend time with friends or in a group.

From May 20 to June 21, the Sun enters Gemini, and you are channeling the spirit of intelligence, communication, and bridge-building. This is a great month for business, contracts, improving relationships with relatives, roommates, neighbors, and people you consider siblings. The next 30 days are good for travel and education.

Between May 20 to 24, Venus trines Mars once again. Romance, love, harmony (the daughter of Venus and Mars), is around you as well as an ability to see people's beautiful side. Great time for making money from things you are passionate about.

Between May 25 to September 1 Saturn enters Aries. Saturn in Aries wishes to rectify how we deal with our identity, body, anger, and vitality. Saturn is now asking you to reexamine all your primary relationships, bringing whatever is going on between you into the spotlight for good and bad.

Between May 26 to June 8 Mercury enters Gemini. Mercury is back to his domicile, and he is happy to unpack and provide his communication services. Information, opportunities, connections, and words flow effortlessly. A good time for travel, teaching, learning and publishing.

The May 27 New Moon in Gemini is a great day to start something new in connection with communication, networking, businesses, marketing, sales, and written projects. This New Moon is blessed by Pluto and Neptune, making it possible for you to link passion and reason, emotions and intellect. A great deal of intimacy and a possibility for a lover coming into your life. A wonderful time to start learning something new.

JUNE

Between June 4 to 8, Venus, Jupiter, Mercury, and Mars are blessing us and each other. Windows of positive opportunities can improve sales, communication, writing, health, education, and art.

On June 6 Venus enters Taurus until July 4. The goddess of love is lending a helping hand in matters of art, finances, relationships, and security.

You will experience your five senses in a much stronger way than regularly, perhaps getting a glimpse of the sixth one as well. A great time to connect to joint artistic and financial projects.

On June 8, Mercury transits Cancer until June 26. Great for healing relationships with family members. Don't be afraid to express your emotions. This transit can help you in your career and professional life as well as your rapport with superiors and bosses.

Between June 9 to 10 we have Mercury squares Neptune and Saturn and Venus squares Pluto. There is deception, lies, theft, and disinformation. Monkey mind is out of the cage, causing you to jump from one subject or project to the other. Breakups, manipulation, and discord with people of power.

On June 9 Jupiter enters Cancer and will stay there until June 30, 2026. A good transit in time of need especially for your career and worldly ambition. This is a great year for real estate, healing familial relationships, connecting to fortune and abundance, and opening new doors. Be careful of overdoing and over commitments.

From June 10 until August 23, Saturn conjuncts with Neptune. While your intuition, ability to meditate, and connect to your dreams are enhanced, so does your self-destructiveness, addictions, and escapism. Tread carefully, watch out for fanaticism or being too attached to your beliefs.

On June 11, the Full Moon is in Sagittarius. A blessed Full Moon in a challenging month. Jupiter, ruler of Sagittarius is exalted, creating what is called Mutual Reception with the Moon, which is auspicious. A wonderful time to complete a cycle of learning and preparation for something new. Great for travel, especially by water or to a location close to the water. Mars gives a boost of energy to the aspect.

From June 17, Mars enters Virgo until August 6. Mars in Virgo gets things done. He is the watchmaker, the engineer, the organizer—here to protect and serve. Conflicts can arise if you are too critical of yourself and others. A good time for diets and a new health regiment. You can make things happen if you stick to a strict routine. There could be PTSD memories from previous lives. Stay away from war zones.

From June 21 the Sun transits in Cancer until July 22. Happy Solstice! Open your heart to your family, and perhaps you might meet family members from past lives. A great month to renovate and remodel your home, relocate, move in with someone, get a new property, or start a family. The Sun joins Jupiter and blesses your career. This trend is magnified on June 25, as the New Moon is in Cancer provides opportunities for a new beginning in your career as well as home and family, real estate, attaining a sense of security and emotional support.

From June 26 until September 3, Mercury is in Leo. This Mercury transit can be extremely creative, entertaining, and exciting. A good time to meet new friends, colleagues and clients. Bring innovation to your workplace if possible.

Between June 27 to 28, Mercury trines Saturn and Neptune. This is a good aspect for making long-term plans and bringing some sanity to a mad mad month. Good for marketing, writing, and sales. It is also a great time for prophetic dreams and practical intuition.

JULY

On July 4 Venus conjuncts Uranus and while relationships can be exciting, they can also show an unpredictable side. There is a need for freedom and exploration of new frontiers with your finances, relationships, and artistic expression. Embrace the original and unique. Be extra aware there could be volatility in the market.

From July 4 Venus flirts with Gemini until July 30 and the next few weeks can bring you in contact with a potential lover or partner at work. A good time to travel and educate yourself. Art and communication come together, a great time for marketing, sales, design, and making new connections.

From July 7 to November 8, Uranus enters Gemini, and your IQ is augmented. However, intelligence and IQ does not mean wisdom or kindness, so take heed not to become a heartless cyborg. You are awakened to a new study topic, or a new culture might pique your interest. However, if you plan to travel take extra heed as there could be twists and turns.

July 10 is the Full Moon in Capricorn. This lunation can bring about a bit of opposition between home and career. The Moon is exiled in Capricorn and can create a sense of emotionality and longing for a paradise lost. However, Mars is sending his troupes to help you, and with a bit of action, determination, and a clear mission, you can disperse the emotional confusion of the Full Moon and get things done.

From July 17 to August 12, Mercury is retrograde in Leo. Avoid signing docs and starting new projects. Especially watch your relationships with friends and communication people in your company.

From July 22 to August 22, Sun enters Leo. Engage in creative, joyful, and heartwarming activities. Generosity, nobility, chivalry, sportsmanship, and enthusiasm are guiding us this month. A great time to connect to a hobby or a new sport. The next 30 days could be good for making new friends, connecting to a new company, as well as updating and upgrading your life with new technologies. This trend is peaking on July 24 as the New Moon in Leo brings a powerful surge of energy. However, this is not an easy New Moon since she falls opposite Pluto and can bring about a confrontation with a powerful figure in your life.

From July 31 to August 25, Venus transits in Cancer and could bring a new artistic element into your career. In addition, Marriage, social events with family members, as well as harmonious flow with family members.

AUGUST

The month starts with a hard aspect on August 1 and 2 between Venus, Saturn and Neptune. Watch out for deception, illusions, and fantasies in your primary relationships as well as financial dealings. Not the best time to start a new relationship. Rapport with people who are older than you can be fraught with discord.

On August 6 Mars enters Libra and stays there until September 22. This is a time to assert yourself, connect to your body, assume a leadership role and take the initiative. There could be legal issues, but it is also a good time for compromise and finding resolutions to conflicts. Between August 7 to 9, Mars trines Uranus bringing about brilliance and originality. Search for innovative and original solutions. Connections with friends can thrive. Action is guided by new approaches.

August 9 is the Full Moon in Aquarius. You might feel a push and pull between the need to spend time with lovers or your children and the demands of your friends or company. It is the Biblical Day of Love, so do something that can bring you joy and love.

On August 12, Mercury finally goes direct in Leo. This is great for your connection to friends as well as dealing with government officials and colleagues in your organization. You can now start plowing ahead, especially since on August 12 and 13, Venus conjuncts Jupiter, which is one of the best aspects this year. Luck, flow in finances, new relationships and maybe a novel love.

Between August 12 to October 27, Uranus trines Pluto. A powerful aspect that can bring about transformation through technology, science, social movements, and revolutions. Changes in government that can, in the long run, bring more prosperity.

From August 22 to September 22 the Sun transits in Virgo. You are asked to focus and refine your diet, health, routine, work, and how we serve. An ideal time to eliminate impediments to health and productivity. A good month to let go, detox, and spend time on your own. This is especially true on August 23's New Moon in Virgo. A great time for a new diet, work project, or service. It is recommended to reorganize your routine and schedule. A bit of chaos is added by a square to Uranus that can awaken the critic and perfectionist in you. Try to channel these propensities into something productive at work.

On August 25, Venus transits in Leo until September 19. The planet of love in the sign of romance is always good news. A platonic friend might become a lover. A good time for artistic projects in a group. It is a very creative time with your inner child, active and playful. A great time to reconnect to a hobby you had in your teens.

SEPTEMBER

On September 1 Saturn returns to Pisces until February 13, 2026. Confusion, floods, conflicts concerning water or in locations that are close to seas, lakes, and rivers. A time to ground your mystical practices, dreams, and intuition. Relationships should become easier as your focus shifts to work, health and diet. A good time for a checkup to make sure all is well.

From September 2 to September 18, Mercury transits into Virgo. Sales, ideas, and information flow effortlessly. A great time for editing projects that need precision, micromanagement, organizing, and purification. A wonderful time for detoxing and a cleanse. Your imagination and subconscious is wide open.

September 7 is the Full Moon in Pisces. The Harvest Full Moon and Lunar Eclipse combo. Momentum builds towards closure especially with work and personal affairs. Now's the time to harvest the fruits of your labor you planted around March/April. Mercury provides a touch of reason to an otherwise very emotional lunation.

From September 18, Mercury transits into Libra until October 6. This Mercury wants peace, compromise, and beauty. A great time for healing relationships and harmonizing the workplace. You can revamp your website, redesign your logo, and come up with new ways to brand yourself and your projects. Mercury in your sign could help you in all aspects of communication. Speak your mind, the world is listening.

From September 19, Venus transits Virgo until October 13. You might feel over critical about your art or your partners as well as be subject to the criticism of others. Good time to be frugal, balance your expenses and income, and detox. Artistic talents you developed in previous life could make an appearance. A good time for couple's therapy and working with your dreams.

September 21 is the Solar Eclipse in Virgo. A great time to balance your diet, start a new work project, and get the energy you need to reach the finish line. The Eclipse is prompting the planets involved in a benevolent aspect to bestow their gifts on you: Pluto (power and intimacy); Saturn (focus); Neptune (imagination and intuition); Uranus (innovation). A great time to start a new meditation practice.

On September 22, the Sun enters Libra until October 23, marking the Equinox. Happy birthday! As one of the four sacred days in the astrological calendar, commemorate it by celebrating relationships, justice, beauty, and art. Over the next 30 days, you should embody Libra traits—diplomacy, balance, art, and attentiveness to partners. A time to connect to your body, shine forward, advance yourself, rebrand and connect to healthy practices.

On September 22, Mars enters Scorpio until November 4. A wonderful time to collaborate on big projects that demand a lot of energy and resources. You might get a raise or promotion but be careful with needless expenditures. Passion, intimacy, and sexuality are on the rise. Great for physical activities in water or reconnecting to sports you are passionate about. An opportune time for research and investigation, as well as fighting for what you believe in.

OCTOBER

On October 6 Mercury transits into Scorpio until October 29. An ideal period for research, finding lost objects or people, and expressing intimacy. Mercury can be your PI and expose hidden information. This is a good transit for clarity with finances, reconnecting to writing talents, and connecting to your gifts.

On October 7 the Full Moon is in Aries. This Full Moon, bordering on a lunar eclipse, is a tad challenging. With Chiron's involvement, it's an occasion for learning, teaching, and shamanistic journeys. While there's an aggressive undertone, it's a good moment to conclude matters and move on. There could be conflicts with partners in life or work.

Between October 11 to 14, Venus is opposite Saturn and Neptune. This can be hard on your relationships and or finances. There is an emotional frustration with partners, especially long-term ones. Illusions as well as dependency and codependency and some disappointment with someone close to you. However, you can use this aspect to connect mysticism and art.

From October 13 to November 6, Venus returns to her sign, Libra, and can help you connect to all that defines you: beauty, diplomacy, justice, relationship, and harmony. You look and feel glorious. This trend is especially strong between October 14–15 as Venus trine Uranus and Pluto. Venus receives much praise from Pluto (intimacy, sexuality, power) and Uranus (innovation, technology, friendships). This is a powerful time for igniting, transforming, balancing and solidifying partnerships in work and personal life.

The New Moon in Libra takes place October 21. Dubbed the "Moon of Peace," the Libra New Moon is a great time to start a relationship or an art project. However, both Jupiter and Pluto are squaring off with the Sun and Moon, creating uncomfortable situations. Be extra cautious and focus on breathwork and meditation.

On October 22, Neptune returns for the last time to his sign, Pisces, until January 27, 2026. A great time to start meditation practice. Dreams, imagination, channeling, mediumship, poetry, and art are enhanced. Please pay extra attention to your immune system and avoid any substances that could be harmful.

On October 23, the Sun enters Scorpio until November 22. Focus on being true to your passion. It is a month of healing, transformation, magic, occult, and assisting others in their talents and finances. A great time for a raise, improving your income and connecting to your talents.

Around October 26 Mars conjuncts Lilith, please be extra careful today as the Mother of Demons hired an assassin. This is a violent and aggressive aspect. Tread cautiously. Someone might want to smear or defame you, take heed and avoid any gossip.

On October 29, Mercury enters Sagittarius until November 19. You might feel a bit absent-minded and distracted. A good time for traveling and doing business with foreigners. Stick to the truth and avoid liars and half-truths. Great for writing, signing contracts, education and publishing.

NOVEMBER

From November 3 to 5 Mars opposes Uranus, therefore, be extra careful of accidents and mishaps involving aggression, impatience, speed or sharp objects. You might experience erratic behavior that doesn't make sense as well as gadgets and machines breaking or malfunctioning. The robot is out of control.

From November 4 to December 15, Mars enters Sagittarius. A call for adventure, as well as an expedition. Your Mars wants you to conquer, hunt, and expend your knowledge. It is an Indiana Jones aspect. Watch out for needless conflicts with relatives, neighbors, and siblings.

November 5 is the Full Moon in Taurus. An opportune time to bring something into completion. Since the lunation is on the 13th degree of Scorpio, it carries a powerful connection to love. Spend time in nature and indulge your five senses.

On November 6, Venus enters Scorpio until November 30. This transit can make you feel alone or unwanted, possessive as well as jealous. A great time for a boost in your income and reconnecting to your skills and talents. Look into your investments as there might be a need to make some adjustments.

From November 8 to April 26, 2026, Uranus returns for the last time to Taurus. Changes in finances, fluctuations in cryptocurrency, new ways of expressing artistic talents. There is an awakening in your passion, sexuality, and intimacy.

From November 9 to December 1 Mercury is stationary and retrograde. Avoid signing documents or starting new projects. This retrograde dances on the cusp of Sagittarius where he is overthinking, to Scorpio where he is too secretive. On November 19, Mercury enters Scorpio until December 10. Watch out for issues with money and or your self-worth. However, it is a good transit for investigations and finding lost objects and people.

November 20 is the New Moon in Scorpio. A great time to investigate your passions, what you really want in life, what you wish to transform, and start today. A New Moon that can benefit projects that need shared resources, talents, or funding. However, since Mercury is retro, you can only start things you already did in the past and failed to bring to completion. An opportune time to initiate healing, therapy, a shamanistic journey, or an investigation. The New Moon is getting a boost from Saturn, Jupiter, and

LIBRA AND LIBRA RISING: I BALANCE

Neptune, which bless this lunation with structure and focus, imagination and inspiration, and a great deal of open-mindedness.

On November 22, the Sun transits in Sagittarius until December 21. Sagittarius is the time of the year when we have the strongest connection to our higher self or guardian angel. This is a month for teaching, mentoring, learning, speaking your truth, mass media, publishing, and connecting to foreigners, and in-laws. This is a good month for marketing, sales, and writing.

On November 28 Venus conjuncts Lilith. Be extra careful with all your relationships and partners in work or in personal life. A three-sided relationship might form around you. Be beware of stalkers, gossip, enemies, and lawsuits. As Venus is your ruler be extra careful today and try to be nice to anyone around you, even those who wish you ill.

From November 30 until December 24 Venus transits in Sagittarius. It is a great time for connecting to educators, foreigners, explore investments and possibilities from travel and abroad. An opportune time to improve relationships with in-laws as well as siblings and relatives.

DECEMBER

December 4 is the Full Moon in Gemini. An optimal moment to finalize projects. As this is the year's last Full Moon.

On December 10, Mercury finally goes direct. It is good for traveling and businesses abroad as well as for studying and teaching. There could be new business opportunities and lucrative contracts coming your way.

From December 15, Mars transits in Capricorn until January 26, 2026. Make sure you give him a mission—something you need help conquering and or mastering. It is a good aspect for leadership and initiation. A call for action is coming, make sure not to refuse the call. A good time for renovation, remodeling, and relocation. However, be mindful of conflicts with family members.

December 20 is the New Moon in Sagittarius. A difficult New Moon with Neptune and Saturn sending squares all over the place. Not the best time to start new projects. Be careful of aggression and anger. A sense of war approaching. Lay low and be vigilant.

From December 20, Lilith enters Sagittarius for nine months. There could be discord with students and teachers, as well as foreigners. Take extra care while traveling. Fear of the foreigner, misinformation, disinformation. There could be negativity coming from or to siblings, relatives, and neighbors. Be extra careful of what you say and publish.

On December 21 the Sun enters Capricorn and will stay there until January 20, 2026. Happy Solstice! The ensuing month calls for Capricorn-like discipline and focus. Strategize the year ahead, bearing in mind that patience is vital. A good month for real estate and spending time with family members. This trend is reinforced from December 24 as Venus transits in Capricorn until January 17, 2026. This transit can help improve relationships with people who are older, long-term partnerships, as well as bosses and superiors. A time to connect art and design to your professional life.

SCORPIO AND
SCORPIO RISING: I TRANSFORM

Finding, Cultivating, and Sharing Joy

♏

Major Trends: Saturn continues teaching you how to be positive and connect to happenings and creativity. A year of focusing on children, grandchildren, as well as your inner child. However, between May to September you are asked to scrutinize your work, routine, how you serve others, as well as your health and diet. The first part of the year can bring expansion with shared assets, investments, your passion, intimacy and sexuality, while the second part of 2025 creates opportunities for travel, education, and defining your philosophy. Since the Black Moon Lilith would be in your sign most of the year, please take care of your image, how people perceive you, and your brand. This intense transit happens once in 9 years.

JANUARY

Between January 1–5, Mars is opposite Pluto, which is not a promising beginning of the year. Not that it's your fault, but these are your two guardians having a fight. In addition, Mars is retrograde therefore, take extra care on the first few days of the year. There is an opposition between your will and that of your community, company, or friends. People around you might experience paranoia, resort to manipulation, conflict and aggression, especially in your career.

On January 3, Venus puts on her swimming suit and dives into Pisces until February 4. Opportunities to improve your finances, relationships as well as artistic gifts. This is a grand transit for romantic love, water sports (ski, sailing, surfing, swimming), creativity, and connection with children.

On January 6, Mars retrogrades into Cancer until April 18. Mars, the warrior, doesn't like to transit in compassionate Cancer, his sign of fall, therefore, be vigilant of accidents, falling (unless it is in love) and issues with or around water such as leaks and floods. Conflict can arise with family members. Be extra mindful if you are traveling.

On January 8 Mercury enters Capricorn until January 28, and this means serious thought, discipline study, lessons coming from mature and experienced figures. Slow your thought, speech, and writing, and be mindful of every word. Great for furthering your career goals and forging long-term plans. This is a good transit for generating business opportunities, signing documents, and writing.

January 13 is the Full Moon in Cancer, a fellow water sign. It could get emotional and a bit aggressive with family and loved ones due to the opposition of retro Mars and Pluto. Take heed of over emotionality and guilt casting.

Between January 18–19, Venus conjuncts Saturn. Finances, values, and your relationships are being scrutinized and audited. This is not necessarily a bad aspect as Venus is exalted and Saturn can ground your talents as well as help you use your gifts in a practical way.

On January 19 the Sun enters Aquarius until February 18. A time to spend with friends, community, as well as immerse yourself in science, technology, and innovation. A great month to focus on home improvements, relocation, and spending time with family members.

Between January 25–26, as Venus trines Mars, the cosmic lovers can bring a new relationship into your life or help you harmonize partnerships you already have.

From January 28 until February 14, Mercury transits in Aquarius, and ideas flow fast as well as new friendships forming with likeminded people. A great time to make new contacts and reconnect to old friendships. An opportune period for real estate and healing relationships with family members. Today is also the New Moon in Aquarius and Chinese New Year. Jupiter is blessing this New Moon with wisdom and synchronicity. A great time to start a study group. Something new is taking place with your family or relationship to your abode or office.

On January 29, the North Node retrogrades into Pisces until August 19, 2026 for the first time in 19 years. Right on the New Moon in Aquarius, the North Node aka "Dragon," is retrograding into the sign of mysticism, intuition, and imagination. For the next 18 months you are asked to practice empathy, meditation, any form of trance or movement practice (yoga, dance, or martial arts). The Dragon can bring romantic love or a child into your life. However, the South Node will be in Virgo asking us to let go of criticism, perfectionism, and overanalytical tendencies.

FEBRUARY

On February 4, Venus enters Aries, until March 27. Conflicts with relationships and partners can arise. Watch impulsiveness with your finances and partnerships. However, this transit of the goddess of art and beauty in your work sector can help workflow as well as improve relationship with coworkers and clients.

Between February 6–12, Mars trines Saturn bringing a weeklong of constructive action, stable effort, and sustained passion. This aspect can give you the endurance to complete a marathon or two.

February 12 is the Full Moon in Leo, and you might feel the pull and push between the gravitational forces of your children or romantic partner versus friends or your company. In addition, there is tension between home life and responsibilities that come from your career. The square with Uranus can cause disruption and lunacy to this lunation.

On Valentine's Day (February 14), Mercury enters Pisces until March 3. Communications can be a bit challenged while intuition and mediumship are on the rise. Trust your gut more than your brain. Make sure to use the words "I feel" or "I imagine" or "I believe," instead of "I think." There is a good flow in creative writing, better rapport with children and or your lovers. This trend is supported by the Sun entering Pisces from February 18 until March 20's Equinox. Imagination, dance, movement, dreaming, meditation, intuition, mysticism, and empathy are heightened. Make sure to guard your boundaries and avoid addictions or self-destructive tendencies.

The month ends with the New Moon in Pisces on February 28. A great day to start something new that involves your imagination, photography, movement, yoga and meditation. There is a tendency to absorb negativity from others so watch what you take in. Be careful of overdoing or illusions. A new love, creative project or perhaps getting pregnant with a child of the mind or a baby.

MARCH

March 1–April 14 Venus stands still and then retrogrades in Aries, her sign of exile. Avoid getting married, starting new relationships, getting engaged, starting lawsuits, signing partnerships agreements. This retrograde might be felt the strongest within your workplace, especially with employees and coworkers, or in health. Exes or lovers from previous lives or this life might return. Be extra mindful with finances, as people tend to lose money or make bad investments.

On March 3, Mercury enters Aries until March 30. Mercury can be a bit impatient when in Aries and favors practical, short, and concise communication. Until the retrograde (March 14) he can help you overcome issues Venus presents in your work and health.

Between March 11–13, the Sun conjunct Saturn while Mercury conjunct Venus. Seriousness, focus, discipline and planning can bring tactical or strategical accomplishments. A good time to improve relations with superiors.

March 14, Pi Day, we have the first Lunar Eclipse of the year. The Full Moon in precise and analytical Virgo. A great time to bring a project to an end, as well as focus on diet, service, and combining your analytical and wholistic perspectives. There could be tension between the need to spend time with your children or lover and friends or company.

March 14–April 8 Mercury is stationary and retrograde. Be extra careful with your anger, impulsiveness, and making rush decisions. As Mercury enters his retro mode be extra careful with your work and health. Projects that you tried to complete and failed in the past could return.

On March 17, the Sun conjuncts North Node. A day to access skills and knowledge from past lifetimes. There could be an encounter with powerful and successful individuals or groups that can further your goals. A mystical and artistic awakening.

On March 20 we have the Equinox and the Sun's transits into Aries until April 19. Happy New Year! A time to focus on your body, health, leadership, as well as your brand and image. In the next 30 days, the Sun brings you in contact with projects or people that could be instrumental for your professional life.

On March 27, Lilith enters Scorpio until December 20. Emotional intensity, powerful desires, fascination with the forbidden, shadow work, possessiveness, and jealousy. Power struggles, manipulation, abuse, distrust, and criminality. Stay clear of any form of gossip. A good time to place a heap of salt in the four corners of your bedroom as protection against negativity. Obviously as a Scorpio, this is not an easy transit which happens every 9 years. Please take care of your image, how people perceive you, and your brand.

On March 29, we have the first Solar Eclipse of the year, and she shines upon Aries. Be mindful of unnecessary aggression and impulsiveness. A good time to initiate something new in your work, diet, or health regime, only if you tried to in the past and failed to complete it.

From March 30 to April 15, Mercury is in Pisces. Mercury retrogrades into his sign of fall, thus, communication can be extra hard as the messenger is not only retro but drowning in subjectivity. Talk and write from your heart rather than mind. Great for intuition and applying imagination to overcome challenges. There could be misunderstandings and miscommunications with your children or romantic lover. Be careful of sports injuries.

From March 30 to October 22, Neptune enters Aries for the first time in 165 years. Confusion can lead to war, be extra careful of fanaticism or aggression triggered by propaganda of misinformation. Watch your immune system, inflammation, and your feet.

APRIL

Between April 5–7, the celestial lovers meet again. Venus is Barbie and Mars in water sign Cancer is Ken, the "simply beach" dude. These are great days for romance, increasing your income from talents you are passionate about, and better relationships with significant others as well as brothers and sisters in arms. This is a wonderful time for you as you are the third water sign needed to have this cosmic "full-house hand". Success, recognition and improved relationships.

From April 5 to 10, Venus conjuncts Saturn. While this aspect can introduce you to someone older that could be helpful with finance and developing your talents, this conjunction can also sit heavy over all your relationships. A time to reassess your primary relationships and how you make money.

On April 8 Mercury finally goes direct and you can begin signing documents and starting new projects. Between April 7–16 Mercury trine Mars and that could give a kick forward to your projects and business. This is especially good for your work, health, and relationships with coworkers.

April 13 is the Full Moon in Libra. This is the day of liberation, coming out of constriction and negativity and marching towards your Promised Land. It is a magical Full Moon where you might connect to your inner Moses, guardian angel, or higher self. You might feel tension between wanting to retreat from life and isolate, and the responsibilities presented by work.

April 14 is a dramatic day when Saturn conjuncts the North Node in Pisces. Positive interactions with groups of powerful individuals or people who are older. You are downloading gifts or connections from previous lives. Good for joining new groups and organizations that share your long-term goals. A lover from a past lifetime or maybe someone who was your child is making an entrance into your life. Do something to honor your inner child—a new hobby, sport, or recreation activity.

From April 16 to May 10 Mercury transits in Aries, speeding things up but also showing signs of impatience. Words can easily be weaponized so be extra careful. A good time for work promotion.

From April 18 to June 17 Mars enters Leo bringing about a great deal of courage and a call for adventure. It is a good time for taking the initiative in your career, reconnecting to your ambition and state clear goals. Be careful not to be over antagonistic to superiors.

On April 19 the Sun enters Taurus and will remain there until May 20. This month you are to indulge your six senses and connect to Mother Nature. It is a good month to tap into your artistic talents and perhaps discover new ones. The next 30 days are focused on partners in work and life. Be careful not to overdo or spread yourself thin.

Between April 22–24, as the Sun square the rulers of Scorpio—Mars and Pluto, take extra heed. This can bring about a great deal of letting go, death, and intense sexuality. Watch your steps these days, things can turn ugly or violent. These aspects are especially hard on you, so take some time off.

April 27 is the exalted New Moon in Taurus. A great time to start a new relationship or partnership in work. A good time for an artistic or financial project.

April 30 Venus reenters Aries until June 6. Venus might be somewhat snappy and can cause hasty decisions and actions with finances and love. However, she can help you with relationships with employees and coworkers. Watch ovaries, kidneys, and try to balance your diet.

MAY

Between May 1 to May 3, Venus conjuncts Neptune and infuses you with romance, creativity, art, improved finances, and intuition.

From May 10 to May 26, Mercury enters Taurus, which can bring a sense of worry and anxiety especially around your primary relationships of partnerships in work. However, it is a good time to communicate and market your talents and gifts.

May 12 is the Full Moon in Scorpio; therefore, it is your Full Moon. A great time for shadow work, reconnecting to your passion, and discovering the light deep within you. A time to focus on your partnerships and if you don't have one, an opportune time to attract a special person. The Sun supports you by transiting in the sector of your chart that relates to partnerships. Because the Moon falls on the 22nd (Master Number) degree of Scorpio, you can build something out of the rubble of an older project or relationship. In this lunation you feel the tug of war between "mine" and "yours."

Between May 17–18, the Sun conjuncts Uranus and everyone's IQ is getting a temporary elevation. A fantastic day for humor, jumping into the unknown, and embracing the original and innovative. Spend time with friends or in a group. There could be a sudden insight into your significant relationships or in connections to adversaries and enemies.

From May 20 to June 21, the Sun enters Gemini, and you are channeling the spirit of intelligence, communication, and bridge-building. This is a great month for business, contracts, improving relationships with relatives, roommates, neighbors, and people you consider your siblings. This transit allows you to follow Orpheus into the underworld and connect to research, investigation, passion, sexuality, intimacy, the occult, healing, and transformation.

Between May 20 to 24, Venus trines Mars once again. Romance, love, harmony (the daughter of Venus and Mars), is around you as well as an ability to see people's beautiful side. Great time for making money from things you are passionate about.

Between May 25 to September 1 Saturn enters Aries. Saturn in Aries wishes to rectify how we deal with our identity, body, anger, and vitality. This is a powerful period to focus on your work, service, health and diet. Watch your knees, joints, skin, and teeth, as these organs could act out. There could also be a need to change the way you work, how you serve people, as well as your diet.

Between May 26 to June 8 Mercury enters Gemini. Mercury is back to his domicile, and he is happy to unpack and share his wit. Information, opportunities, connections, and words flow effortlessly. This is a magical transit where you can become a healer as well as healed. This is especially strong on the New Moon in Gemini taking place May 27. A wonderful day to start something new in connection with communication, networking, businesses, marketing, sales, and written projects. This New Moon is blessed by Pluto, your ruler, and Neptune, making it possible for you to link passion and reason, emotions and intellect. A great deal of intimacy and a possibility for a lover coming into your life.

JUNE

Between June 4 to 8, Venus, Jupiter, Mercury, and Mars are blessing you and each other. Windows of positive opportunities can improve sales, communication, writing, health, education, and art.

On June 6 Venus enters Taurus until July 4. The goddess of love is lending a helping hand in matters of art, finances, relationships, and security. Venus blesses your relationships and might help you attract a potential partner or a new close friend. Venus in your opposite sign connects you to your five senses, perhaps getting a glimpse of the sixth one as well. A great time to connect to an artistic project or a talent, reconnect with your gifts and translate them into income.

On June 8, Mercury transits Cancer until June 26. Great for healing relationships with family members. Don't be afraid to express your emotions. A wonderful time for education, publishing and traveling.

Between June 9 to 10 Mercury squares Neptune and Saturn and Venus squares Pluto. A bundle of challenging aspects come together. There is deception, lies, theft, and disinformation. Monkey mind is out of the cage, causing you to jump from one subject or project to the other. Breakups, manipulation, and discord with people of power.

On June 9 Jupiter enters Cancer and will stay there until June 30, 2026. This is great news for you being a fellow water sign. This is a great year for real estate, healing familial relationships, connecting to fortune and abundance, and opening new doors. Be careful of overdoing and over commitments. If there are any lawsuits, you might get a favorable ruling. Focus on education, learning a language, traveling, publishing, and teaching. You might get closer to an in-law or get closer to a foreigner.

From June 10 until August 23, Saturn conjuncts with Neptune. While your intuition, ability to meditate, and connect to your dreams are enhanced, so does your self-destructiveness, addictions, and escapism. Tread carefully, watch out for fanaticism or being too attached to your beliefs.

On June 11, the Full Moon is in Sagittarius. A blessed Full Moon in a challenging month. Jupiter, ruler of Sagittarius is exalted, creating what is called Mutual Reception with the Moon, which is auspicious. A wonderful time to complete a cycle of learning in preparation for something new. Great for travel, especially by water or to a location close to the water. Mars gives a boost of energy to the aspect. There could be tension between your talents and money and that of your partner's.

From June 17, Mars enters Virgo until August 6. Mars in Virgo gets things done. He is the watchmaker, the engineer, the organizer—here to protect and serve. Conflicts can arise if you are too critical of yourself or others. A good time for diets and a new health regiment. You can make things happen if you stick to a strict routine. Be careful of conflicts with friends, clients, government officials, or colleagues.

From June 21 the Sun transits Cancer until July 22. Happy Solstice! Open your heart to your family, and perhaps you might meet family members from past lives. A great month to renovate and remodel your home, relocate, move in with someone, purchase a property, or start a family. This is a month full of optimism and flow, a wonderful time for adventure and traveling. This is strongest on June 25's New Moon is in Cancer, providing a new beginning that involves home and family, real estate, security, and emotional support. With Jupiter, exalted in Cancer, blessing the union of the Sun and Moon, it is an opportune period to start new projects that involves education, wisdom, travel, or truth. Besides Pluto, there are no planets retrograde, so full swim ahead!

From June 26 until September 3, Mercury is in Leo. This Mercury transit can be extremely creative, entertaining, and exciting. A powerful time for career advancement and improving your communication with superiors.

Between June 27 to 28, Mercury trines Saturn and Neptune. This is a good aspect for making long-term plans and bringing some sanity to a mad mad month. Good for marketing, writing, and sales. It is also a great time for prophetic dreams and practical intuition.

JULY

On July 4 Venus conjuncts Uranus and while relationships can be exciting, they can also show an unpredictable side. There is a need for freedom and exploration of new frontiers with your finances, relationships, and artistic expression. Embrace the original and unique. Be extra aware there could be volatility in the market. There could be unexpected revelations regarding partners or relationships in work or life.

From July 4 Venus flirts with Gemini until July 30 and the next few weeks can bring you in contact with a potential lover or partner at work. A wonderful time for marketing, sales, design, and making new connections. In addition, investments and working on joint artistic and financial projects are favored.

From July 7 to November 8, Uranus enters Gemini, and your IQ is augmented. This is a time to experiment and awaken your sexuality, passion, as well as let go of things that block or hinder you.

July 10 is the Full Moon in Capricorn. This lunation can bring about a bit of opposition between home and career. The Moon is exiled in Capricorn and can create a sense of emotionality and longing for a paradise lost. However, Mars is sending his troupes to help us, and with a bit of action, determination, and a clear mission, you can disperse the emotional confusion of the Full Moon and get things done.

From July 17 to August 12, Mercury is retrograde in Leo. Avoid signing docs and starting new projects. Especially watch your relationships and communication with kids, lovers, and people with big egos. Be extra careful of how you deal or speak with superiors or coworkers. A time to reexamine your career and trajectory in professional life.

From July 22 to August 22, Sun enters Leo. Engage in creative, joyful, and heartwarming activities. Generosity, nobility, chivalry, sportsmanship, and enthusiasm are guiding us this month. A great time to connect to a hobby or a new sport. The Sun shines upon your career and can further your goals, however, be aware of the retrograding Mercury.

Between July 23–25, the Sun trine Saturn and Neptune creating a wonderful flow and help with vitality, intuition, healing, and the ability to bring some new structure into our lives. This is a glorious aspect, and you can benefit from creative visualizations, meditation, dance and self-expression.

On July 24 the New Moon is in Leo. This is not an easy New Moon since it is smack opposite to Pluto and can bring about a confrontation with a powerful figure in your life whose motivations are unclear. With Mercury retrograding in Leo, it is not the best time to start something new in your career, however, you could initiate a project you already tried before and failed to complete.

From July 31 to August 25, Venus transits in Cancer. Marriage, social events with family members, as well as harmonious flow with family members. Finances could improve through education, traveling, or connecting with people from different countries.

AUGUST

The month starts with a hard aspect on August 1 and 2 between Venus, Saturn and Neptune. Watch out for deception, illusions, and fantasies in your primary relationships as well as financial dealings. Not the best time to start a new relationship. Rapport with people who are older than you can be fraught with discord. Try a new approach to an old problem.

On August 6 Mars enters Libra and stays there until September 22. There could be some legal issues but also a good time for compromise and finding resolutions to conflicts. You might have echoes of PTSD from previous lives or from ancestral traumas. However, between August 7 to 9, Mars trines Uranus bringing about brilliance and originality. Search for innovative and original solutions. Connections with friends can thrive.

Watch it between August 8 to 10 as Mars opposites both Saturn and Neptune. Accidents, mishaps, and physical challenges especially since Mercury is retrograding. Stay away from arguments with superiors. The opposition with Neptune adds more hardships to the already difficult few days. Stay away from stormy seas (metaphysically and physically speaking).

August 9 is the Full Moon in Aquarius. You might feel a push and pull between the need to spend time with lovers or your children and demands presented by your friends or company. Something in your family or professional life is coming to completion.

On August 12, Mercury finally goes direct in Leo. You can now start plowing ahead, especially since on August 12 and 13, Venus conjuncts Jupiter, which is one of the best aspects this year. Luck, flow in finances, new relationships and maybe a novel love. You will see your career taking off now.

Between August 12 to October 27, Uranus trines Pluto. A powerful aspect that can bring about transformation through technology, science, social movements, and revolutions. Changes in government that can, in the long run, bring more prosperity.

From August 22 to September 22 the Sun transits in Virgo. You are asked to focus and refine your diet, health, routine, work, and how you serve. An ideal time to eliminate impediments to health and productivity. This is a month to focus on your friends, altruism, as well as the company or clubs you belong to. This is especially true on August 23 when the New Moon is in Virgo. A great time for a new diet, work project, or service. It is recommended to reorganize your home and office or home office. A bit of chaos is added by a square to Uranus that can awaken the critic and perfectionist in you. Try to channel these propensities into something productive at work. You might make a new friend today or connect with a new client.

On August 25, Venus transits in Leo until September 19. Great time for career advancement as well as improving relationships with people in your work sphere. Try adding an artistic or creative element to your professional life. The planet of love in the sign of romance is always good news. Just be careful of a romance outside your relationship if you are already in one. It is a very creative time with your inner child, active and playful. A great time to reconnect to a hobby you had in your teens.

SEPTEMBER

On September 1, Saturn returns to Pisces until February 13, 2026. Confusion, floods, conflicts about water or in locations that are close to seas, lakes, and rivers. A time to ground your mystical practices, dreams, and intuition. There could be renewed worry or focus on your children or romantic partner. A time to remove any obstacles that stand in the way of your happiness and creativity.

From September 2 to September 18, Mercury transits into Virgo. Improved communication and flow within your company or with friends. Good time for fixing issues you might have with government officials. Sales, ideas, and information flow effortlessly. A great time for editing projects that need precision, micromanagement, organizing, and purification. The best time for detoxing and cleansing.

September 7 is the Full Moon in Pisces. The Harvest Full Moon and Lunar Eclipse combo. Momentum builds towards closure especially with work and personal affairs. Now's the time to harvest the fruits of your labor from March/April. Mercury provides a touch of reason to an otherwise very emotional lunation.

From September 18, Mercury transits into Libra until October 6. This Mercury wants peace, compromise, and beauty. A great time for healing relationships and harmonizing the workplace. Art and business are coming together. You can revamp your website, redesign your logo, and come up with new ways to brand yourself and your projects. Your imagination is working overtime, and you can access visions and dreams. Talents you had in past lifetime are revisited.

From September 19, Venus transits Virgo until October 13. You might feel over critical about your art or your partners as well as feel the criticism of others directed towards you. Good time to be frugal, balance your expenses and income, and detox.

September 21 is the Solar Eclipse in Virgo. A great time to balance your diet, start a new work project, and get the energy you need to reach the finish line. The Eclipse is giving a push allowing all the planets involved in a good aspect to bestow their gifts on you: Pluto (power and intimacy); Saturn (focus); Neptune (imagination and intuition); Uranus (innovation).

On September 22, the Sun enters Libra until October 23, marking the Equinox! Over the next 30 days, you should embody Libra traits—diplomacy, balance, and attentiveness to partners. A month of connection to mysticism, intuition, memories and people from previous life and a great deal of letting go.

On September 22, Mars enters Scorpio until November 4. A wonderful time to collaborate on big projects that demand a lot of energy and resources. Passion, intimacy and sexuality are on the rise. Great for physical activities in water or reconnecting to sports you are passionate about. An opportune time for research and investigation, as well as fighting for what you believe in. Mars, your ruler, is coming back home. You are full of vitality and passion and able to move mountains. Watch out for injuries or overdoing.

Between September 23–25, tread cautiously as Mars squares Pluto. Since both heavenly bodies are your rulers, you might feel that you are torn between two options, or two people. Aggression and manipulative folks are around you. Take extra heed in general. Actions can be easily misconstrued.

OCTOBER

On October 6 Mercury transits into Scorpio until October 29. That is great news for the start of the month. It is as if you hired a celestial public relations team to work on your behalf. An ideal period for research, finding lost objects or people, and expressing intimacy. An opportune period to explore investments and collaborations with other people's assets and talents.

On October 7 the Moon reaches her fullness in Aries. With Chiron's involvement, it's an occasion for learning, teaching, and shamanistic journeys. Something in your work or health is coming to completion. While there's an aggressive undertone, it's a good moment to conclude matters and move on. There could be conflicts with partners in life or work.

Between October 11 to 14, Venus is opposite Saturn and Neptune. This can be hard on your relationships and or finances. There is an emotional frustration with partners, especially long-term ones. Illusions as well as dependency and codependency and some disappointment with someone close to you. However, you can use this aspect to connect mysticism and art.

From October 13 to November 6, Venus returns to her sign, Libra, and can help you connect to beauty, diplomacy, justice, relationship, and harmony. This is especially strong between October 14–15 as Venus trine Uranus and Pluto. Venus receives much praise from Pluto (intimacy, sexuality, power) and Uranus (innovation, technology, friendships). This is another benevolent aspect that carries you upward with Venus (finances, relationships) leading the way. This is a powerful time for igniting, transforming, balancing and solidifying partnerships in work and personal life. You could access your imagination and bring beauty and art into your life.

The New Moon in Libra takes place October 21. Dubbed the "Moon of Peace," the Libra New Moon is a great time to start a relationship or an art project. However, both Jupiter and Pluto are squaring off with the Sun and Moon, creating uncomfortable situations. Be extra cautious and focus on breathwork and meditation. A great time to explore your mystical side, maybe a meeting with someone you've known in previous lives.

On October 22, Neptune returns for the last time to his sign, Pisces, until January 27, 2026. A great time to start meditation practice that can be facilitated by the ruler of mysticism. Dreams, imagination, channeling, mediumship, poetry, and art are enhanced, as well as your intuition. A great time to connect to hobbies and sports that relate to water. Dance, yoga, and martial arts are perfect activities and in addition, your creativity is heightened.

On October 23, the Sun enters Scorpio until November 22. Focus on being true to your passion. It is a month of healing, transformation, magic, occult, and assisting others in their talents, finances, and endeavors. Happy birthday! This is a month to shine forth and share your talents and magic with the world. A good time to reinvent and rebrand yourself.

Around October 26 Mars conjuncts Lilith, please be extra careful today as the Mother of Demons hired an assassin. This is a violent and aggressive aspect. Tread cautiously. Be extra careful since this drama is taking place in your domain. Stay away from sharp objects, be careful of explosions (real and metaphorical).

On October 29, Mercury enters Sagittarius until November 19. You might feel a bit absent-minded and distracted. A good time for traveling and doing business with foreigners. Stick to the truth and avoid liars and half-truths. Great for education and publishing. For you Scorpio, this is a great time to promote your talents and gifts. Great for writing and sales.

NOVEMBER

From November 3 to 5 Mars opposes Uranus, therefore, be extra careful of accidents and mishaps involving aggression, impatience, speed or sharp objects. You might act in an erratic way and gadgets and machines around you might malfunction. The robot is out of control.

From November 4 to December 15, Mars enters Sagittarius. A call for adventure, as well as an expedition. Your Mars wants you to conquer, hunt, and expend your knowledge. It is an Indiana Jones aspect. Renewed energy and passion return to the sector if your chart that relates to money, talents, self-worth, and values. Time to fight for what you believe in. A good time for promotion and asserting your worth.

November 5 is the Full Moon exalted in Taurus. An opportune time to bring something into completion. Since the lunation is on the 13th degree of Scorpio, it carries a powerful connection to love. Spend time in nature and indulge your five senses. The Moon can shine upon a potential partner in work and life. A day later, November 6, Venus enters your sign, Scorpio, until November 30. You look, feel, and appear beautiful and radiating. A good time to focus on your partner's money and talents rather than your own. Look into your investments as there might be a need to make some adjustments. A great time to get a new outfit, reconnect to the artist in you, and beautify yourself.

From November 8 to April 26, 2026, Uranus returns for the last time to Taurus. Changes in finances, fluctuations in cryptocurrency, new ways of expressing artistic talents. Since 2018 Uranus has been causing havoc in your relationships, awakening you to the cons and pros of your significant others. This is the last time Uranus will be shaking your relationship sector of your chart and could expose an enemy or someone who plots against you as well as potential good allies.

From November 9 to December 1 Mercury is stationary and retrograde. This retrograde dances on the cusp of Sagittarius where he is overthinking to Scorpio where he is secretive. Avoid signing documents, starting new projects, and initiating anything unless you tried to do so before and failed to accomplish it.

On November 19, Mercury enters Scorpio until December 10. Mercury returns to your sign as he retrogrades back into the underworld. Good for investigations and finding lost objects and people.

November 20 is the New Moon in Scorpio. A great time to investigate your passions, what you really want in life, what you wish to transform, and start today. A good New Moon to initiate projects that need shared resources, talents, or funding. However, since Mercury is retro be selective in what you initiate. An opportune time to initiate healing, therapy, a shamanistic journey, or an investigation. The New Moon is getting a boost from Saturn, Jupiter, and Neptune, which bless this lunation with structure and focus, imagination and inspiration, and a great deal of open-mindedness.

On November 22, the Sun transits in Sagittarius until December 21. Sagittarius is the time of the year when we have the strongest connection to our higher self or guardian angel. This is a month for teaching, mentoring, learning, speaking your truth, mass media, publishing, and connecting to foreigners, and in-laws. This month you might experience an increase in your income and reconnection to talents and self-worth.

November 23 is an interesting day when the Sun trines Neptune; Mercury trines Jupiter and Saturn; Jupiter trines Saturn. This day can further your goals in almost all aspects of your life.

On November 28 Venus conjuncts Lilith. Be extra careful with all your relationships and partners in work or in personal life. A three-sided relationship might form around you. Be beware of stalkers, gossip, enemies, and lawsuits.

From November 30 until December 24 Venus transits in Sagittarius. It is a great time for connecting to educators, foreigners, explore investments and possibilities from travel and abroad. You can now improve relationships with in-laws and mentors. A great month for your finances and self-esteem.

DECEMBER

The month starts with a Full Moon in Gemini, December 4, an optimal moment to finalize projects. However, there is an opposition between your talent and money and those of others.

On December 10, Mercury finally goes direct, and life can return to normal. It is good for traveling and businesses abroad as well as for philosophy. Mercury can help you increase your income and find new ways to be compensated for your talents.

From December 15, Mars transits in Capricorn until January 26, 2026. Make sure you give him a mission—something you need help conquering and or mastering. It is a good aspect for leadership and initiation. A call for action is coming, make sure not to refuse the call. A great time to assert yourself and your communication, just don't over do it. Mars wants you to be more forceful and aggressive in your business dealings, sales, writing, and marketing.

December 20 is the New Moon in Sagittarius. A good time to initiate something new around your finances and talents. However, it is a difficult New Moon with Neptune and Saturn sending squares all over the place. Be careful of aggression and anger. A sense of war approaching. Lay low and be vigilant.

From December 20, Lilith enters Sagittarius for nine months. There could be discord with students and teachers, as well as foreigners. Take extra care when traveling. Fear of the foreigner, misinformation, disinformation. You are all to happy to hand over the Mother of Demons to Sagittarius after having to host her for 9 months.

On December 21 the Sun enters Capricorn and will stay there until January 20, 2026. Happy Solstice! The ensuing month calls for Capricorn-like discipline and focus. Strategize the year ahead, bearing in mind that patience is vital. A great month for writing, communication, signing documents, and improving relationships with relatives, neighbors, and roommates. This trend continues from December 24, as Venus transits in Capricorn until January 17, 2026. This transit of Venus can help you improve relationships with people who are older, long-term partnerships, as well as bosses and superiors. A time to connect art and design to your professional life.

SAGITTARIUS AND SAGITTARIUS RISING: I SEE

The Journey Homeward

General Trends: In 2025 your pivot towards home and family continues. 2025 should be dedicated to settling down, healing ancestral traumas, and practicing parenthood. Jupiter, your ruler, can help you find a partner or heal your current relationships in the first part of the year, while in the second part of 2025, Jupiter connects you to your talents, promising to increase your finances, improve investments, or benefiting from your partner's income and talent. There could be enemies that were hidden before, raising their heads. Therefore, avoid gossip or getting into other people's drama.

JANUARY

Between January 1–5, Mars is opposite his Scorpio coruler, Pluto, which is not a promising beginning of the year. There is an opposition between your will and that of your community, company, or friends. People around you might experience paranoia, resort to manipulation, conflict and aggression. If you are traveling pay extra attention to needless conflicts and accidents. There also could be issues with your teachers or students.

On January 3, Venus puts on her swimming suit and dives into Pisces until February 4. There are plenty of opportunities to improve your finances, as well as heal or attract partnerships. Creative visualization can be extremely potent. A great time to remodel your home, beautify your abode and or office, and invest in real estate.

On January 6, Mars retrogrades into Cancer until April 18. Be vigilant of accidents, falling (unless it is in love) and issues with or around water such as leaks and floods. Conflict can arise with family members. Be extra careful with investments.

On January 8 Mercury enters Capricorn until January 28, and this means serious thought, discipline study, lessons coming from mature and experienced figures. Slow your thought, speech, and writing, and be mindful of every word. Great for furthering your career goals and forging long-term plans. This is a great time to market your talents and skills.

January 13 is the Full Moon in Cancer, and it could get emotional and a bit aggressive with family and loved ones due to the opposition of retro Mars and Pluto. Take heed of over emotionality and guilt casting. There could be tension between your talents and money and those of your partner.

Between January 18–19, Venus conjuncts Saturn. Finances, values, and your relationships are being scrutinized and audited. This is not necessarily a bad aspect as Venus is exalted and Saturn can ground your talents as well as help you use your gifts in a practical way. Whatever is going on in your personal and professional relationships are galvanized and crystallized, for good or bad.

On January 19 the Sun enters Aquarius until February 18. A time to spend with friends, community, as well as immerse yourself in science, technology, and innovation. A month long of improved communication, attract lucrative contracts, and increase sales and or business. Immerse yourself in writing and communication.

Between January 25–26, as Venus trines Mars, the cosmic lovers can bring a new relationship into your life or help you harmonize partnerships you already have.

From January 28 until February 14, Mercury transits in Aquarius, and ideas flow fast as well as new friendships forming with likeminded people. You are a messenger and surrounded by other connectors. January 29 is also the New Moon in Aquarius and Chinese New Year. Time to welcome to the Year of the Earth Snake. Jupiter is blessing this New Moon with wisdom and synchronicity. A great time to start a study group. A new friend or group from whom you can learn a great deal is making an entrance into your life.

On January 29, the North Node retrogrades into Pisces until August 19, 2026, for the first time in 19 years. Right on the New Moon in Aquarius, the North Node aka "Dragon," is retrograding into the sign of mysticism, intuition, and imagination. For the next 18 months we are asked to practice empathy, meditation, any form of trance or movement practice (yoga, dance, or martial arts). However, the South Node will be in Virgo asking us to let go of criticism, perfectionism, and overanalytical tendencies. The next 18 months are good for relocation, buying a property, starting or expanding your family.

FEBRUARY

On February 4, Venus enters Aries, until March 27. While it is true Venus is in exile in Aries, but as a loyal fellow fire sign, you can benefit from this long track of the goddess of love in the sector of your chart associated with romantic adventures. You feel creative, enthusiastic, and energetic. Watch impulsiveness with your finances. This is taken to the next level between February 6–12, as Mars trines Saturn bringing a weeklong of constructive action, stable effort, and sustained passion. This aspect can give you the endurance to complete a marathon or two.

On February 12 the Moon is reaching her fullness in Leo, and you might feel the pull and push between the gravitational forces of your children or romantic partner versus friends or your company. A good time for traveling and education, however, the square with Uranus can cause disruption and lunacy to this lunation.

On Valentine's Day (February 14), Mercury enters Pisces until March 3. This transit can benefit healing in the household as well as real estate opportunities. Communications can be a bit challenged while intuition and mediumship are on the rise. Trust your gut feeling more than your brain. Make sure to use the words "I feel" or "I imagine" or "I believe," instead of "I think." This trend is supported by the Sun entering Pisces from February 18 until March 20's Equinox. A great time to relocate, remodel, and focus on family members. Imagination, dance, movement, dreaming, meditation, intuition, mysticism, and empathy are heightened. Just make sure to guard your boundaries and avoid addictions or self-destructive tendencies.

The month ends with the New Moon in Pisces on February 28. A great day to start something new that involves your home, family, imagination, photography, movement, yoga and meditation. There is a tendency to absorb negativity from others so watch what you take in. Be careful of overdoing or illusions.

MARCH

Between March 1 to April 14, Venus stands still and then retrogrades in Aries, her sign of exile. While she is still blessing the area in your chart associated with romantic love, creativity and children, there could be issues coming up in these aspects of your life due to her retrograde motion. Avoid getting married, starting new relationships, getting engaged, starting lawsuits, signing partnerships agreements. Exes or lovers from previous lives or this life might return. Be extra mindful with finances, as people tend to lose money or make bad investments.

On March 3, Mercury joins Venus and enters Aries until March 30. Mercury can be a bit impatient when in Aries and favors practical and short and concise communication. Mercury can help improve your communication with your children as well as romantic lovers. Sports that demand a great deal of cardio are favored.

Between March 11–13, Sun conjunct Saturn while Mercury conjunct Venus. Seriousness, focus, discipline and planning can bring tactical or strategical accomplishments. A good time to improve relations with superiors.

March 14, Pi Day, we undergo the first Lunar Eclipse of the year. The Full Moon is in precise and analytical Virgo. Since this lunation squares your sign, it can be a bit more emotional. A great time to bring a project to an end, as well as focus on diet, service, and combining your analytical and wholistic aspects in life.

March 14–April 8 Mercury is stationary and retrograde. Since it is happening in Aries this month, be extra careful with anger, impulsiveness, and rush decisions. A great time to go back to a creative projects you abandoned in the past.

On March 17, the Sun conjuncts North Node. A day to access skills and knowledge from past lifetimes. There could be an encounter with powerful and successful individuals or groups that can further your goals. A good time to reconnect to talents that run down in your family, perhaps gifts etched in your genes.

March 20 is the Equinox and the Sun transits into Aries until April 19. Happy New Year! A time to focus on your body, health, leadership, as well as your brand and image. This is a great month for love, happiness, sports, creativity and connecting to your inner child as well as kids in general.

On March 27, Lilith enters Scorpio until December 20. Emotional intensity, powerful desires, fascination with the forbidden, shadow work, possessiveness, and jealousy. BE careful of power struggles, manipulation, abuse, distrust, and criminality. Stay clear of any form of gossip. A good time to place a heap of salt in the four corners of your bedroom as protection against negativity. Take extra care from hidden enemies or people who pretend to be on your side but plot against you.

March 29 is the first Solar Eclipse of the year, and she shines upon Aries. Be mindful of unnecessary aggression and impulsiveness. A great time to try to spend with children.

From March 30 to April 15, Mercury is in Pisces. Mercury retrogrades into his sign of fall, therefore, communication can be extra hard as the messenger is not only retro but drowning in subjectivity. Talk and write from your heart rather than mind. Great for intuition and applying imagination to overcome challenges. There could be misunderstandings with family members.

From March 30 to October 22, Neptune enters Aries for the first time in 165 years. Confusion can lead to war, be extra careful of fanaticism or aggression triggered by propaganda of misinformation. Watch your immune system, inflammation, and your head. This is a very creative transit combining mysticism and happiness. A good time for yoga, dance, movement, water sports, and inspiration.

APRIL

Between April 5–7, the celestial lovers meet again. Venus is Barbie and Mars in water sign Cancer is Ken, the "simply beach" dude. These are great days for romance, increasing your income from talents you are passionate about, and better relationships with significant others as well as brothers and sisters in arms.

From April 5 to 10, Venus conjuncts Saturn. While this aspect can introduce you to someone older that could be helpful with finance and developing your talents, this conjunction can also sit heavy over all your relationships. A time to reassess your primary relationships and how you make money.

On April 8 Mercury finally goes direct and you can begin signing documents and starting new projects. There could be increased interest in real estate or relocation. Between April 7–16 Mercury trine Mars and that could give a kick forward to your projects and business.

On April 13 the Moon is Full in Libra. This is the day of liberation, coming out of constriction and negativity and marching towards your Promised Land. It is a magical Full Moon where you can connect to your inner Moses, guardian angel, or higher self. A great time to spend with friends.

April 14 is a dramatic day when Saturn conjuncts the North Node in Pisces. Positive interactions with groups of powerful individuals or people who are older. You are downloading some gifts or connections from previous lives. Good for joining new groups and organizations that share your long-term goals. You are able to fix ancestral karma and tap into the gifts that run down your family line.

From April 16 to May 10 Mercury transits in Aries, speeding things up but also showing signs of impatience. Words can easily be weaponized so be extra careful. This is the time to communicate your needs to your lover. If you have children, this transit can help dealing with any issues they might have.

From April 18 to June 17 Mars enters Leo bringing about a great deal of courage and a call for adventure. Great for entertainment, sports, creativity, and reconnecting to your inner child. An opportune time for education, traveling, and fighting for what you believe in. Walk the talk.

On April 19 the Sun enters Taurus and will remain there until May 20. This month you are to indulge your six senses and connect to Mother Nature. It is a good month to tap into your artistic talents and perhaps discover new ones. The Sun now shines upon your work and health. An opportune time for promotion, raise, taking on a leadership in your workplace as well as improving your health and wellbeing.

Between April 22–24, as the Sun square the rulers of Scorpio—Mars and Pluto, take extra heed. This can bring about a great deal of letting go, death, and intense sexuality. Watch your steps these days, things can turn ugly or violent.

April 27 is the exalted New Moon in Taurus. A great time to start a new artistic or financial project. Spend time in nature, connect to your senses and do something that can symbolize rooting yourself. A good time to initiate something new in your work as well as health and diet. This trend continues April 30 as Venus enters Aries until June 6. There could be more conflict and confusion in your primary relationships. In her sign of exile, Venus might be somewhat snappy and can cause hasty decisions and actions with finances and love.

MAY

Between May 1 to May 3, Venus conjuncts Neptune and infuses us with romance, creativity, art, improved finances and intuition. Love is in the air and can inspire all aspects of your life.

From May 10 to May 26, Mercury enters Taurus, which can bring a sense of worry and anxiety. However, it is a good time to communicate and market your talents and gifts. Speak your mind without attachment or inflexibility. This transit is great for your work and professional life. A time to market yourself and your projects.

May 12 is the Full Moon in Scorpio, and while the Moon is fallen, it is still a great time for shadow work, dealing with any temptation you might have, and discovering the light in you. Tension could arise between the need to focus on your work and wanting to rest or isolate. Because the Moon falls on the 22nd (Master Number) degree of Scorpio, we can build something out of the rubble of an older project or relationship. In this lunation you feel the tug of war between "mine" and "yours."

Between May 17–18, the Sun conjuncts Uranus and everyone's IQ is getting a temporary elevation. A fantastic day for humor, jumping into the unknown, and embracing the original and innovative. Spend time with friends or in a group.

From May 20 to June 21, the Sun enters Gemini, and we are all channeling the spirit of intelligence, communication, and bridge-building. This is a great month for business, contracts, improving relationships with relatives, roommates, neighbors, and people you consider siblings who didn't share a womb. Since the Sun is in your opposite sign, he shines upon your partnerships in work and life. A great time to find a partner and harmonize the ones you have.

Between May 20 to 24, Venus trines Mars once again. Romance, love, harmony (the daughter of Venus and Mars), is around you as well as an ability to see people's beautiful side. Great time for making money from things you are passionate about.

On May 24, as Mercury conjunct Uranus, we have a day of ingeniousness. You can get new insights and ideas that can help you in business, communication, and better connect to people around you.

Between May 25 to September 1 Saturn enters Aries. Saturn in Aries wishes to rectify how we deal with our identity, body, anger, and vitality. There is renewed focus on issues you might be dealing with your children, creative projects, or romantic lover. A good time to be disciplined with hobbies, sports, and having fun.

Between May 26 to June 8 Mercury enters Gemini. Mercury is back to his domicile, and he is happy to unpack and inspire you. Information, opportunities, connections, and words flow effortlessly. Improved communication with relationships and good luck with legal issues.

The May 27 New Moon in Gemini is a great day to start something new in connection with your partnerships. In addition, this lunation is a good time to initiate something that relates to communication, networking, businesses, marketing, sales, and written projects. This New Moon is blessed by Pluto and Neptune, making it possible for you to link passion and reason, emotions and intellect. A great deal of intimacy and a possibility for a lover coming into your life.

JUNE

Between June 4 to 8, Venus, Jupiter, Mercury, and Mars are blessing us and each other. Windows of positive opportunities can improve sales, communication, writing, health, education, and art.

On June 6 Venus enters Taurus until July 4. The goddess of love is lending a helping hand in matters of art, finances, relationships, and security. You will experience your five senses in a much stronger way than regularly, perhaps getting a glimpse of the sixth one as well. This is wonderful news for your workplace. There could be a promotion as well as the addition of an artistic element to your work.

On June 8, Mercury transits Cancer until June 26. Great for healing relationships with family members. Don't be afraid to express your emotions. It is also a good time for research, investigation, and benefiting from shared resources and projects that necessitate financial and artistic collaborations.

Between June 9 to 10, Mercury squares Neptune and Saturn while Venus squares Pluto. A bundle of challenging aspects come together. There is deception, lies, theft, and disinformation. Monkey mind is out of the cage, causing us to jump from one subject or project to the other. Breakups, manipulation, and discord with people of power.

On June 9 Jupiter, your ruler, enters Cancer, where he is exalted, and will stay there until June 30, 2026. This is great news for all aspects of your life, but especially for joint artistic and financial affairs, reconnecting to your passion, sexuality, and intimacy. An opportune time to exercise the wizard, healer, and enchantress in you. Try to let go of things that hinder your growth. In addition, this is a great year for real estate, healing familial relationships, and connecting to fortune and abundance. Be careful of overdoing and over commitments.

From June 10 until August 23, Saturn conjuncts with Neptune. While your intuition, ability to meditate, and connect to your dreams are enhanced, so does your self-destructiveness, addictions, and escapism. Tread carefully, watch out for fanaticism or being too attached to your beliefs.

On June 11, the Full Moon is in Sagittarius—a blessed Moon in a challenging month. Jupiter, ruler of Sagittarius, your sign, is forming what is called "Mutual Reception" with the Moon, which is highly auspicious. A wonderful time to complete a cycle of learning and preparation for something new. Great for travel, especially by water or to a location close to the water. Mars gives a boost of energy to the aspect. There could be a great deal of back and forth with partners in work and life. Keep a balance attitude between the "I" and "we."

From June 17, Mars enters Virgo until August 6. Mars in Virgo gets things done. He is the watchmaker, the engineer, the organizer—here to protect and serve. Conflicts can arise if you are too critical of yourself and others. You can make things happen if you stick to a strict routine. This is an especially powerful period for pushing your professional life forward and exploring new career horizons.

From June 21 the Sun transits Cancer until July 22. Happy Solstice! Open your heart to your family, and perhaps you might meet family members from past lives. A great month to renovate and remodel your home, relocate, move in with someone, get a new property, or start a family. This is the month for healing, letting go of whatever blocks your development, and focusing on investments. It is a time of transformation. This trend is especially strong on June 25's New Moon is in Cancer, providing a new beginning that involves home and family, real estate, security, and emotional support. With Jupiter, exalted in Cancer, blessing the union of the Sun and Moon, this is a great time to start new projects. Besides Pluto, there are no planets retrograde. Full swim ahead!

From June 26 until September 3, Mercury is in Leo. This Mercury transit can be extremely creative, entertaining, and exciting. A great time for education, travel, and improving communication with in-laws, as well as foreigners.

Between June 27 to 28, Mercury trines Saturn and Neptune. This is a good aspect for making long-term plans and bringing some sanity to a mad mad month. Good for marketing, writing, and sales. It is also a great time for prophetic dreams and practical intuition.

JULY

On July 4 Venus conjuncts Uranus and while relationships can be exciting, they can also show an unpredictable side. There is a need for freedom and exploration of new frontiers with your finances, relationships, and artistic expression. Embrace the original and unique. Be extra aware there could be volatility in the market.

From July 4 Venus flirts with Gemini until July 30 and the next few weeks can bring you in contact with a potential lover or partner at work. A time for marketing, sales, design, and making new connections. This is one of the best times this year to harmonize as well as attract a partnership. Love is in the air!

From July 7 to November 8, Uranus enters Gemini, and your IQ is augmented. Since Gemini is your opposite sign, Uranus is awakening your relationship for good and bad. Expect twists and changes in most of your partnerships. You or your partner might need freedom. In addition, there could be revelations about people who strive against you. Humor and lightheartedness can be the cure for most ails.

July 10 is the Full Moon in Capricorn. This lunation can bring about a bit of opposition between home and career. The Moon is exiled in Capricorn and can create a sense of emotionality and longing for a paradise lost. However, Mars is sending his troupes to help you, and with a bit of action, determination, and a clear mission, you can disperse the emotional confusion of the Full Moon. There could be tension between your needs and those of your partner's.

From July 17 to August 12, Mercury is retrograde in Leo. Avoid signing docs and starting new projects. Especially watch your relationships and communication with kids, lovers, and people with big egos. Be extra vigilant if you are traveling abroad.

From July 22 to August 22, Sun enters Leo. Engage in creative, joyful, and heartwarming activities. Generosity, nobility, chivalry, sportsmanship, and enthusiasm are guiding us this month. A great time to connect to a hobby or a new sport. This is a month which is especially strong for you as the Sun lights issues you care about: travel, truth, education, publishing, and mass media. A good time for an adventure.

Between July 23–25, the Sun trine Saturn and Neptune creating a wonderful flow and help with vitality, intuition, healing, and the ability to bring some new structure into our lives. This is a glorious aspect, and you can benefit from creative visualizations, meditation, dance and self-expression.

July 24 is the New Moon in Leo. This is not an easy New Moon since it is smack opposite to Pluto and can bring a confrontation with a powerful figure in your life whose motivations are unclear. With Mercury retrograding in Leo, it is not the best time to start something new, however, you could initiate a project you already tried before and failed to complete. A good time to start learning something you tried in the past and failed, could be anything from a language, an instrument, or a skill.

From July 31 to August 25, Venus transits in Cancer. Marriage, social events with family members, as well as harmonious flow with family members. Your connection to intimacy and sexuality is enhanced.

AUGUST

The month starts with a hard aspect on August 1 and 2 between Venus, Saturn and Neptune. Watch out for deception, illusions, and fantasies in your primary relationships as well as financial dealings. Not the best time to start a new relationship. Rapport with people who are older than you can be fraught with discord. Try a new approach to an old problem.

On August 6 Mars enters Libra and stays there until September 22. Not Mars' favorite position unless he can be given the mission to fight or defend peace. There could be some legal issues but also a good time for compromise and finding resolutions to conflicts. Be extra cautious with all your dealings with government officials, corporations, and friends. However, between August 7 to 9, Mars trines Uranus bringing about brilliance and originality. Connections with friends can thrive. Action is guided by new approaches.

Watch it between August 8 to 10 as Mars opposes both Saturn and Neptune. Accidents, mishaps, and physical challenges especially since Mercury is retrograding. Stay away from arguments with superiors. Stay calm and try to do less.

August 9 is the Full Moon in Aquarius. You might feel a push and pull between the need to spend time with lovers or your children and your friends or company. There could be tension rising between your relatives and those of your partner.

On August 12, Mercury finally goes direct in Leo. You can now start plowing ahead, especially since on August 12 and 13, Venus conjuncts Jupiter, which is one of the best aspects this year. Luck, flow in finances, new relationships and maybe a novel love.

Between August 12 to October 27, Uranus trines Pluto. A powerful aspect that can bring about transformation through technology, science, social movements, and revolutions. Changes in government that can, in the long run, bring more prosperity.

From August 22 to September 22 the Sun transits in Virgo. This is a wonderful transit for your career and worldly ambition. We are asked to focus and refine our diet, health, routine, work, and how we serve. An ideal time to eliminate impediments to health and productivity. This is especially true on August 23 when we have the New Moon in Virgo. A great time to start something new in your career. In addition, it is a good time for a new diet, work project, or acts of service. A bit of chaos is added by a square to Uranus that can awaken the critic and perfectionist in you. Try to channel these propensities into something productive at work.

On August 25, Venus transits in Leo until September 19. A great time to lean an artistic skill as well as connect to foreigners and educators. The planet of love in the sign of romance is always good news. Just be careful of extra martial affairs. It is a very creative time with your inner child active and playful.

SEPTEMBER

On September 1, Saturn returns to Pisces until February 13, 2026. Lord Karma is revisiting the sector of your chart that relates to home, family, genetics, and real estate. This is a good time to heal from traumas that run down the generation, relocate, change homes, and experience the changes you need to be able to feel and connect to your emotions. In general, it is a g time to ground your mystical practices, dreams, imagination, and intuition.

From September 2 to September 18, Mercury transits into Virgo. A good time for your career as well as an increase in sales and for coming up with new ideas. Information flows effortlessly. A great time for editing projects that need precision, micromanagement, organizing, and purification. A wonderful time for detoxing and a cleanse.

September 7 is the Lunar eclipse in Pisces, which is also dubbed the Harvest Full Moon. Momentum builds towards closure especially with work and personal affairs. There could be tension between home life and career responsibilities. Now's the time to harvest the fruits of your labor from March/April. Mercury provides a touch of reason to an otherwise very emotional lunation.

From September 18, Mercury transits into Libra until October 6. This Mercury wants peace, compromise, and beauty especially with your friends and within your company. A great time for healing relationships and harmonizing the workplace. Art and business are coming together. You can revamp your website, redesign your logo, and come up with new ways to brand yourself and your projects.

From September 19, Venus transits Virgo until October 13. Try to add an artistic element to your career. Any form of partnership can further your professional life. However, you might feel over critical about your partners as well as feel the criticism of others towards you.

September 21 is the Solar Eclipse in Virgo. A great time to balance your diet, start a new work project, and get the energy you need to reach the finish line. An opportune time to start something new in your career. In addition, the Eclipse is aided by a gang of planets: Pluto (power and intimacy); Saturn (focus); Neptune (imagination and intuition); Uranus (innovation).

On September 22, the Sun enters Libra until October 23, marking the Equinox! For the next 30 days the Sun shines upon your friendships and your organization or company. A great time to update and upgrade yourself and reconnect to technology and innovation. Over the next 30 days, you should embody Libra traits—diplomacy, balance, and attentiveness to partners.

On September 22, Mars enters Scorpio until November 4. A wonderful time to collaborate on big projects that demand a lot of energy and resources. Passion, intimacy and sexuality are on the rise. Since Mars is transiting the sector of your chart that relates to past lifetime, isolation, hospitals and confinements, be extra careful and tread cautiously.

Between September 23–25, Mars squares Pluto. Aggression and manipulative folks are around you. Take extra heed in general. Your actions can be easily misconstrued.

OCTOBER

On October 6 Mercury transits into Scorpio until October 29. An ideal period for research, finding lost objects or people, and expressing intimacy. It's a good time to move on, let bygones be bygones, bury the zombies in your life, and explore investments and collaborations with other people's assets and talents. A great time for therapy and reconnecting to your subconscious as well as receiving messages from your dreams.

October 7 is the Lunar eclipse in Aries and is a tad challenging. With Chiron's involvement, it's an occasion for learning, teaching, and shamanistic journeys. While there's an aggressive undertone, it's a good moment to conclude matters and move on. There could be conflicts with partners in life or work. Since you are a fire sign, this eclipse can open a path for a new love, hobby, or physical activity. A great time to get pregnant with a child or an idea.

Between October 11 to 14, Venus is opposite Saturn and Neptune. This can be hard on your relationships and or finances. There is an emotional frustration with partners, especially long-term ones. Illusions as well as dependency and codependency and some disappointment with someone close to you. However, you can use this aspect to connect mysticism and art.

From October 13 to November 6, Venus returns to her sign, Libra, and can help us connect to beauty, diplomacy, justice, relationship, and harmony. A friendship can transform into romantic love or maybe you will be meeting with someone that could open your heart. A wonderful time for artistic exploration in a group or with friends. This is especially strong between October 14–15 as Venus trine Uranus and Pluto. Venus receives much praise from Pluto (intimacy, sexuality, power) and Uranus (innovation, technology, friendships). This is a powerful time for igniting, transforming, balancing and solidifying partnerships in work and personal life.

The New Moon in Libra takes place October 21. Dubbed the "Moon of Peace," the Libra New Moon is a great time to start a relationship or an art project. However, both Jupiter and Pluto are squaring off with the Sun and Moon, creating uncomfortable situations. Be extra cautious and focus on breathwork and meditation.

On October 22, Neptune returns for the last time to his sign, Pisces, until January 27, 2026. A great time to start meditation practice that can be facilitated by the ruler of mysticism. Dreams, imagination, channeling, mediumship, poetry, and art are enhanced, as well as your intuition. Watch for leaks in your home or water damage. A wonderful time to transform your home into a sacred place.

On October 23, the Sun enters Scorpio until November 22. Focus on being true to your passion. It is a month of healing, transformation, magic, occult, and assisting others in their talents, finances, and endeavors. This is a month that propels you to let go and detox from people, substances, or attitudes. These are 30 days that are good for meditation, mysticism, healing, and shamanic work.

Around October 26 Mars conjuncts Lilith, please be extra careful today as the Mother of Demons hired an assassin. This is a violent and aggressive aspect. Avoid war zones.

On October 29, Mercury enters Sagittarius until November 19. You might feel a bit absent-minded and distracted. A good time for traveling and doing business with foreigners. Stick to the truth and avoid liars and half-truths. Great for education and publishing. Mercury in your sign can help you reinvent yourself, take the initiative and become a leader. .

NOVEMBER

From November 3 to 5 Mars opposes Uranus, therefore, be extra careful of accidents and mishaps involving aggression, impatience, speed or sharp objects. You might experience erratic behavior that doesn't make sense as well as gadgets and machines breaking or malfunctioning. The robot is out of control.

From November 4 to December 15, Mars enters Sagittarius, setting you on fire with passion, strength, vitality and leadership abilities. A call for adventure, as well as an expedition. Your Mars wants you to conquer, hunt, and expend your knowledge. It is an Indiana Jones aspect. Be careful of not overdoing it or injuries die to impatience. There is a call for action, adhere it if you can. A time to assert yourself and tap into your leadership abilities.

November 5 is the Full Moon in Taurus. An opportune time to bring something into completion. Since the lunation is on the 13th degree of Scorpio, it carries a powerful connection to love. Spend time in nature and indulge your five senses. A time of tension between the reed for rest and work responsibilities.

On November 6, Venus enters Scorpio until November 30. This transit can make you feel a bit isolated. However, it is a good time to focus on your partner's money and talents rather than your own. Look into your investments as there might be a need to make some adjustments. A wonderful time for creative visualization, projecting to the universe what you need to end the year in a glorious way. Your dream life as well as imagination is enhanced.

From November 8 to April 26, 2026, Uranus returns for the last time to Taurus. Changes in finances, fluctuations in cryptocurrency, new ways of expressing artistic talents. Watch for injuries or sudden aliments that are hard to diagnose. Try to implement new technology and innovation in your workplace.

From November 9 to December 1 Mercury is stationary and retrograde. This retrograde dances on the cusp of Sagittarius where he is overthinking to Scorpio where he is secretive. Avoid signing documents, starting new projects, and initiating anything unless you tried to do so before and failed to accomplish it. This can be extra challenging for you as Mercury retro can add to the general confusion. Avoid making big decisions.

On November 19, Mercury enters Scorpio until December 10. Mercury returns to Scorpio as he retrogrades back into the underworld. Good for investigations and finding lost objects and people. You are receiving messages from the beyond as well as past lifetimes. A great time for therapy.

November 20 is the New Moon in Scorpio. A great time to investigate your passions, what you really want in life, what you wish to transform, and start today. A good New Moon to initiate projects that involve shared resources, combined talents, or large fundings. However, since Mercury is retro, you can only start things you already did in the past and failed to bring to completion. An opportune time to initiate healing, therapy, a shamanistic journey, or an investigation. The New Moon is getting a boost from Saturn, Jupiter, and Neptune, which bless this lunation with structure and focus, imagination and inspiration, and a great deal of open-mindedness.

On November 22, the Sun transits in Sagittarius until December 21. Happy Birthday! This is your time to shine since the Sun is supporting your endeavors. You are attractive and attracting opportunities. This is a month for teaching, mentoring, learning, speaking your truth, mass media, publishing, and connecting to foreigners, and in-laws.

On November 28 Venus conjuncts Lilith. Be extra careful with all your relationships and partners in work or in personal life. A three-sided relationship might form around you. Be beware of stalkers, gossip, enemies, and lawsuits.

From November 30 until December 24 Venus transits in Sagittarius. It is a great time for connecting to educators, foreigners, explore investments and possibilities from travel and abroad. A good time to improve relationships with in-laws. You look, feel, and appear beautiful. Venus blesses you with creativity and grace. A great time to try new outfits, hairdo, and style.

DECEMBER

December 4 is the Full Moon in Gemini. An optimal moment to finalize projects. As this is the year's last Full Moon. There could be tension between you and your partner.

On December 10, Mercury finally goes direct. A good period for traveling and businesses abroad as well as for philosophy. Now is the time to communicate your needs and receive from the universe the answers you have been waiting for.

From December 15, Mars transits in Capricorn until January 26, 2026. Make sure you give him a mission—something you need help conquering and or mastering. It is a good aspect for leadership and initiation. A wonderful time to get a raise, promotion, and initiate projects that could increase your finances.

December 20 is the New Moon in Sagittarius. A difficult New Moon with Neptune and Saturn sending squares all over the place. Be careful of aggression and anger. However, this is your New Moon, for good or bad, a time you can initiate projects that could help you take control over your life and present yourself in new ways.

From December 20, Lilith enters Sagittarius for nine months. There could be discord with students and teachers, as well as foreigners. Take extra care when traveling. Fear of the foreigner, misinformation, disinformation. Hosting the strife-bound Mother of Demons for 9 months is not an easy task. Stay away from gossip and getting between people's wars and conflicts.

On December 21 the Sun enters Capricorn and will stay there until January 20, 2026. Happy Solstice! The ensuing month calls for Capricorn-like discipline and focus. Strategize the year ahead, bearing in mind that patience is vital. A good month to focus on your finances, talents, and gifts. This trend is supported by Venus transiting in Capricorn between December

24 to January 17, 2026. This transit of Venus can help you improve relation-ships with people who are older, long-term partnerships, as well as bosses and superiors. A time to connect art and design to your professional life.

CAPRICORN AND CAPRICORN RISING: I USE

First was the Word and the Word was God

General Trends: Saturn, your ruler, continues rectifying the way you communicate, write, conduct your business, and deal with relatives. However, in the middle of the year you will be asked to take a closer look at your home, real estate, and family relationships, as commitments and extra responsibilities in relation to your abode will occupy the center stage. The first part of the year, you will be experiencing expansion in your work and health while the second part of 2025 promises good news with your relationships in work or life. While Capricorn favor their professional life, 2025 can connect you to your personal life as well. In addition, 2025 is a year to listen carefully to your intuition, dreams, and psychic hits.

JANUARY

Between January 1–5, Mars is opposite his Scorpio coruler, Pluto, which is not a promising beginning of the year. There is an opposition forming between your will and that of your community, company, or friends. People around you might experience paranoia, resort to manipulation, conflict and aggression.

On January 3, Venus puts on her swimming suit and dives into Pisces until February 4. You could experience opportunities to improve your finances, relationships as well as artistic gifts. Creative visualization can be extremely potent. A great time for combining art with your communication and healing relationships with relatives.

On January 6, Mars retrogrades into Cancer, your opposite sign, until April 18. Be vigilant of accidents, falling (unless it is in love) and issues with or around water such as leaks and floods. Conflict can arise with family members as well as partners in work or life.

On January 8 Mercury enters Capricorn until January 28, and this means serious thought, discipline study, lessons coming from mature and experienced figures. Slow your thought, speech, and writing. Great for furthering your career goals and forging long-term plans. An opportune time for marketing and promoting yourself and projects that are close to your heart.

January 13 is the Full Moon in Cancer, where she loves to be. It could get emotional and a bit volatile with family and loved ones due to the opposition of retro Mars and Pluto. Take heed of over emotionality and guilt casting. There could be attraction to someone new as well as some tensions between you are your partners in work or life.

Between January 18–19, Venus conjuncts Saturn, your ruler. Finances, values, and your relationships are being scrutinized and audited. This is not necessarily a bad aspect as Venus is exalted and Saturn can ground your talents as well as help you use your gifts in a practical way. Whatever is going on in your personal and professional relationships are galvanized and crystallized, for good or bad.

On January 19 the Sun enters Aquarius until February 18. A time to spend with friends, community, as well as immerse yourself in science, technology, and innovation. As a Capricorn, this transit is wonderful for your finances and talents. There could be an award, recognition of your talents and skills, as well as opportunities to feel better about yourself.

Between January 25–26, as Venus trines Mars, the cosmic lovers can bring a new relationship into your life or help you harmonize partnerships you already have.

From January 28 until February 14, Mercury transits in Aquarius, and ideas flow fast. A great time to make new contacts and reconnect to old friendships. January 29 is also the New Moon in Aquarius and Chinese New Year. Time to welcome to the Year of the Earth Snake. Jupiter is blessing this New Moon with wisdom and synchronicity. A great time to start a study group. A new friend or group from whom you can learn a great deal is making an entrance into your life. An opportune time to start a new business.

On January 29, the North Node retrogrades into Pisces until August 19, 2026, for the first time in 19 years. Right on the New Moon in Aquarius, the North Node aka "Dragon," is retrograding into the sign of mysticism, intuition, and imagination. For the next 18 months you are asked to practice empathy, meditation, and any form of movement (yoga, dance, or martial arts). Your intuition, channeling abilities, and mediumship are being enhanced by the North Node. However, the South Node will be in Virgo asking us to let go of criticism, perfectionism, and overanalytical tendencies.

FEBRUARY

On February 4, Venus enters Aries, until March 27. A great time to beautify your home or office. Relationships with family members can be healed or improved. Focus on real estate or remodeling. Watch impulsiveness with your finances.

Between February 6–12, Mars trines Saturn bringing a weeklong of constructive action, stable effort, and sustained passion. This aspect can give you the endurance to complete a marathon or two.

February 12 is the Full Moon in Leo, and you might feel the pull and push between the gravitational forces of your children or romantic partner versus the needs of your friends or community. The square with Uranus can cause disruption and lunacy to this lunation. There could be issues in investments or conflicts between your finances and that of your partner.

On Valentine's Day (February 14), Mercury enters Pisces until March 3. Communications can be a bit challenged while intuition and mediumship are on the rise. Trust your gut feeling rather than your brain. Make sure to use the words "I feel" or "I imagine" or "I believe," instead of "I think." This is the best time in 2025 for writing, communication, sales, marketing, and coming up with great ideas. This trend is supported by the Sun entering Pisces from February 18 until March 20's Equinox. Imagination, dance, movement, dreaming, meditation, intuition, mysticism, and empathy are heightened. Just make sure to guard your boundaries and avoid addictions or self-destructive tendencies.

The month ends with the New Moon in Pisces on February 28. A great day to start something new that involves your business, writing, communication, and business especially if it can be incorporated with imagination, photography, movement, yoga and meditation. There is a tendency to absorb negativity from others so watch what you take in. Be careful of overdoing or illusions.

MARCH

March 1–April 14 Venus stands still and then retrogrades in Aries, her sign of exile. Avoid getting married, starting new relationships, getting engaged, starting lawsuits, signing partnerships agreements. Exes or lovers from previous lives or this life might return. Be extra mindful with finances, as people tend to lose money or make bad investments. This retrograde is not a good time to invest in real estate, and it can also create challenges between family members, so take heed.

On March 3, Mercury enters Aries until March 30. Until the retrograde on March 14, Mercury could offset some of the familial issues that could arise from Venus' retrograde. Mercury can be a bit impatient when in Aries and favors practical, short, and concise communication.

Between March 11–13, Sun conjunct Saturn while Mercury conjunct Venus. Seriousness, focus, discipline and planning can bring tactical or strategical accomplishments. A good time to improve relations with superiors.

On March 14, Pi Day, the first Lunar Eclipse of the year shines on. The Full Moon in precise and analytical Virgo. A great time to bring a project to an end, as well as focus on diet, service, and combining your analytical and wholistic perspectives in life. There could be tension when you travel in your own country as well as abroad. Watch your communication and what you write, post, text or promote.

March 14–April 8 Mercury stationary and retrograde. Be extra careful with anger, impulsiveness, and rush decisions. Now that both Venus and Mercury are retrograding in the sector of your chart associated with home and family, be extra mindful, especially in your personal life.

On March 17, the Sun conjuncts North Node. A day to access skills and knowledge from past lifetimes. There could be an encounter with powerful and successful individuals or groups that can further your goals.

March 20 is the Equinox and the Sun's transits into Aries until April 19. Happy New Year! A time to focus on your body, health, leadership, as well as your brand and image. You might travel or be connected to a place that you would one day call "home." The Sun can help shine light on your family and homestead.

On March 27, Lilith enters Scorpio until December 20. Emotional intensity, powerful desires, fascination with the forbidden, shadow work, possessiveness, and jealousy. Lilith could also bring about power struggles, manipulation, abuse, distrust, and criminality. Stay clear of any form of gossip. A good time to place a heap of salt in the four corners of your bedroom as protection against negativity. Be extra careful with government officials, taxes, permits, as well as your friends and colleagues in your company.

March 29 is the first Solar Eclipse of the year, and she shines upon Aries. Be mindful of unnecessary aggression and impulsiveness. A secret about your family or home might be revealed.

From March 30 to April 15, Mercury is in Pisces. Mercury retrogrades into his sign of fall, thus, communication can be extra hard as the messenger is not only retro but drowning in subjectivity. Talk and write from your heart rather than mind. Great for intuition and applying imagination to overcome challenges. While regular communications might experience glitches, channeling, intuition and synchronicities abound.

From March 30 to October 22, Neptune enters Aries for the first time in 165 years. Confusion can lead to war, be extra careful of fanaticism or aggression triggered by propaganda of misinformation. Watch your immune system, inflammation, and your head. Once again, the theme of intuition and imagination is enhanced. There could be deception and illusion coming from neighbors, siblings, or roommates. Read every document and contract many times before you sign anything.

APRIL

Between April 5–7, the celestial lovers meet again. Venus is Barbie and Mars in water sign Cancer is Ken, the "simply beach" dude. These are great days for romance, increasing your income from talents you are passionate about, and experiencing better relationships with significant others as well as brothers and sisters in arms.

From April 5 to 10, Venus conjuncts Saturn, your ruler. While this aspect can introduce you to someone older that could be helpful with finances and developing your talents. A time to reassess your primary relationships and how you make money.

On April 8 Mercury finally goes direct and you can begin signing documents and starting new projects. This is great for all your businesses and communications. Between April 7–16 Mercury trine Mars and that could give a kick forward to your projects and business.

April 13 is the Full Moon in Libra. This is the day of liberation, coming out of constriction and negativity and marching towards your Promised Land. It is a magical Full Moon where you might connect to your inner Moses, guardian angel, or higher self. This lunation can create tension between home and career.

April 14 is a dramatic day when Saturn conjuncts the North Node in Pisces. Positive interactions with groups of powerful individuals or people who are older. You are downloading some gifts or connections from previous lives. Good for joining new groups and organizations that have long term goals.

From April 16 to May 10 Mercury transits in Aries, speeding things up but also showing signs of impatience. Words can easily be weaponized so be extra careful. Sanity is returning to your home and family, and it is a great time for feeling safe again.

From April 18 to June 17 Mars enters Leo bringing about a great deal of courage and a call for adventure. Great for entertainment, sports, creativity, and reconnecting to your inner child. A wonderful time for investments, rekindling your passion, intimacy and sexuality. A wonderful time to work with other people's talents and money.

On April 19 the Sun enters Taurus and will remain there until May 20. This month you are to indulge your six senses. It is a good month to tap into your artistic talents and perhaps discover new ones. The Sun's transit in a fellow earth sign is wonderful news for you and can bring about love, creativity, happiness, as well as reconnection to a sport or hobby. Romance is in the air as well as an improved connection to your kids or children in general.

Between April 22–24, as the Sun square the rulers of Scorpio—Mars and Pluto, take extra heed. This can bring about a great deal of letting go, death, and intense sexuality. Watch your steps these days, things can turn ugly or violent.

April 27 is the exalted New Moon in Taurus. A great time to start a new artistic or financial project. Spend time in nature, connect to your senses and do something that can symbolize rooting yourself. This trend continues April 30 as Venus enters Aries until June 6. There could be a bit more conflict and aggression in your primary relationships. In her sign of exile, Venus might be somewhat snappy and can cause hasty decisions and actions with finances and love. A possibility for a new love or a new creative project.

MAY

Between May 1 to May 3, Venus conjuncts Neptune and infuses us with romance, creativity, art, improved finances, and intuition. Use this mystical touch to manifest a new relationship in your life or a new artistic project.

From May 10 to May 26, Mercury enters Taurus, which can bring a sense of worry and anxiety. However, it is a good time to communicate and market your talents and gifts. Speak your mind without attachment or inflexibility. This is a wonderful transit in a fellow earth sign that promises a renewed connection to your children, romantic partner, or creative endeavor.

May 12 is the Full Moon in Scorpio, and while the Moon is fallen, it is still a great time for shadow work, dealing with temptation, and discovering the light within you. Because the Moon falls on the 22nd (Master Number) degree of Scorpio, you can build something out of the rubble of an older project or relationship. In this lunation you feel the tug of war between "mine" and "yours." There could be conflicts arising with your partner over shared resources.

Between May 17–18, the Sun conjuncts Uranus and everyone's IQ is getting a temporary elevation. A fantastic day for humor, jumping into the unknown, and embracing the original and innovative. Spend time with friends or in a group.

From May 20 to June 21, the Sun enters Gemini, and you are channeling the spirit of intelligence, communication, and bridge-building. This is a great month for business, contracts, improving relationships with relatives, roommates, neighbors, and people you consider siblings. The next 30 days are a blessing for your work, health, and ability to serve yourself and others.

Between May 20 to 24, Venus trines Mars once again. Romance, love, harmony (the daughter of Venus and Mars), is around you as well as an ability to see people's beautiful side. Great time for making money from things you are passionate about.

Between May 25 to September 1 Saturn enters Aries. Saturn in the ram's sign wishes to rectify how you deal with your identity, body, anger, and vitality. This is a time to focus on your home, family, real estate, and fix issues that come from your genetics, ancestral karma and traumas that run down the generation. There could be a need for relocation, change homes, commit to creating a family or having children.

Between May 26 to June 8 Mercury enters Gemini. Mercury is back to his domicile, and he is happy to unpack and share his intelligence. Information, opportunities, connections, and words flow effortlessly. This transit can help get things done with your work, diet, and health. This trend peaks on the New Moon in Gemini taking place May 27. A great day to start something new in connection with communication, networking, businesses, marketing, sales, and written projects. This New Moon is blessed by Pluto and Neptune, making it possible for you to link passion and reason, emotions and intellect. A great deal of intimacy and a possibility for a lover coming into your life.

JUNE

Between June 4 to 8, Venus, Jupiter, Mercury, and Mars are blessing us and each other. Windows of positive opportunities can improve sales, communication, writing, health, education, and art.

On June 6 Venus enters Taurus until July 4. The goddess of love is lending a helping hand in matters of art, finances, relationships, and security. You will experience your five senses in a much stronger way than usual, perhaps getting a glimpse of the sixth one as well. A great time to connect to an artistic project or a talent, reconnect with your gifts and translate them into income. An opportune time for creativity, falling in love, engaging in a hobby or sports that is associated with a partner, and increasing your happiness and fun.

On June 8, Mercury transits Cancer until June 26. Great for healing relationships with family members. Don't be afraid to express your emotions. The transit of the messenger of the gods and goddesses in your opposite sign brings clarity and improved communications with partners in work and life.

Between June 9 to 10 Mercury squares Neptune and Saturn and Venus squares Pluto. A bundle of challenging aspects come together. There is deception, lies, theft, and disinformation. Monkey mind is out of the cage, causing us to jump from one subject or project to the other. Breakups, manipulation, and discord with people of power.

On June 9 Jupiter enters Cancer and will stay there until June 30, 2026. This is a wonderful time for attracting, maintaining, and harmonizing relationships both in work and personal life. An opportune time to get married, overcome challenges posed by enemies or competitors, and win court cases. In addition, this is a great year for real estate, healing familial relationships, connecting to fortune and abundance, and opening new doors. Be careful of overdoing and over commitments.

From June 10 until August 23, Saturn, your ruler, conjuncts with Neptune. While your intuition, ability to meditate, and connect to your dreams are enhanced, so does your self-destructiveness, addictions, and escapism. Tread carefully, watch out for fanaticism or being too attached to your beliefs. On June 11, the Full Moon is in Sagittarius. A wonderful time to complete a cycle of learning and preparation for something new. Great for travel, especially by water or to a location close to the water. Mars gives a boost of energy to the aspect. You will be flooded with memories from past lives as well as messages from dreams.

From June 17, Mars enters Virgo until August 6. Mars in Virgo gets things done. He is the watchmaker, the engineer, the organizer—here to protect and serve. Conflicts can arise if you are too critical of yourself and others. A good time for diets and a new health regiment. You can make things happen if you stick to a strict routine. One of the best transits for education as well as traveling. Be careful of needless conflicts with in-laws.

From June 21 the Sun transits Cancer until July 22. Happy Solstice! Open your heart to your family. Perhaps you might meet family members from past lives. A great month to renovate and remodel your home, relocate, move in with someone, get a new property, or start a family. This transit helps you shine on your partnerships and improve your relationships with your significant others. This trend is peaking on the New Moon in Cancer, July 25, providing a new beginning that involves home and family, real estate, security, and emotional support. With Jupiter, exalted in Cancer, blessing the union of the Sun and Moon, this is a great time to start new projects. Besides Pluto, there are no planets retrograde, so full swim ahead!

From June 26 until September 3, Mercury is in Leo. This Mercury transit can be extremely creative, entertaining, and exciting. An opportune time for investments as well as connecting and increasing your passion, intimacy, and sexuality.

Between June 27 to 28, Mercury trines Saturn and Neptune. This is a good aspect for making long-term plans and bringing some sanity to a mad mad month. Good for marketing, writing, and sales. It is also a great time for prophetic dreams and practical intuition.

JULY

On July 4 Venus conjuncts Uranus and while relationships can be exciting, they can also show an unpredictable side. There is a need for freedom and exploration of new frontiers with your finances, relationships, and artistic expression. Embrace the original and unique. Be extra aware there could be volatility in the market.

From July 4 Venus flirts with Gemini until July 30 and the next few weeks can bring you in contact with a potential lover or partner at work. Art and communication come together, a great time for marketing, sales, design, and making new connections. A great time to implement design, art, and creativity into your workplace and routine. This transit can also help improve relationships with clients and coworkers. However, be careful with your diet, a tendency to medicate yourself with food can arise.

From July 7 to November 8, Uranus enters Gemini, and your IQ is augmented. This transit can bring disruptions in your health and work; however, it is also a transit of awakening into new possibilities. Be extra careful of mishaps and accidents.

July 10 is the Full Moon in Capricorn. The Full Moon can bring about a bit of opposition between home and career. The Moon is exiled in Capricorn and can create a sense of emotionality and longing for a paradise lost. However, Mars is sending his troupes to help you, and with a bit of action, determination, and a clear mission, you can disperse the emotional confusion of the Full Moon and get things done. This is your Full Moon and brings tension between your needs and those of your partner.

From July 17 to August 12, Mercury is retrograde in Leo. Avoid signing docs and starting new projects. Especially watch your relationships and communication with kids, lovers, and people with big egos. Avoid making big investments. Intimate partners from the past might return, it doesn't mean you need to let them in.

From July 22 to August 22, Sun enters Leo. Engage in creative, joyful, and heartwarming activities. Generosity, nobility, chivalry, sportsmanship, and enthusiasm are guiding us this month. A great time to connect to a hobby or a new sport. The Sun is asking you to go down into the Underworld and do a bit of shadow work. A great time for therapy, investigation, research, and finding lost objects and talents.

Between July 23–25, the Sun trines Saturn and Neptune, creating a wonderful flow and help with vitality, intuition, healing, and the ability to bring some new structure into your lives. This is a glorious aspect, and you can benefit from creative visualizations, meditation, dance and self-expression. Practical messages from dreams, meditations, and visions are coming into your consciousness.

On July 24 the New Moon is in Leo. This is not an easy New Moon since it is smack opposite to Pluto and can bring about a confrontation with a powerful figure in your life whose motivations are unclear. With Mercury retrograding in Leo, it is not the best time to start something new, however, you could initiate a project you already tried before and failed to complete.

From July 31 to August 25, Venus transits in Cancer. Marriage, social events with family members, as well as harmonious flow with family members. One of the best times for your partnerships and contractual relationships. A wonderful time to heal relationships with your significant others. A new love might come into your life.

AUGUST

The month starts with a hard aspect on August 1 and 2 between Venus, Saturn and Neptune. Watch out for deception, illusions, and fantasies in your primary relationships as well as financial dealings. Rapport with people who are older than you can be fraught with discord. Try a new approach to an old problem.

On August 6 Mars enters Libra and stays there until September 22. There could be some legal issues but also a good time for compromise and finding resolutions to conflicts. Nevertheless, Mars can help you get a raise, assert your position in your career, and initiate new projects. You are gathering your troupes to conquer something new. Between August 7 to 9, Mars trines Uranus bringing about brilliance and originality. Search for innovative and original solutions. Connections with friends can thrive. Action is guided by new approaches.

Watch it between August 8 to 10 as Mars opposites both Saturn and Neptune. Accidents, mishaps, and physical challenges, especially with Mercury retrograding. Stay away from arguments with superiors. The opposition with Neptune adds more hardships to already difficult few days. Stay away from stormy seas (metaphysically and physically speaking).

August 9 is the Full Moon in Aquarius. You might feel a push and pull between the need to spend time with lovers or your children and the needs of your friends or company. A time to balance your talents and money with that of your partner.

On August 12, Mercury finally goes direct in Leo. You can now start plowing ahead, especially since on August 12 and 13, Venus conjuncts Jupiter, which is one of the best aspects this year. Luck, flow in finances, new relationships and maybe a novel love.

Between August 12 to October 27, Uranus trines Pluto. A powerful aspect that can bring about transformation through technology, science, social movements, and revolutions. Changes in government that can, in the long run, bring more prosperity.

From August 22 to September 22 the Sun transits in Virgo. You are asked to focus and refine our diet, health, routine, work, and how you serve. An ideal time to eliminate impediments to health and productivity. A great time for travel, education, and fighting for what you believe in. This is especially true on August 23 when the New Moon is in Virgo. It is recommended to reorganize your home and office or home office. A bit of chaos is added by a square to Uranus that can awaken the critic and perfectionist in you. Try to channel these propensities into something productive at work.

On August 25, Venus transits in Leo until September 19. The planet of love in the sign of romance is always good news. Just be careful of extra marital affairs. It is a very creative time with your inner child fully active and playful. Try to reconnect to a hobby you had in your teens. An opportune time to help other people tap into their financial potential and talents. You are now attracting people and opportunities, as your sex appeal is higher than normal.

SEPTEMBER

On September 1 Saturn returns to Pisces until February 13, 2026. Confusion, floods, conflicts about water or in locations that are close to seas, lakes, and rivers. A time to ground your mystical practices, dreams, and intuition. The last transit of Saturn, the rectifier, in the area of your chart that is associated with communication, relatives, and businesses. It is a perfect time to add discipline, planning, and strategy to all forms of messaging and information. You are fixing your messages, how you deliver them, and to whom.

From September 2 to September 18, Mercury transits into Virgo. Sales, ideas, and information flow effortlessly. A great time for editing projects that need precision, micromanagement, organizing, and purification. A wonderful time for detoxing and a cleanse. It is also a period you can dedicate to traveling, building bridges with foreigners, mass media, as well as all forms of education.

September 7 is the Full Moon in Pisces and a Lunar Eclipse. Momentum builds towards closure especially with work and personal affairs. Now's the time to harvest the fruits of your labor from March/April. Mercury provides a touch of reason to an otherwise very emotional lunation.

From September 18, Mercury transits into Libra until October 6. This Mercury wants peace, compromise, and beauty. A great time for healing relationships and harmonizing the workplace as well as how you relate to people in your career. Art and business are coming together. You can revamp your website, redesign your logo, and come up with new ways to brand yourself and your projects.

From September 19, Venus transits Virgo until October 13. You might feel over critical about your talents or your partner's as well as feel the criticism of others. Good time to be frugal, balance your expenses and income. Engage in study, teaching., and pursuit of justice. Relationships with in-laws can improve.

September 21 is the Solar Eclipse in Virgo. A great time to balance your diet, start a new work project, and get the energy you need to reach the finish line. The Eclipse is involved with a beneficial aspect, bringing their energies together: Pluto (power and intimacy); Saturn (focus); Neptune (imagination and intuition); Uranus (innovation).

On September 22, the Sun enters Libra until October 23, marking the Equinox! As one of the four sacred days in the astrological calendar, commemorate it by celebrating relationships, justice, beauty, and art. Over the next 30 days, you should embody Libra traits—diplomacy, balance, and attentiveness to partners. A great time for career advancement and success in your worldly ambition.

On September 22, Mars enters Scorpio until November 4. A wonderful time to collaborate on big projects that demand a lot of energy and resources. Passion, intimacy and sexuality are on the rise. Great for physical activities in water or reconnecting to sports you are passionate about. Try to immerse in some form of research and investigation. A time to assert your position in your company and take the initiative.

Between September 23–25, tread cautiously as Mars squares Pluto. Aggression and manipulative folks are around you. Take extra heed in general. Actions can be easily misconstrued.

OCTOBER

On October 6 Mercury transits into Scorpio until October 29. An ideal period for research, finding lost objects or people, and expressing intimacy. It's a good time to move on, let bygones be bygones, bury the zombies in your life, and explore investments and collaborations with other people's assets and talents. Mercury can be your private investigator and expose hidden information. A good time to heal issues with friends or people you work with you in the same company. Update and upgrade your digital environment.

October 7 is the Full Moon in Aries. This Full Moon, bordering on a lunar eclipse, is a tad challenging. With Chiron's involvement, it's an occasion for learning, teaching, and shamanistic journeys. While there's an aggressive undertone, it's a good moment to conclude matters and move on. There could be conflicts between family obligations and career responsibilities.

Between October 11 to 14, Venus is opposite Saturn and Neptune. This can be hard on your relationships and or finances. There is an emotional frustration with partners, especially long-term ones. Illusions as well as dependency and codependency and some disappointment with someone close to you. However, you can use this aspect to connect mysticism and art.

From October 13 to November 6, Venus returns to her sign, Libra, and can help us connect to beauty, diplomacy, justice, relationship, and harmony. You will feel this transit the strongest in your career and professional life as well as with your superiors. This is especially strong between October 14–15 as Venus receives much praise from Pluto (intimacy, sexuality, power) and Uranus (innovation, technology, friendships). This is another kite that carries us upward with Venus (finances, relationships) leading the way. This is a powerful time for igniting, transforming, balancing and solidifying partnerships in work and personal life.

The New Moon in Libra takes place October 21. Dubbed the "Moon of Peace," the Libra New Moon is a great time to start a relationship or an art project. However, both Jupiter and Pluto are squaring off with the Sun and Moon, creating uncomfortable situations. Be extra cautious and focus on breathwork and meditation. A great time to start something new in your career.

On October 22, Neptune returns for the last time to his sign, Pisces, until January 27, 2026. A great time to start meditation practice that can be facilitated by the ruler of mysticism. Dreams, imagination, channeling, mediumship, poetry, and art are enhanced, as well as your intuition. Make an effort to listen to your intuition, connect to poetry, imagination, and adhere to messages coming from your dreams.

On October 23, the Sun enters Scorpio until November 22. Focus on being true to your passion. It is a month of healing, transformation, magic, occult, and assisting others in their talents, finances, and endeavors. A wonderful month to form friendships and improve relationships with clients and colleagues.

Around October 26 Mars conjuncts Lilith, please be extra careful today as the Mother of Demons hired an assassin. This is a violent and aggressive aspect. Tread cautiously, especially with friends and clients.

On October 29, Mercury enters Sagittarius until November 19. You might feel a bit absent-minded and distracted. A good time for traveling and doing business with foreigners. Stick to the truth and avoid liars and half-truths. Great for education and publishing. An opportune time to focus on therapy and receiving messages from the beyond.

NOVEMBER

From November 4 to December 15, Mars enters Sagittarius. A call for adventure, as well as an expedition. Your Mars wants you to conquer, hunt, and expend your knowledge. It is an Indiana Jones aspect. There could be flashback from PTSD from past lives or ancestors' traumas family.

November 5 is the Full Moon exalted in Taurus. An opportune time to bring something into completion. Since the lunation is on the 13th degree of Scorpio, it carries a powerful connection to love. Spend time in nature and indulge your five senses. There could be tension between your need to spend time with your children or lovers and your community or friends.

On November 6, Venus enters Scorpio until November 30. This transit can make you feel alone or unwanted, possessive as well as jealous. However, it is a good time to focus on your partner's money and talents rather than your own. Look into your investments as there might be a need to make some adjustments. A friend could transform into a lover or vis versa.

From November 8 to April 26, 2026, Uranus returns for the last time to Taurus. Changes in finances, fluctuations in cryptocurrency, new ways of expressing artistic talents. There could be an unexpected pregnancy, or a sudden love affair. Be careful of taking unnecessary risks.

From November 9 to December 1 Mercury is stationary and retrograde. This retrograde dances on the cusp of Sagittarius where he is overthinking to Scorpio where he is secretive. Avoid signing documents, starting new projects, and initiating anything unless you tried to do so before and failed to accomplish it. Be extra careful with this retrograde since it can create a sense of isolation, sadness, and abandonment. Deep meditations and cardio can help overcome morbidness.

On November 19, Mercury enters Scorpio until December 10. Mercury returns to Scorpio as he retrogrades back into the underworld. Good for investigations and finding lost objects and people. A friend you had a falling out with could come back into your life but watch for misunderstandings with members of your community or company.

On November 20, we have the New Moon in Scorpio. A great time to investigate your passions, what you really want in life, what you wish to transform, and start today. A good New Moon to initiate projects that need shared resources, talents, or funding. However, since Mercury is retro, you can only start things you already tried in the past and failed to bring to completion. An opportune time to initiate healing, therapy, a shamanistic journey, or an investigation. The New Moon is getting a boost from Saturn, Jupiter, and Neptune, which bless this lunation with structure and focus, imagination and inspiration, and a great deal of open-mindedness.

On November 22, the Sun transits in Sagittarius until December 21. Sagittarius is the time of the year when you have the strongest connection to your higher self or guardian angel. This is a month for teaching, mentoring, learning, speaking your truth, mass media, publishing, and connecting to foreigners, and in-laws. A time to go deeper into the mystical realms, meditation, past lifetimes, and imagination.

November 23 is an interesting day when the Sun trines Neptune; Mercury trines Jupiter and Saturn; Jupiter trines Saturn. This day can further your goals in almost all aspects of your life.

On November 28 Venus conjuncts Lilith. Be extra careful with all your relationships and partners in work or in personal life. A three-sided relationship might form around you. Be beware of stalkers, gossip, enemies, and lawsuits.

From November 30 until December 24 Venus transits in Sagittarius. It is a great time for connecting to educators, foreigners, explore investments and possibilities from travel and abroad. A good time to improve relationships with in-laws. Talents and artistic abilities from previous lives are making an entrance into your life. You also might meet people you have known in past lifetimes.

DECEMBER

December 4 is the Full Moon in Gemini. An optimal day to finalize projects. As this is the year's last Full Moon. There could be tension between the need to rest and obligation at work.

On December 10, Mercury finally goes direct. A good time for traveling and businesses abroad as well as for philosophy.

From December 15, Mars transits in Capricorn until January 26, 2026. Mars in your sign is exalted and all too eager to get things done. You are attracting loads of energy and can focus on your body, leadership, and initiation. Make sure you give Mars a mission—something you need help conquering and or mastering. It is a good aspect for leadership and initiation.

December 20 is the New Moon in Sagittarius. A difficult New Moon with Neptune and Saturn sending squares all over the place. Not the best time to start new projects. Be careful of aggression and anger. A sense of war approaching. Lay low and be vigilant.

From December 20, Lilith enters Sagittarius for nine months. There could be discord with students and teachers, as well as foreigners. Take extra care when traveling. Fear of the foreigner, misinformation, disinformation. The Mother of Demons can empower your hidden enemies, so be extra vigilant and stay away from gossip or defaming.

On December 21 the Sun enters Capricorn and will stay there until January 20, 2026. Happy Solstice and happy birthday! The ensuing month calls for Capricorn-like discipline and focus. Strategize the year ahead, bearing in mind that patience is vital. Along with Mars in your sign, the Sun helps you shine your skills and abilities. In addition, from December

24 Venus joins the Sun and Mars and transits in Capricorn until January 17, 2026. This transit of Venus can help you improve relationships with people who are older, long-term partnerships, as well as bosses and superiors. A time to connect art and design to your professional life. You look and feel gorgeous. A wonderful time to rebrand and reimagine yourself.

AQUARIUS AND AQUARIUS RISING: I KNOW (THAT I DON'T KNOW)

Money Can't Buy Me Love (But it sure can other things)

General Trends: Saturn, the rectifier, continues fixing and focusing on your values, talents, skills, and financial responsibilities. In the middle of the year, he would also want you to focus on how you communicate, your business endeavors, and finding the message you need to deliver to the world. In the first part of the year your expansion comes from children, love, and hobbies, while the second part of 2025 promises expansion at work, in health, as well as the ability to serve others. With the Dragon coming into the sector of your chart relating to money, you can expect opportunities to increase your finances as long as you stick to your values and believe you deserve abundance.

JANUARY

Between January 1–5, Mars is opposite his Scorpio coruler, Pluto, which is not a promising beginning of the year. In addition, Mars is retrograde therefore, take extra care on the first few days of the year. There is an opposition between your will and that of your community, company, or friends. People around you might experience paranoia, resort to manipulation, conflict and aggression.

On January 3, Venus puts on her swimming suit and dives into Pisces until February 4. This mystical plunge is great news especially for your finances, connection to talents, sharing your skills, and receiving awards for your hard work. Creative visualization focused on improving your income can be extremely successful.

On January 6, Mars retrogrades into Cancer until April 18. This is a time to take the initiative in your workplace as well as with your health and diet. Time to demand the raise you deserve, take a leadership role, and assume more responsibility. In addition, conflict can arise with family members.

On January 8 Mercury enters Capricorn until January 28, and this means serious thought, discipline study, lessons coming from mature and experienced figures. Slow your thought, speech, and writing, and be mindful of every word. Great for furthering your career goals and forging long-term plans. This is a good time for therapy, going deeper into your subconscious and connecting to skills and people from previous lives.

January 13 is the Full Moon in Cancer, where she loves to be. It could get emotional and a bit aggressive with family and loved ones due to the opposition of retro Mars and Pluto. There could be tension between the need to rest and responsibilities at work.

Between January 18–19, Venus conjuncts Saturn. Finances, values, and your relationships are being scrutinized and audited. This is not necessarily a bad aspect as Venus is exalted and Saturn can ground your talents as well as help you use your gifts in a practical way. Whatever is going on in your personal and professional relationships are galvanized and crystallized, for good or bad.

On January 19 the Sun enters Aquarius until February 18. Happy birthday! A time to spend with friends, community, as well as immerse yourself in science, technology, and innovation. All aspects of your life can shine forth this month. An opportune time to rebrand yourself and invest in self-development.

Between January 25–26, as Venus trines Mars, the cosmic lovers can bring a new relationship into your life or help you harmonize partnerships you already have.

From January 28 until February 14, Mercury transits in Aquarius, and ideas flow fast as well as new friendships form. A wonderful time to shine your brilliance and ideas. Your communication skills are enhanced—the Universe is responding favorably. January 29 is also the New Moon in Aquarius and Chinese New Year. Time to welcome to the Year of the Earth Snake. Jupiter is blessing this New Moon with wisdom and synchronicity. A great time to start a study group. A great time to start something new that could connect you to your body, image, looks, and health. This is your time to shine.

On January 29, the North Node retrogrades into Pisces until August 19, 2026, for the first time in 19 years. Right on the New Moon in Aquarius, the North Node aka "Dragon," is retrograding into the sign of mysticism, intuition, and imagination. For the next 18 months we are asked to practice empathy, meditation, any form of trance or movement practice (yoga, dance, or martial arts). This period can also help you tap into new talents and invest in your skills. However, the South Node will be in Virgo asking us to let go of criticism, perfectionism, and overanalytical tendencies.

FEBRUARY

On February 4, Venus enters Aries, until March 27. Watch impulsiveness with your finances. Be mindful of how you communicate, write, post, text, or tweet.

Between February 6–12, Mars trines Saturn bringing a weeklong of constructive action, stable effort, and sustained passion. This aspect can give you the endurance to complete a marathon or two.

February 12 is the Full Moon in Leo, and you might feel the pull and push between the gravitational forces of your children or romantic partner versus friends or your company. The square with Uranus can cause disruption and lunacy to this lunation. There could be tension rising between you and your partners in work or life.

On Valentine's Day (February 14), Mercury enters Pisces until March 3. Communications can be a bit challenged while intuition and mediumship are on the rise. Trust your gut feeling rather than your brain. Make sure to use the words "I feel" or "I imagine" or "I believe," instead of "I think." This is a good time to get intellectual clarity regarding your income, finances, and talents. This trend is supported by the Sun entering Pisces from February 18 until March 20's Equinox. Imagination, dance, movement, dreaming, meditation, intuition, mysticism, and empathy are heightened. Make sure to guard your boundaries and avoid addictions or self-destructive tendencies.

The month ends with the New Moon in Pisces on February 28. A great day to start something new that involves your imagination, photography, movement, yoga and meditation. There is a tendency to absorb negativity from others so watch what you take in. Be careful of overdoing or illusions. A wonderful time to start something new in relation to your talents and skill development.

MARCH

March 1–April 14 Venus stands still and then retrogrades in Aries, her sign of exile. Avoid getting married, starting new relationships, getting engaged, starting lawsuits, signing partnerships agreements. However, exes or lovers from previous lives or this life might return. Be extra mindful with finances, as people tend to lose money or make bad investments. In this retrograde pay extra attention to your communications as well as how you deal with relatives, siblings, roommates, and neighbors. Avoid signing contracts if possible.

On March 3, Mercury enters Aries until March 30. Mercury can be a bit impatient when in Aries and favors practical, short, and concise communication.

Between March 11–13, Sun conjunct Saturn while Mercury conjunct Venus. Seriousness, focus, discipline and planning can bring tactical or strategical accomplishments. A good time to improve relations with superiors.

March 14, Pi Day, is also the first Lunar Eclipse of the year. The Full Moon in precise and analytical Virgo. A great time to bring a project to an end, as well as focus on diet, service, and combining your analytical and wholistic sides. There could be tension between your assets and those of your partner.

March 14–April 8 Mercury is stationary and retrograde. Since it is happening in Aries this month, be extra careful with anger, impulsiveness, and rush decisions. This retrograde can be extra hard on your business, contracts, and communication, so take heed.

On March 17, the Sun conjuncts North Node. A day to access skills and knowledge from past lifetimes. There could be an encounter with powerful and successful individuals or groups that can further your goals.

March 20 is the Equinox and the Sun transits into Aries until April 19. Happy New Year! A time to focus on your body, health, leadership, as well as your brand and image. Start a writing project or a new business you tried in the past but failed to complete.

On March 27, Lilith enters Scorpio until December 20. Emotional intensity, powerful desires, fascination with the forbidden, shadow work, possessiveness, and jealousy. In addition there are power struggles, manipulation, abuse, distrust, and criminality. The dark side of the Force. Stay clear of any form of gossip. A good time to place a heap of salt in the four corners of your bedroom as protection against negativity. Watch out for enemies or saboteurs in your career. There could be a boss or a superior that is negative or difficult.

March 29 is the first solar eclipse of the year, and she shines upon Aries. Be mindful of unnecessary aggression and impulsiveness.

From March 30 to April 15, Mercury is in Pisces. Mercury retrogrades into his sign of fall, thus, communication can be extra hard as the messenger is not only retro but drowning in subjectivity. Talk and write from your heart rather than mind. Great for intuition and applying imagination to overcome challenges. A good time to reconnect to talents you abandoned in the past.

From March 30 to October 22, Neptune enters Aries for the first time in 165 years. Confusion can lead to war, be extra careful of fanaticism or aggression triggered by propaganda of misinformation. Watch your immune system, inflammation, and your head. Your intuition is off the roof and can provide you with a lot of psychic hits. However, there could be issues with relatives, especially siblings and their children or family.

APRIL

Between April 5–7, the celestial lovers meet again. Venus is Barbie and Mars, in the water sign Cancer, is Ken, the "simply beach" dude. These are great days for romance, increasing your income from talents you are passionate about, and better relationships with significant others as well as brothers and sisters in arms.

From April 5 to 10, Venus conjuncts Saturn. While this aspect can introduce you to someone older that could be helpful with finance and developing your talents, this conjunction can also sit heavy over all your relationships. A time to reassess your primary relationships and how you make money.

On April 8 Mercury finally goes direct and you can begin signing documents and starting new projects. This is great news for all aspects of your finances. Between April 7–16, Mercury trines Mars and that could give a kick forward to your projects and business.

April 13 is the Full Moon in Libra. This is the day of liberation, coming out of constriction and negativity and marching towards your Promised Land. It is a magical Full Moon where you might connect to your inner Moses, guardian angel, or higher self. Communications that were going through a great deal of scrutiny are now going to flow easily.

April 14 is a dramatic day when Saturn conjuncts the North Node in Pisces. Positive interactions with groups of powerful individuals or people who are older. You are downloading gifts or connections from previous lives. Good for joining new groups and organizations that share your long-term goals.

From April 16 to May 10 Mercury transits in Aries, speeding things up but also showing signs of impatience. Words can easily be weaponized so be extra careful. A wonderful time to start new businesses as well as writing projects.

From April 18 to June 17 Mars enters Leo bringing about a great deal of courage and a call for adventure. Great for entertainment, sports, creativity, and reconnecting to your inner child. Watch out for needless conflicts with neighbors, roommates, and siblings.

On April 19 the Sun enters Taurus and will remain there until May 20. This month you are to indulge your six senses and connect to Mother Nature. It is a good month to tap into your artistic talents and perhaps discover new ones. This is a month to focus on your home and family. A wonderful time for relocation, remodeling, and purchasing real estate.

Between April 22-24, as the Sun square the rulers of Scorpio—Mars and Pluto, take extra heed. This can bring about a great deal of letting go, death, and intense sexuality. Watch your steps these days, things can turn ugly or violent.

April 27 is the exalted New Moon in Taurus. A great time to start a new artistic or financial project. Spend time in nature, connect to your senses and do something that can symbolize rooting yourself. A great time to start a family, get pregnant, and initiate a project at home.

On April 30, Venus enters Aries until June 6. Art and communication come together. However, Venus might be somewhat snappy and can cause hasty decisions and actions with finances and love. However, it is a good time for sales, and creative writing.

MAY

Between May 1 to May 3, Venus conjuncts Neptune and infuses us with romance, creativity, art, improved finances and intuition.

From May 10 to May 26, Mercury enters Taurus, which can bring a sense of worry and anxiety. However, it is a good time to communicate and market your talents and gifts. Speak your mind without attachment or inflexibility. This transit is good for real estate transactions, as well as improved relationships with family members.

May 12 is the Full Moon in Scorpio, and while the Moon is fallen, it is still a great time for shadow work, dealing with temptation and rediscovering the light in you. Because the Moon falls on the 22nd (Master Number) degree of Scorpio, you can build something out of the rubble of an older project or relationship. In this lunation you feel the tug of war between "mine" and "yours." There could be tension between the need to spend time at home and career demands.

Between May 17–18, the Sun conjuncts Uranus and everyone's IQ is getting a temporary elevation. A fantastic day for humor, jumping into the unknown, and embracing the original and innovative. Spend time with friends or in a group.

From May 20 to June 21, the Sun enters Gemini, and you are channeling the spirit of intelligence, communication, and bridge-building. This is a great month for business, contracts, improving relationships with relatives, roommates, neighbors, and people you consider siblings. These 30 days are great for love, happiness, creativity, embracing your inner child as well as improving relations with children.

Between May 20 to 24, Venus trines Mars once again. Romance, love, harmony (the daughter of Venus and Mars), is around you as well as an ability to see people's beautiful side. Great time for making money from things you are passionate about.

On May 24, as Mercury conjunct Uranus, your modern ruler, we have a day of ingeniousness. You can get new insights and ideas that can help you in business, communication, and better connect to people around you.

Between May 25 to September 1 Saturn enters Aries. Saturn in Aries rectifies how you deal with your identity, body, anger, and vitality. A period when you must connect to your message, what do you wish to say, communicate, write, and what form these communications take. If you were a country, you would be investing in your infrastructure. You might have to take extra responsibility over your siblings, relatives, and possible issues with neighbors.

Between May 26 to June 8 Mercury enters Gemini. Mercury is back to his domicile, and he is happy to unpack and share his gifts. Information, opportunities, connections, and words flow effortlessly. A wonderful time for creative writing as well as businesses that involve entertainment, sports, creativity, and children. This trend peaks on the May 27 New Moon in Gemini. A great day to start something new in connection with communication, networking, businesses, marketing, sales, and written projects. This New Moon is blessed by Pluto and Neptune, making it possible for you to link passion and reason, emotions and intellect. A great deal of intimacy and a possibility for a lover coming into your life. A wonderful time to start a new hobby, conceive, and start a new physical activity. Have fun!

JUNE

Between June 4 to 8, Venus, Jupiter, Mercury, and Mars are blessing us and each other. Windows of positive opportunities can improve sales, communication, writing, health, education, and art.

On June 6 Venus enters Taurus until July 4. The goddess of love is lending a helping hand in matters of art, finances, relationships, and security. You will experience your five senses in a much stronger way than usual, perhaps getting a glimpse of the sixth one as well. A great time to connect to an artistic project or a talent, reconnect with your gifts and translate them into income. The best time of the year to beautify, remodel, and improve your home or office.

On June 8, Mercury transits Cancer until June 26. Great for healing relationships with family members. Don't be afraid to express your emotions. An opportune time for work, marketing yourself and your project and improving relationships with employees, clients, and coworkers.

Between June 9 to 10, Mercury squares Neptune and Saturn and Venus squares Pluto. A bundle of challenging aspects come together. There is deception, lies, theft, and disinformation. Monkey mind is out of the cage, causing you to jump from one subject or project to the other. Breakups, manipulation, and discord with people of power.

On June 9 Jupiter enters Cancer and will stay there until June 30, 2026. A good transit in time of need. This is a great year for real estate, healing familial relationships, connecting to fortune and abundance, and opening new doors. Be careful of overdoing and over commitments. This yearlong transit of Jupiter can take your work life, your health, diet, and opportunities to serve to the next level, infusing you with purpose and sense of worth. Try to increase the amount of water intake. Watch your liver, thighs, and hips.

From June 10 until August 23, Saturn conjuncts with Neptune. While your intuition, ability to meditate, and connect to your dreams are enhanced, so does your self-destructiveness, addictions, and escapism. Tread carefully, watch out for fanaticism or being too attached to your beliefs.

On June 11, the Full Moon is in Sagittarius. A blessed Full Moon in a challenging month. Jupiter, ruler of Sagittarius is exalted, creating what is called Mutual Reception with the Moon, which is auspicious. A wonderful time to complete a cycle of learning and preparation for something new. Great for travel, especially by water or to a location close to the water. Mars gives a boost of energy to the aspect. There could be tension rising between the need to spend time with your children or lover and the demands of your friends or company.

From June 17, Mars enters Virgo until August 6. Mars in Virgo gets things done. He is the watchmaker, the engineer, the organizer—here to protect and serve. Conflicts can arise if you are too critical of yourself and others. A good time for diets and a new health regiment. You can make things happen if you stick to a strict routine. A powerful period of increased passion, sexuality, and drive.

From June 21 the Sun transits Cancer until July 22. Happy Solstice! Open your heart to your family, and perhaps you might meet family members from past lives. A great month to focus on your work, diet, and health as the Sun joins Jupiter and brings a new purpose into your workplace. This trend peaks on June 25, the New Moon is in Cancer, providing a new beginning that involves home and family, real estate, security, and emotional support. With Jupiter, exalted in Cancer, blessing the union of the Sun and Moon, this is a great time to start new projects. Besides Pluto, there are no planets retrograde, so full swim ahead!

From June 26 until September 3, Mercury is in Leo, your opposite sign. This Mercury transit can be extremely creative, entertaining, and exciting. This transit can improve your communication with partners in work and life, however in July it can get a bit testy when Mercury retrogrades.

Between June 27 to 28, Mercury trines Saturn and Neptune. This is a good aspect for making long-term plans and bringing some sanity to a mad mad month. Good for marketing, writing, and sales. It is also a great time for prophetic dreams and practical intuition.

JULY

On July 4 Venus conjuncts Uranus, your ruler, and while relationships can be exciting, they can also show an unpredictable side. There is a need for freedom and exploration of new frontiers with your finances, relationships, and artistic expression. Embrace the original and unique. Be extra aware there could be volatility in the market.

From July 4 Venus flirts with Gemini until July 30 and the next few weeks can bring you in contact with a potential lover or partner at work. Art and communication come together, a great time for marketing, sales, design, and making new connections. The goddess of love in the area of your chart associated with romantic love and creativity is a great option of experiencing love and happiness. A great time to spend with kids, yours and others.

From July 7 to November 8, Uranus enters Gemini, and your IQ is augmented. This is an interesting transit that would become more dominant in 2026. Uranus is the awakener and could bring twists and turns with your romantic love, children, and projects you consider "your babies." If you have kids, they might act more rebelliously. A wonderful time to merge creativity and technology.

July 10 is the Full Moon in Capricorn. This lunation can bring an opposition between home and career. The Moon is exiled in Capricorn and can create a sense of emotionality and longing for a paradise lost. However, Mars is sending his troupes to help us, and with a bit of action, determination, and a clear mission, you can disperse the emotional confusion of the Full Moon and get things done. Watch your health and be mindful of injuries or accidents.

From July 17 to August 12, Mercury is retrograde in Leo. Avoid signing docs and starting new projects. Especially watch your relationships and communication with children, lovers, and people with big egos. These three weeks could be extra challenging with your partners in work and life. Especially between July 21 to 24, when Venus Squares Mars. You might need to exercise compassion towards your significant others and those surrounding you. Don't make rash decisions regarding breakups or unions with partners.

From July 22 to August 22, Sun enters Leo. Engage in creative, joyful, and heartwarming activities. Generosity, nobility, chivalry, sportsmanship, and enthusiasm are guiding us this month. A great time to connect to a hobby or a new sport.

Between July 23–25, the Sun trine Saturn and Neptune creating a wonderful flow and help with vitality, intuition, healing, and the ability to bring some new structure into our lives. This is a glorious aspect, and you can benefit from creative visualizations, meditation, dance and self-expression.

On July 24 the New Moon is in Leo. This is not an easy New Moon since it is smack opposite to Pluto and can bring about a confrontation with a powerful figure in your life whose motivations are unclear. A new process is beginning in your primary relationships.

From July 31 to August 25, Venus transits in Cancer. Marriage, social events with family members, as well as harmonious flow with family members.

AUGUST

The month starts with a hard aspect on August 1 and 2 between Venus, Saturn and Neptune. Watch out for deception, illusions, and fantasies in your primary relationships as well as financial dealings. Not the best time to start a new relationship. Rapport with people who are older than you can be fraught with discord. Try a new approach to an old problem.

On August 6 Mars enters Libra and stays there until September 22. There could be some legal issues but also a good time for compromise and finding resolutions to conflicts. Time for travel and education but be mindful of your relationship with in-laws or your mentors.

Between August 7 to 9, Mars trines Uranus bringing about brilliance and originality. Search for innovative and original solutions. Connections with friends can thrive. Action is guided by new approaches.

Watch it between August 8 to 10 as Mars opposites both Saturn and Neptune. Accidents, mishaps, and physical challenges especially since Mercury is retrograding. Stay away from arguments with superiors. Stay calm and try to do less. The opposition with Neptune adds more hardships to the already difficult few days. Stay away from stormy seas (metaphysically and physically speaking).

August 9 is the Full Moon in Aquarius. You might feel a push and pull between the need to spend time with lovers or your children and responsibilities toward your friends or company.

On August 12, Mercury finally goes direct in Leo. You can now start plowing ahead, especially since on August 12 and 13, Venus conjuncts Jupiter, which is one of the best aspects this year. Luck, flow in finances, new relationships and maybe a novel love. Mercury's change of direction can improve your relationship and communication with your partner.

Between August 12 to October 27, Uranus trines Pluto. A powerful aspect that can bring about transformation through technology, science, social movements, and revolutions. Changes in government that can, in the long run, bring more prosperity. Of all the signs, this aspect can help you tremendously.

From August 22 to September 22 the Sun transits in Virgo. You are asked to focus and refine your diet, health, routine, work, and how you serve. An ideal time to eliminate impediments to health and productivity. This transit can help tap into shared resources, your intimacy and passion. This is especially true on August 23 when the New Moon is in Virgo. A great time for a new diet, work project, or service. It is recommended to reorganize your home and office or home office. A bit of chaos is added by a square to Uranus that can awaken the critic and perfectionist in you. Try to channel these propensities into something productive at work.

On August 25, Venus transits in Leo until September 19. The planet of love in the sign of romance is always good news. Just be careful of extra marital affairs. A great time to reconnect to a hobby you had in your teens. Venus can help you attract, harmonize, and perfect your intimate relationships as well as bring balance into your life.

SEPTEMBER

On September 1 Saturn returns to Pisces until February 13, 2026. Confusion, floods, conflicts about water or in locations that are close to seas, lakes, and rivers. A time to ground your mystical practices, dreams, and intuition. Saturn, the rectifier, will now revisit the sector of your chart associated with finances, asking you to connect your talents, values, and self-esteem in order to make a living with integrity and authenticity. It is a great time to be disciplined regarding balancing the sheets, making sure you are coming out of any debts and ready for a new financial cycle.

From September 2 to September 18, Mercury transits into Virgo. Sales, ideas, and information flow effortlessly. A great time for editing projects that need precision, micromanagement, organizing, and purification. A wonderful time for detoxing and a cleanse. Try to reexamine your investments and how you work with shared resources.

September 7 is the Full Moon in Pisces. The Harvest Full Moon and Lunar Eclipse combo. Momentum builds towards closure especially with work and personal affairs. Now's the time to harvest the fruits of your labor from March/April. Mercury provides a touch of reason to an otherwise very emotional lunation. There could be tension between your money and talents and those of your partners in work or life.

From September 18, Mercury transits into Libra until October 6. This Mercury wants peace, compromise, and beauty. A great time for healing relationships and harmonizing the workplace. Art and business are coming together. You can revamp your website, redesign your logo, and come up with new ways to brand yourself and your projects. An opportune time for travel, publishing, teaching, and learning.

From September 19, Venus transits Virgo until October 13. You might feel over critical about your talents or your partner's as well as feel the criticism of others. Good time to be frugal, balance your expenses and income, and detox. Venus is blessing the sector of your chart associated with intimacy, passion, sexuality, as well as joint financial and artistic affairs.

September 21 is the Solar Eclipse in Virgo. A great time to balance your diet, start a new work project, and get the energy you need to reach the finish line. The Eclipse is quickening a benevolent aspect allowing all the planets involved to bestow their gifts on you: Pluto (power and intimacy); Saturn (focus); Neptune (imagination and intuition); Uranus (innovation). A great time to start a big project that demands shared resources.

On September 22, the Sun enters Libra until October 23, marking the Equinox! Today, the masculine phase of the year gracefully transitions into its feminine counterpart. As one of the four sacred days in the astrological calendar, commemorate it by celebrating relationships, justice, beauty, and art. Over the next 30 days, you should embody Libra traits—diplomacy, balance, and attentiveness to partners. The best time of the year for traveling, publishing, teaching, and learning.

On September 22, Mars enters Scorpio until November 4. A wonderful time to collaborate on big projects that demand a lot of energy and resources. Passion, intimacy and sexuality are on the rise. Great for physical activities in water or reconnecting to sports you are passionate about. An opportune time for research and investigation, as well as fighting for what you believe in. This is the time to assert yourself in your career, take on a leadership role, and ask for a raise or promotion. However, between September 23–25, tread cautiously as Mars squares Pluto. Aggression and manipulative folks are around you. Take extra heed in general. Actions can be easily misconstrued.

OCTOBER

On October 6 Mercury transits into Scorpio until October 29. An ideal period for research, finding lost objects or people, and expressing intimacy. Mercury is known as the psychopomp—the guide of souls to the realm of the dead. It's a good time to move on, let bygones be bygones, bury the zombies in your life, and explore investments and collaborations with other people's assets and talents. Mercury can be your private investigator and expose hidden information. This is a great time for career advancement, and improved relationships with superiors, bosses, and coworkers.

October 7 is the Full Moon in Aries. This Full Moon, bordering on a lunar eclipse, is a tad challenging. With Chiron's involvement, it's an occasion for learning, teaching, and shamanistic journeys. While there's an aggressive undertone, it's a good moment to conclude matters and move on. There could be conflicts with partners in life or work.

Between October 11 to 14, Venus is opposite Saturn and Neptune. This can be hard on your relationships and or finances. There is an emotional frustration with partners, especially long-term ones. Illusions, dependency and codependency as well as disappointment with someone close to you. However, you can use this aspect to connect mysticism and art.

From October 13 to November 6, Venus returns to her sign, Libra, and can help you connect to beauty, diplomacy, justice, relationship, and harmony. A good time to heal or improve relationships with mentors and in-laws. This is especially strong between October 14–15 as Venus trine Uranus and Pluto. Venus receives much praise from Pluto (intimacy, sexuality, power) and Uranus (innovation, technology, friendships). This benevolent aspect carries us upward with Venus (finances, relationships) leading the way. This is a powerful time for igniting, transforming, balancing and solidifying partnerships in work and personal life.

The New Moon in Libra takes place October 21. Dubbed the "Moon of Peace," the Libra New Moon is a great time to start a relationship or an art project. However, both Jupiter and Pluto are squaring off with the Sun and Moon, creating uncomfortable situations. Be extra cautious and focus on breathwork and meditation.

On October 22, Neptune returns for the last time to his sign, Pisces, until January 27, 2026. A great time to start meditation practice that can be facilitated by the ruler of mysticism. Dreams, imagination, channeling, mediumship, poetry, and art are enhanced, as well as your intuition. Be extra careful of Ponzi schemes or financial frauds. A good time to connect to talents or income streams that relate to mysticism, dance, movement, meditation, photography, yoga, and imagination.

On October 23, the Sun enters Scorpio until November 22. Focus on being true to your passion. It is a month of healing, transformation, magic, occult, and assisting others in their talents, finances, and endeavors. This is the month for you to take your career and professional life to the next level.

Around October 26 Mars conjuncts Lilith, please be extra careful today as the Mother of Demons hired an assassin. This is a violent and aggressive aspect. Tread cautiously.

On October 29, Mercury enters Sagittarius until November 19. You might feel a bit absent-minded and distracted. A good time for traveling and doing business with foreigners. Stick to the truth and avoid liars and half-truths. Great for education and publishing. Spend time with friends, change companies, connect to your favorite charity, and dive deeper into innovation and technology.

NOVEMBER

From November 4 to December 15, Mars enters Sagittarius. A call for adventure, as well as an expedition. Your Mars wants you to conquer, hunt, and expend your knowledge. It is an Indiana Jones aspect. A good time to take the lead if you work in a group of a company. Be extra careful of needless arguments and discord with friends or people in your community.

November 5 is the Full Moon in Taurus. An opportune time to bring something into completion. Since the lunation is on the 13th degree of Scorpio, it carries a powerful connection to love. Spend time in nature and indulge your five senses. There could be tension between the need to spend time at home and career responsibilities.

On November 6, Venus enters Scorpio until November 30. This transit can make you feel alone or unwanted, possessive as well as jealous. However, it is a good time to focus on your partner's money and talents rather than your own. Look into your investments as there might be a need to make some adjustments. A great time for partnerships in your career and professional life as well as adding an artistic touch to your career.

From November 8 to April 26, 2026, Uranus returns for the last time to Taurus. Changes in finances, fluctuations in cryptocurrency, new ways of expressing artistic talents. Unexpected guests or change or location. A family member might act out of character or in an erratic way.

From November 9 to December 1 Mercury is stationary and retrograde. This retrograde dances on the cusp of Sagittarius where he is overthinking to Scorpio where he is secretive. Avoid signing documents, starting new projects, and initiating anything unless you tried before and failed to accomplish. Be extra careful of misunderstanding and miscommunication in your career and among colleagues, clients, and friends.

On November 19, Mercury enters Scorpio until December 10. Mercury returns to Scorpio as he retrogrades back into the underworld. Good for investigations and finding lost objects and people.

November 20 is the New Moon in Scorpio. A great time to investigate your passions, what you really want in life, what you wish to transform, and start today. A good New Moon to initiate projects that need shared resources, talents, or funding. However, since Mercury is retro, you can only start things you already did in the past and failed to bring to completion. An opportune time to initiate healing, therapy, a shamanistic journey, or an investigation. The New Moon is getting a boost from Saturn, Jupiter, and Neptune, which bless this lunation with structure and focus, imagination and inspiration, and a great deal of open-mindedness.

On November 22, the Sun transits in Sagittarius until December 21. Sagittarius is the time of the year when you have the strongest connection to your higher self or guardian angel. This is a month for teaching, mentoring, learning, speaking your truth, mass media, publishing, and connecting to foreigners, and in-laws. The Sun shines on your friendships and communities, new friends are coming into your life, and your status in your company increases.

November 23 is an interesting day when the Sun trines Neptune; Mercury trines Jupiter and Saturn; Jupiter trines Saturn. This day can further your goals in almost all aspects of your life.

On November 28 Venus conjuncts Lilith. Be extra careful with all your relationships and partners in work or in personal life. A three-sided relationship might form around you. Be beware of stalkers, gossip, enemies, and lawsuits.

From November 30 until December 24 Venus transits in Sagittarius. It is a great time for connecting to educators, foreigners, explore investments and possibilities from travel and abroad. A good time to improve relationships with in-laws. A friend might become a romantic partner but in general artistic activities in a group are favored.

DECEMBER

December 4 is the Full Moon in Gemini. An optimal moment to finalize projects. You might feel the opposition between the need to spend time with your children or lover and demands from friends or your company.

On December 10, Mercury finally goes direct, it is good for traveling and businesses abroad as well as for philosophy.

From December 15, Mars transits in Capricorn until January 26, 2026. Make sure you give him a mission—something you need help conquering and or mastering. It is a good aspect for leadership and initiation. A call for action is coming, make sure not to refuse the call. PTSD from past lives might appear in the form of nightmares, panic attacks, or time spent in hospitals. One way to avoid it is to meditate longer, connect to trancework, and go to therapy.

December 20 is the New Moon in Sagittarius. A difficult New Moon with Neptune and Saturn sending squares all over the place. Not the best time to start new projects. Be careful of aggression and anger. A sense of war approaching. Lay low and be vigilant.

From December 20, Lilith enters Sagittarius for nine months. There could be discord with students and teachers, as well as foreigners. Take extra care when traveling. Fear of the foreigner, misinformation, disinformation. There could be strife and discord within your community or with a specific friend. Avoid gossip and intrigues within your friend group or company.

On December 21 the Sun enters Capricorn and will stay there until January 20, 2026. Happy Solstice! The ensuing month calls for Capricorn-like discipline and focus. Strategize the year ahead, bearing in mind that patience is vital. A good month to chill out and relax, sleep more, and meditate. Memories from previous lives could become more prevalent. This is supported by Venus transiting into Capricorn between December 24 and January 17, 2026. This transit of Venus can help you improve relationships with people who are older, long-term partnerships, as well as bosses and superiors. A time to connect art and design to your professional life.

PISCES AND
PISCES RISING: I IMAGINE
Rebranding—From Fish to Dolphin

General Trends: This year you continue hosting Saturn, Lord Karma, who is asking you to focus on your body, identity, direction in life, and reimagining your future goals. However, between May—August, Saturn will take a look at your finances and self-worth and start fixing these aspects of your life. The first part of the year offers an expansion in your home, family and real estate while the second part of 2025 you will experience opportunities and growth in love, happiness, children, and creativity. In addition, this year you are becoming the Dragon Master, and you will ride the North Node towards success and recognition. Be fearless and jump onto new opportunities.

JANUARY

Between January 1–5, Mars is opposite his Scorpio coruler, Pluto, which is not a promising beginning of the year. There is an opposition between your will and that of your community, company, or friends. People around you might experience paranoia, resort to manipulation, conflict and aggression.

On January 3, Venus puts on her swimming suit and dives into Pisces until February 4. This is great news for you, as you will feel and look beautiful. A great time to reimagine and rebrand yourself. Opportunities to improve your finances, relationships as well as artistic gifts come into the light. You are a child of the goddess of love in the next few weeks.

On January 6, Mars retrogrades into Cancer until April 18. Be vigilant of accidents, falling (unless it is in love) and issues with or around water such as leaks and floods. Conflict can arise with family members. However, for you Pisces, Mars provides you with passion and energy for creative projects, hobbies, romantic love and sports.

On January 8 Mercury enters Capricorn until January 28, and this means serious thought, discipline study, lessons coming from mature and experienced figures. Slow your thought, speech, and writing, and be mindful of every word. Great for furthering your career goals and forging long-term plans. This is a great time to advance yourself in your company, make new friends, and connect to clients and colleagues.

January 13 is the Full Moon in Cancer. It could get emotional and tumultuous with family and loved ones due to the opposition of retro Mars and Pluto. Take heed of not being over emotional and guilt casting. There could be push and pull between the need to spend time with your children or lover and the demands of friends or your company.

Between January 18–19, Venus conjuncts Saturn. Finances, values, and your relationships are being scrutinized and audited. This is not necessarily a bad aspect as Venus is exalted and Saturn can ground your talents as well as help you use your gifts in a practical way.

On January 19 the Sun enters Aquarius until February 18. A time to spend with friends, community, as well as immerse yourself in science, technology, and innovation. This is a month for your mystical pursuits, meditations, helping people in need, and retreats.

Between January 25–26, as Venus trines Mars, the cosmic lovers can bring a new relationship into your life or help you harmonize partnerships you already have.

From January 28 until February 14, Mercury transits in Aquarius, and ideas flow fast as well as new friendships enter your life. A wonderful time to dive into your famous imagination. January 29 is also the New Moon in Aquarius and Chinese New Year. Time to welcome to the Year of the Earth Snake. Jupiter is blessing this New Moon with wisdom and synchronicity. A great time to start a study group. A new friend or group from whom you can learn a great deal is making an entrance into your life.

On January 29, the North Node retrogrades into Pisces until August 19, 2026, for the first time in 19 years. This is a big deal for you as you are asked to host the North Node, the bringer of good karma, in your sign for the next 18 months. This is happening right on the New Moon in Aquarius, and it is time to teach as well as practice empathy, meditation, any form of trance or movement (yoga, dance, or martial arts). However, the South Node will be in Virgo asking us to let go of criticism, perfectionism, and overanalytical tendencies. The next year and a half you are asked to focus on yourself (without being self-centered) and less on trying to please others.

FEBRUARY

On February 4, Venus enters Aries, until March 27. Conflicts and discord with relationships and partners can arise. Watch impulsiveness with your finances. This is wonderful for your finances, talents, and self-worth. There could be a raise or promotion.

Between February 6–12, Mars trines Saturn bringing a weeklong of constructive action, stable effort, and sustained passion. This aspect can give you the endurance to complete a marathon or two.

February 12 is the Full Moon in Leo, and you might feel the pull and push between the need to spend time on your own or rest and the demands of work. The square with Uranus can cause disruption and lunacy to this lunation.

On Valentine's Day (February 14), Mercury enters Pisces until March 3. Communications can be a bit challenged while intuition and mediumship are on the rise. Trust your gut feeling rather than your brain. Make sure to use the words "I feel" or "I imagine" or "I believe," instead of "I think." This trend is supported by the Sun entering Pisces from February 18 until March 20's Equinox. Happy birthday! This is your month, and you need to focus on leadership, initiation and rebranding yourself. Just make sure to guard your boundaries and avoid addictions or self-destructive tendencies.

The month ends with the New Moon in Pisces on February 28. A great day to start something new that involves your imagination, photography, movement, yoga and meditation. There is a tendency to absorb negativity from others so watch what you take in. Be careful of overdoing or illusions. Something new is coming into your life. Let it in!

MARCH

March 1–April 14 Venus stands still and then retrogrades in Aries, her sign of exile. Avoid getting married, starting new relationships, getting engaged, starting lawsuits, and signing partnerships agreements. Since Venus retrogrades in the sector of your chart associated with finances, take extra care of your assets and money. You might need to reevaluate your values and decide to invest in new talents. A good time for refinancing.

On March 3, Mercury enters Aries until March 30. Mercury can be a bit impatient when in Aries and favors practical, short, and concise communication.

Between March 11–13, Sun conjunct Saturn while Mercury conjunct Venus. Seriousness, focus, discipline and planning can bring tactical or strategical accomplishments. A good time to improve relations with superiors.

March 14, Pi Day, is the first Lunar Eclipse of the year. The Full Moon is in precise and analytical Virgo. A great time to bring a project to an end, as well as focus on diet, service, and combining your analytical and wholistic aspects in life. This is your eclipse, and you might feel a push and pull between you and your partners in work and life.

March 14–April 8 Mercury is stationary and retrograde. Since it is happening in Aries, be extra careful with anger, impulsiveness, and rush decisions. With Venus and Mercury retrograding together take extra heed with all your financial decisions.

On March 17, the Sun conjuncts North Node. A day to access skills and knowledge from past lifetimes. There could be an encounter with powerful and successful individuals or groups that can further your goals.

March 20 is the Equinox and the Sun's transits into Aries until April 19. Happy New Year! A time to focus on your body, health, leadership, as well as your brand and image. You might discover hidden talents, gifts, and skills that you could use once the retrogrades are done to increase your income.

On March 27, Lilith enters Scorpio until December 20. Emotional intensity, powerful desires, fascination with the forbidden, shadow work, possessiveness, and jealousy. There could also be power struggles, manipulations, abuse, distrust, and criminality. Stay clear of any form of gossip. A good time to place a heap of salt in the four corners of your bedroom as protection against negativity. Take extra care while traveling or your dealings with teachers and students. In-laws might cause strife.

March 29 is the first Solar Eclipse of the year, and she shines upon Aries. Be mindful of unnecessary aggression and impulsiveness, especially with your finances.

From March 30 to April 15, Mercury is in Pisces. Mercury retrogrades into his sign of fall, thus, communication can be extra hard as the messenger is not only retro but drowning in subjectivity. Talk and write from your heart rather than mind. Great for intuition and applying imagination to overcome challenges. This can be a hard one for you, but you can still manage if you avoid starting new projects and stick to old ones you tried in the past and failed to accomplish.

From March 30 to October 22, Neptune, your ruler, leaves your sign and enters Aries for the first time in 165 years. Confusion can lead to war, be extra careful of fanaticism or aggression triggered by propaganda of misinformation. Mystical and healing talents can come to the front, like martial arts, dance, yoga, and any activity that demands imagination. Avoid any shortcuts with finances as there could be a lot of schemes and illusions around money-making possibilities. Creative visualization can bring about abundance.

APRIL

Between April 5–7, the celestial lovers meet again. Venus is Barbie and Mars in water sign Cancer is Ken, the "simply beach" dude. These are great days for romance, increasing your income from talents you are passionate about, and better relationships with significant others as well as brothers and sisters in arms.

From April 5 to 10, Venus conjuncts Saturn. While this aspect can introduce you to someone older that could be helpful with finance and developing your talents, this conjunction can also sit heavy over all your relationships. A time to reassess your primary relationships and how you make money.

On April 8 Mercury finally goes direct and you can begin signing documents and starting new projects. A great time to get clarity about money and start feeling better about yourself after all these retrogrades. Between April 7–16, Mercury trines Mars and that could give a kick forward to your projects and business.

April 13 is the Full Moon in Libra. This is the day of liberation, coming out of constriction and negativity and marching towards your Promised Land. It is a magical Full Moon where you might connect to your inner Moses, guardian angel, or higher self. There could be tension between your assets or values and those of your partner's. Avoid arguments and try to find compromises

April 14 is a dramatic day when Saturn conjuncts the North Node in Pisces. Positive interactions with groups of powerful individuals or people who are older. You are downloading some gifts or connections from previous lives. Good for joining new groups and organizations that share your long-term goals.

From April 16 to May 10 Mercury transits in Aries, speeding things up but also showing signs of impatience. Words can easily be weaponized so be extra careful. A great time to communicate your worth, ask for a raise, and tap into your writing skills.

From April 18 to June 17 Mars enters Leo bringing about a great deal of courage and a call for adventure. Great for entertainment, sports, creativity,

and reconnecting to your inner child. A great time to ask for a raise or promotion in your work. Be extra careful from overdoing, pushing yourself too hard, and burnouts.

On April 19 the Sun enters Taurus and will remain there until May 20. This month you are to indulge your six senses and connect to Mother Nature. It is a good month to tap into your talents and perhaps discover new ones. A month for marketing, sales, making new connections, and signing lucrative contracts.

Between April 22–24, as the Sun square the rulers of Scorpio—Mars and Pluto, take extra heed. This can bring about a great deal of letting go, death, and intense sexuality. Watch your steps these days, things can turn ugly or violent.

April 27 is the exalted New Moon in Taurus. A great time to start a new artistic or financial project. Spend time in nature, connect to your senses and do something that can symbolize rooting yourself. A great time for a new business or writing project. This trend continues April 30 as Venus enters Aries until June 6. There could be a bit more conflict and aggression in your primary relationships. In her sign of exile, Venus might be somewhat snappy and can cause hasty decisions and actions with finances and love.

MAY

Between May 1 to May 3, Venus conjuncts Neptune and infuses us with romance, creativity, art, improved finances, and intuition.

From May 10 to May 26, Mercury enters Taurus and transits in the area of your chart associated with communication, businesses, contracts, and writing. This is a good time to connect to new people as well as become a connector to others. A powerful time for sales, marketing, and promotion.

May 12 is the Full Moon in Scorpio. A great time for shadow work, overcoming temptation, and discovering the light within you. Because the Moon falls on the 22nd (Master Number) degree of Scorpio, you can build something out of the rubble of an older project or relationship. In this lunation you feel the tug of war between "mine" and "ours."

Between May 17–18, the Sun conjuncts Uranus and everyone's IQ is getting a temporary elevation. A fantastic day for humor, jumping into the unknown, and embracing the original and innovative. Spend time with friends or in a group.

From May 20 to June 21, the Sun enters Gemini, and you are channeling the spirit of intelligence, communication, and bridge-building. This is a great month for business, contracts, improving relationships with relatives, roommates, neighbors, and people you consider siblings. You could also benefit from the Sun shining on your home, family, and real estate.

Between May 20 to 24, Venus trines Mars once again. Romance, love, harmony (the daughter of Venus and Mars), is around you as well as an ability to see people's beautiful side. Great time for making money from things you are passionate about.

Between May 25 to September 1 Saturn enters Aries. Saturn in Aries wishes to rectify how we deal with our identity, body, anger, and vitality. This is a preview of things to come between 2026—2028. Saturn wishes you to focus on your finances, and attitude towards failure and success, self-worth, your values, and talents. It is a time to invest patience, faith, time and money in your talents so they can become the core of how you make your income.

Between May 26 to June 8 Mercury enters Gemini. Mercury is back to his domicile, and he is happy to unpack and share his skills. Information, opportunities, connections, and words flow effortlessly. This is a great time to heal relationships with family members as well as for real estate and relocation. This trend peaks May 27's New Moon in Gemini. A great day to start something new in connection with communication, networking, businesses, marketing, sales, and written projects. This New Moon is blessed by Pluto and Neptune, making it possible for you to link passion and reason, emotions and intellect. A great deal of intimacy and a possibility for a lover coming into your life.

JUNE

Between June 4 to 8, Venus, Jupiter, Mercury, and Mars are blessing us and each other. Windows of positive opportunities can improve sales, communication, writing, health, education, and art.

On June 6 Venus enters Taurus until July 4. The goddess of love is lending a helping hand in matters of art, any talent you possess, finances, relationships, and security. You will experience your five senses in a much stronger way than regularly, perhaps getting a glimpse of the sixth one as well. A great time to connect to an artistic project or a talent and translate them into income. Try to link design and communications, art with marketing. Relationships with relatives and neighbors could improve.

On June 8, Mercury transits Cancer until June 26. Great for healing relationships with family members. Don't be afraid to express your emotions. This is an opportune time for creative writing, as well as improving communication with children or lovers.

Between June 9 to 10 we have Mercury squares Neptune and Saturn and Venus squares Pluto. A bundle of challenging aspects come together. There is deception, lies, theft, and disinformation. Monkey mind is out of the cage, causing us to jump from one subject or project to the other. Breakups, manipulation, and discord with people of power.

On June 9 Jupiter, your traditional ruler, enters Cancer and will stay there until June 30, 2026. This is a great year for real estate, healing familial relationships, connecting to fortune and abundance, and opening new horizons. One of the best years to conceive, give birth to a creative project or a baby, attract a romantic love, and find a new sport or hobby. Be careful of overdoing and over commitments.

From June 10 until August 23, Saturn conjuncts with Neptune. While your intuition, ability to meditate, and connection to your dreams are enhanced, so could be your self-destructiveness, addictions, and escapism. Tread carefully, watch out for fanaticism or being too attached to your beliefs.

On June 11, the Full Moon is in Sagittarius. A blessed Full Moon in a challenging month. Jupiter, ruler of Sagittarius is exalted, creating what is called Mutual Reception with the Moon, which is auspicious. A wonderful time to complete a cycle of learning and preparation for something new. Great for travel, especially by water or to a location close to the water. Mars gives a boost of energy to the aspect. There could be tension between home life and your career.

From June 17, Mars enters Virgo until August 6. Mars in Virgo gets things done. He is the watchmaker, the engineer, the organizer—here to protect and serve. Conflicts can arise if you are too critical of yourself and others. A good time for diets and a new health regiment. You can make things happen if you stick to a strict routine. There could be unnecessary conflicts with your partners in work and life.

From June 21 the Sun transits Cancer until July 22. Happy Solstice! Open your heart to your family, and perhaps you might meet family members from past lives. A great month to renovate and remodel your home, relocate, move in with someone, get a new property, or start a family. Love is in the air as well as creativity and happiness. This trend increases on June 25's New Moon is in Cancer, providing a new beginning that involves home and family, real estate, security, and emotional support. With Jupiter, exalted in Cancer, blessing the union of the Sun and Moon, this is a great time to start new projects. Besides Pluto, there are no planets retrograde, so full swim ahead!

From June 26 until September 3, Mercury is in Leo. This Mercury transit can be extremely creative, entertaining, and exciting. A great time to focus on your work, health, and diet.

Between June 27 to 28, Mercury trines Saturn and Neptune. This is a good aspect for making long-term plans and bringing some sanity to a mad mad month. Good for marketing, writing, and sales. It is also a great time for prophetic dreams and practical intuition.

JULY

On July 4 Venus conjuncts Uranus and while relationships can be exciting, they can also show an unpredictable side. There is a need for freedom and exploration of new frontiers with your finances, relationships, and artistic expression. Embrace the original and unique. Be extra aware there could be volatility in the market.

From July 4 Venus flirts with Gemini until July 30 and the next few weeks can bring you in contact with a potential lover or partner at work. Art and communication come together, a great time for marketing, sales, design, and making new connections. One of the best time this year to beautify your abode, office, and improve relationships with family members.

From July 7 to November 8, Uranus enters Gemini, and your IQ is augmented. However, intelligence and IQ does not mean wisdom or kindness, so take heed not to become a heartless cyborg. There could be unexpected gusts, breaking from ancestral karma, and need for freedom from homelife. In addition, Uranus the awakener could manifest as sudden change of location, and unpredictable twists and turns around your family and real estate.

On July 10 we have the Full Moon in Capricorn. The lunation can bring about a bit of opposition between home and career. The Moon is exiled in Capricorn and can create a sense of emotionality and longing for a paradise lost. However, Mars is sending his troupes to help us, and with a bit of action, determination, and a clear mission, you can disperse the emotional confusion of the Full Moon and get things done. There could be tension between the need to focus on your children or lover and responsibilities towards your company or friends.

From July 17 to August 12, Mercury is retrograde in Leo. Avoid signing docs and starting new projects. Especially watch your relationships and communication with kids, lovers, and people with big egos.

From July 22 to August 22, Sun enters Leo. Engage in creative, joyful, and heartwarming activities. Generosity, nobility, chivalry, sportsmanship, and enthusiasm are guiding us this month. A great time to connect to a hobby or a new sport. This is the best month to improve your health, as well as connect to the right diet. You will feel an urge to serve people and follow a stricter routine.

Between July 23–25, the Sun trine Saturn and Neptune creating a wonderful flow and help with vitality, intuition, healing, and the ability to bring some new structure into our lives. This is a glorious aspect, and you can benefit from creative visualizations, meditation, dance and self-expression.

On July 24, the New Moon is in Leo. This is not an easy New Moon since she is opposite to Pluto and can bring about a confrontation with a powerful figure in your life whose motivations are unclear. With Mercury retrograding in Leo, it is not the best time to start something new, however, you could initiate a project you already tried before and failed to complete. A good time to start a diet or work project you tried in the past and failed to accomplish.

From July 31 to August 25, Venus transits in Cancer. Marriage, social events with family members, as well as harmonious flow with family members.

AUGUST

The month starts with a hard aspect on August 1 and 2 between Venus, Saturn and Neptune. Watch out for deception, illusions, and fantasies in your primary relationships as well as financial dealings. Not the best time to start a new relationship. Communications with people who are older than you can be fraught with discord. Try a new approach to an old problem.

On August 6 Mars enters Libra and stays there until September 22. There could be legal issues, but it is also a good time for compromise and finding resolutions to conflicts. This is a good time to connect to your passion, intimacy, and sexuality. Between August 7 to 9, Mars trines Uranus bringing about brilliance and originality. Search for innovative and original solutions. Connections with friends can thrive. Action is guided by new approaches.

Watch it between August 8 to 10 as Mars opposites both Saturn and Neptune. Accidents, mishaps, and physical challenges especially since Mercury is retrograding. Stay away from arguments with superiors. Stay calm and try to do less. The opposition with Neptune adds more hardships to the already difficult few days. Stay away from stormy seas (metaphysically and physically speaking).

August 9 is the Full Moon in Aquarius. You might feel a push and pull between the need to spend time with lovers or your children and your friends or company. A great time to let go, start a diet, detox, and cut away from people or attitudes that block your path.

On August 12, Mercury finally goes direct in Leo. You can now start plowing ahead, especially since on August 12 and 13, Venus conjuncts Jupiter, which is one of the best aspects this year. Luck, flow in finances, new relationships and maybe a novel love. This is great news for your health, work, and ability to serve and be served.

Between August 12 to October 27, Uranus trines Pluto. A powerful aspect that can bring about transformation through technology, science, social movements, and revolutions. Changes in government that can, in the long run, bring more prosperity.

From August 22 to September 22 the Sun transits in Virgo. You are asked to focus and refine your diet, health, routine, work, and how you serve. An ideal time to eliminate impediments to health and productivity. The next 30 days are wonderful for focusing on your relationships, partners in work and life and victories over enemies or competitors. This is especially true on August 23, and the Moon is new in Virgo. A great time to start a new diet, work project, or service. It is recommended to reorganize your home and office or home office. A bit of chaos is added by a square to Uranus that can awaken the critic and perfectionist in you.

On August 25, Venus transits in Leo until September 19. The planet of love in the sign of romance is always good news. Just be careful of extra marital affairs. It is a very creative time with your inner child, active and playful. You can ask for a raise or promotion, as Venus blesses your workplace. Be mindful of your kidneys, ovaries, and overly rich diets.

SEPTEMBER

On September 1 Saturn returns to Pisces until February 13, 2026. Confusion, floods, conflicts about water or in locations that are close to seas, lakes, and rivers. A time to ground your mystical practices, dreams, and intuition. This is the last transit of the Lord Karma in your sign, therefore, pay extra attention to your body, image, and status in your community. Reconnect with your true passions and start a path that could help you define what you would like to become in the next three decades.

From September 2 to September 18, Mercury transits into Virgo. Sales, ideas, and information flow effortlessly. A great time for editing projects that need precision, micromanagement, organizing, and purification. A wonderful time for detoxing and a cleanse. Communication with your primary relationships improves. A good time to speak your mind and your need to your business and life partners.

September 7 is the Full Moon in Pisces. The Harvest Full Moon and Lunar Eclipse combo. Momentum builds towards closure especially with work and personal affairs. Now's the time to harvest the fruits of your labor from March/April. Mercury provides a touch of reason to an otherwise very emotional lunation.

From September 18, Mercury transits into Libra until October 6. This Mercury wants peace, compromise, and beauty. A great time for healing relationships and harmonizing the workplace. Art and business are coming together. You can revamp your website, redesign your logo, and come up with new ways to brand yourself and your projects. A good time for investments, helping your partners in work and life with their finances, and working on joint artistic and financial projects.

From September 19, Venus transits Virgo until October 13. You might feel over critical about your art or your partners as well as feel the criticism of others. This is one of the best times in the year to attract partners in work or life, win legal challenges, and overcome negativity from others.

September 21 is the Solar Eclipse in Virgo. A great time to balance your diet, start a new work project, and get the energy you need to reach the finish line. The eclipse gives a benevolent aspect a push, supporting all the planets involved in bestowing their gifts upon you: Pluto (power and intimacy); Saturn (focus); Neptune (imagination and intuition); Uranus (innovation). A good time to start something new with your partner or attract a new relationship.

On September 22, the Sun enters Libra until October 23, marking the Equinox! As one of the four sacred days in the astrological calendar, commemorate it by celebrating relationships, justice, beauty, and art. Over the next 30 days you are connecting to your passion, intimacy, sexuality, and bury the zombies in your life, as in, half-dead project, friendships, or relationships. Great for research and investigation.

On September 22, Mars enters Scorpio until November 4. A wonderful time to collaborate on big projects that demand a lot of energy and resources. As you can see, the theme of passion, intimacy and sexuality are on the rise. Great for physical activities in water or reconnecting to sports you are passionate about. An opportune time for research and investigation, as well as fighting for what you believe in. Immerse yourself in studying, teaching, and traveling.

Between September 23–25, tread cautiously as Mars squares Pluto. Aggression and manipulative folks are around you. Take extra heed in general. Actions can be easily misconstrued.

OCTOBER

On October 6 Mercury transits into Scorpio until October 29. An ideal period for research, finding lost objects or people, and expressing intimacy. Mercury is known as the psychopomp—the guide of souls to the realm of the dead. It's a good time to move on, let bygones be bygones, bury the zombies in your life, and explore investments and collaborations with other people's assets and talents. You can make new affiliations with multinational corporations, foreigners, and teachers.

October 7 is the Full Moon in Aries. This Full Moon, bordering on a lunar eclipse, is a tad challenging. With Chiron's involvement, it's an occasion for learning, teaching, and shamanistic journeys. While there's an aggressive undertone, it's a good moment to conclude matters and move on. There could be conflicts with partners in life or work.

Between October 11 to 14, Venus is opposite Saturn and Neptune. This can be hard on your relationships and or finances. There is an emotional frustration with partners, especially long-term ones. Illusions as well as dependency and codependency and some disappointment with someone close to you. However, you can use this aspect to connect mysticism and art.

From October 13 to November 6, Venus returns to Libra and can help you connect to beauty, diplomacy, justice, relationship, and harmony.

This is especially strong between October 14–15 as Venus trine Uranus and Pluto. Venus receives much praise from Pluto (intimacy, sexuality, power) and Uranus (innovation, technology, friendships). This is another helpful aspects with Venus (finances, relationships) leading the way. This is a powerful time for igniting, transforming, balancing and solidifying partnerships in work and personal life.

The New Moon in Libra takes place October 21. Dubbed the "Moon of Peace," the Libra New Moon is a great time to start a relationship or an art project. However, both Jupiter and Pluto are squaring off with the Sun and Moon, creating uncomfortable situations. Be extra cautious and focus on breathwork and meditation.

On October 22, Neptune returns for the last time to his sign, Pisces, until January 27, 2026. A great time to start meditation practice that can be facilitated by the ruler of mysticism. Dreams, imagination, channeling, mediumship, poetry, and art are enhanced, as well as your intuition. Neptune has been in your sign since 2012 and soon will move away. It is a good time to connect to yoga, dance, meditation, and any mystical activity. Your imagination, which is already strong, is getting even more potent.

On October 23, the Sun enters Scorpio until November 22. Focus on being true to your passion. It is a month of healing, transformation, magic, occult, and assisting others in their talents, finances, and endeavors. A month you can connect to foreigners, improve relationships with in-laws and focus on learning and teaching.

Around October 26 Mars conjuncts Lilith, please be extra careful today as the Mother of Demons hired an assassin. This is a violent and aggressive aspect.

On October 29, Mercury enters Sagittarius until November 19. You might feel a bit absent-minded and distracted. A good time for traveling and doing business with foreigners. Stick to the truth and avoid liars and half-truths. Great for education and publishing. Mercury can really help you push your career to the next level. Focus on marketing and promoting yourself. Don't be afraid to ask for help.

NOVEMBER

From November 3 to 5 Mars opposes Uranus, therefore, be extra careful of accidents and mishaps involving aggression, impatience, speed or sharp objects. You might experience erratic behavior that doesn't make sense as well as gadgets and machines breaking or malfunctioning. The robot is out of control.

From November 4 to December 15, Mars enters Sagittarius. A call for adventure, as well as an expedition. Your Mars wants you to conquer, hunt, and expend your knowledge, especially in your career and professional life.

November 5 is the Full Moon in Taurus. An opportune time to bring something into completion. Since the lunation is on the 13th degree of Scorpio, it carries a powerful connection to love. Spend time in nature and indulge your five senses.

On November 6, Venus enters Scorpio until November 30. This transit can make you feel alone or unwanted, possessive as well as jealous. However, it is a good time to focus on your partner's money and talents rather than your own. Look into your investments as there might be a need to make some adjustments. A wonderful time to study and publish anything to do with art and design.

From November 8 to April 26, 2026, Uranus returns for the last time to Taurus. Changes in finances, fluctuations in cryptocurrency, new ways of expressing artistic talents. There could be unpredictable situations taking place with or with your relatives, neighbors, and siblings. Any businesses that have to do with innovation, technology and high-tech are favored.

From November 9 to December 1 Mercury is stationary and retrograde. This retrograde dances on the cusp of Sagittarius where he is overthinking to Scorpio where he is secretive. Avoid signing documents, starting new projects, and initiating anything unless you tried to do so before and failed to accomplish it. Be extra careful if you travel. Misunderstandings can arise in your career or with superiors.

On November 19, Mercury enters Scorpio until December 10. Mercury returns to Scorpio as he retrogrades back into the underworld. Good for investigations and finding lost objects and people. A good time to go back to something you studied and dropped.

November 20 is the New Moon in Scorpio. A great time to investigate your passions, what you really want in life, what you wish to transform, and start today. A good Moon to initiate projects that need shared resources, talents, or funding. However, since Mercury is retro, you can only start things you already did in the past and failed to bring to completion. An opportune time to initiate healing, therapy, a shamanistic journey, or an investigation. The New Moon is getting a boost from Saturn, Jupiter, and Neptune, which bless this lunation with structure and focus, imagination and inspiration, and a great deal of open-mindedness.

On November 22, the Sun transits in Sagittarius until December 21. Sagittarius is the time of the year when we have the strongest connection to our higher self or guardian angel. This is a month to focus your efforts on your career where you could see the most amount of advancement and success.

November 23 is an interesting day when the Sun trines Neptune; Mercury trines Jupiter and Saturn; Jupiter trines Saturn. This day can further your goals in almost all aspects of your life.

On November 28 Venus conjuncts Lilith. Be extra careful with all your relationships and partners in work or in personal life. A three-sided relationship might form around you. Be beware of stalkers, gossip, enemies, and lawsuits.

From November 30 until December 24 Venus transits in Sagittarius. It is a great time for connecting to educators, foreigners, explore investments and possibilities from travel and abroad. A good time to improve relationships with in-laws. Great for forming affiliations, partnerships, and collaborations in your career. Try to add an artistic element to your professional life.

DECEMBER

December 4 is the Full Moon in Gemini. An optimal moment to finalize projects. As this is the year's last Full Moon.

On December 10, Mercury finally goes direct. A good for traveling and businesses abroad as well as for philosophy. Projects in your career are pushed forward by both the Sun and Mercury on your side.

From December 15, Mars transits in Capricorn until January 26, 2026. Make sure you give him a mission—something you need help conquering and or mastering. It is a good aspect for leadership and initiation. A call for action is coming within your company or among your friends. A good time for team sports and collaboration with brothers and sisters in arms.

December 20 is the New Moon in Sagittarius. A difficult New Moon with Neptune and Saturn sending squares all over the place. Not the best time to start new projects. Be careful of aggression and anger. However, you can still start something new in your career.

From December 20, Lilith enters Sagittarius for nine months. There could be discord with students and teachers, as well as foreigners. Take extra care when traveling. Fear of the foreigner, misinformation, disinformation. The Mother of Demons could hinder your relationships with superiors, clients, or people you meet in your career. There could be enemies showing up among your coworkers.

On December 21 the Sun enters Capricorn and will stay there until January 20, 2026. Happy Solstice! As one of the four sacred astrological days, your spiritual connection peaks. The ensuing month calls for Capricorn-like discipline and focus. Strategize the year ahead, bearing in mind that patience is vital. A great time to approach new companies, make new friends and increase your status in your community.

From December 24 Venus transits in Capricorn until January 17, 2026. This transit of Venus can help you improve relationships with people who are older, long-term partnerships, as well as bosses and superiors. A time to connect art and design to your professional life. A wonderful time to create art in a group.

Made in the USA
Columbia, SC
30 December 2024

50921488R00200